Rather than taking a standard public administration approach to local government, Hijino focuses on the relationship between local and national parties and politicians. This approach generates many new insights and exciting new research agendas. It also makes the study of local government much more relevant to the study of Japanese politics and should thus be of interest to a very wide audience.

Steven R. Reed, *Professor in the Faculty of Policy Studies, Chuo University. Author of* Japanese prefectures and policymaking; *"Structure and behaviour: Extending Duverger's Law to the Japanese case"; and editor/co-author of* Japan Decides 2014: The Japanese General Election

This book is a masterpiece of Japanese local and multi-level politics in English. Hijino not only shows how intensely integrated intergovernmental relations have been dismantled over the past twenty years, but also clearly analyses how and why this transformation has changed the Japanese polity in comparative perspectives. He makes a valuable contribution by introducing the essence of works by Japanese scholars for English readers, as well as by showing the usefulness of regarding Japanese multi-level politics as a case comparable with other industrialized countries like Canada and Germany.

Satoshi Machidori, *Professor in the Faculty of Law, Kyoto University. Author of* Shusho Seiji no Seido Bunseki: Gendai Nihon Seiji no Kenryoku Kiban Keisei *[The Japanese Premiership: An Institutional Analysis of the Power Relations]; co-author of* Nihon no Chiho Seiji: Nigen Daihyosei Seifu no Seisaku Sentaku *[Japan's Local Politics: Continuity and Change in the Presidential System]; contributor of* Examining Japan's Lost Decades

Local Politics and National Policy

This book is about why and how central and local governments clash over important national policy decisions. Its empirical focus is on the local politics of Japan which has significantly shaped, and been shaped by, larger developments in national politics. The book argues that since the 1990s, changes in the national political arena, fiscal and administrative decentralization, as well as broader socio-economic developments have led to a decoupling of once closely integrated national and local party systems in Japan. Such decoupling has led to a breakdown of symbiotic relations between the centre and regions. In its place are increasing strains between national and local governments leading to greater intra-party conflict, inter-governmental conflicts, and more chief executives with agendas and resources increasingly autonomous of the national ruling party.

Although being a book primarily focused on the Japanese case, the study seeks to contribute to a broader understanding of how local partisans shape national policy-making. The book theorizes and investigates how the degree of state centralization, vertical integration for party organizations, and partisan congruence in different levels of government affect inter-governmental relations.

Japan's experience is compared with Germany, Canada, and the UK to explore sources of multi-level policy conflict.

Ken Victor Leonard Hijino is Associate Professor at the Graduate School of Law in Kyoto University, Japan.

Routledge Contemporary Japan Series

58 **Decision-Making Reform in Japan**
The DPJ's Failed Attempt at a Politician-led Government
Karol Zakowski

59 **Examining Japan's Lost Decades**
Edited by Yoichi Funabashi and Barak Kushner

60 **Japanese Women in Science and Engineering**
History and Policy Change
Naonori Kodate and Kashiko Kodate

61 **Japan's Border Issues**
Pitfalls and Prospects
Akihiro Iwashita

62 **Japan, Russia and Territorial Dispute**
The Northern Delusion
James D.J. Brown

63 **Fukushima and the Arts in Japan**
Negotiating Disaster
Edited by Barbara Geilhorn and Kristina Iwata-Weickgenannt

64 **Social Inequality in Post-Growth Japan**
Transformation during Economic and Demographic Stagnation
Edited by David Chiavacci and Carola Hommerich

65 **The End of Cool Japan**
Ethical, Legal, and Cultural Challenges to Japanese Popular Culture
Edited by Mark McLelland

66 **Regional Administration in Japan**
Departure from Uniformity
Shunsuke Kimura

67 **Japanese Media at the Beginning of the 21st Century**
Consuming the Past
Katsuyuki Hidaka

68 **Intercultural Communication in Japan**
Theorizing Homogenizing Discourse
Edited by Satoshi Toyosaki and Shinsuke Eguchi

68 **Local Politics and National Policy**
Multi-level Conflicts in Japan and Beyond
Ken Victor Leonard Hijino

Local Politics and National Policy
Multi-level Conflicts in Japan and Beyond

Ken Victor Leonard Hijino

LONDON AND NEW YORK

First published 2017
by Routledge

2 Park Square, Milton Park, Abingdon, Oxfordshire OX14 4RN
52 Vanderbilt Avenue, New York, NY 10017

Routledge is an imprint of the Taylor & Francis Group, an informa business

First issued in paperback 2018

Copyright © 2017 Ken Victor Leonard Hijino

The right of Ken Victor Leonard Hijino to be identified as author of this
work has been asserted by him in accordance with sections 77 and 78 of
the Copyright, Designs and Patents Act 1988.

All rights reserved. No part of this book may be reprinted or reproduced or
utilised in any form or by any electronic, mechanical, or other means, now
known or hereafter invented, including photocopying and recording, or in
any information storage or retrieval system, without permission in writing
from the publishers.

Notice:
Product or corporate names may be trademarks or registered trademarks,
and are used only for identification and explanation without intent to infringe.

British Library Cataloguing in Publication Data
A catalogue record for this book is available from the British Library

Library of Congress Cataloging-in-Publication Data
A catalog record for this book has been requested

ISBN: 978-1-138-64041-2 (hbk)
ISBN: 978-0-367-14186-8 (pbk)

Typeset in Gaillard
by Wearset Ltd, Boldon, Tyne and Wear

Contents

List of figures		viii
List of tables		ix
Acknowledgements		x
	Introduction	1
1	Theories of local power and multi-level conflict	14
2	Local autonomy and partisan linkages in post-war Japan	35
3	Campaigning against the capital: multi-level conflicts within the LDP	57
4	The politics of local opposition: multi-level conflicts under the DPJ	80
5	Governors and governments: multi-level policy conflicts between executives	100
6	Multi-level conflicts in Canada, Germany, and the UK	128
	Conclusion	149
	Index	162

Figures

I.1	Structure and overview of book	8
1.1	Local autonomy and partisan congruence shaping multi-level conflict	27
2.1	Regional inequality as measured by per capita prefectural income	36
2.2	Perceived expansion of regional inequalities in Japan	37
2.3	Ratio of locally raised revenues, current account to expenditure, and debt-to-expenditure for prefectural governments	41
2.4	Proportion of all incumbents, LDP incumbents, and first-time candidates for the House Representative with experience in local politics (prefectural or municipal)	48
2.5	Partisan affiliation of governors (LDP, non-LDP, or Independent)	51
2.6	National volatility vs local stability in electoral outcomes for the LDP and main opposition party	52
3.1	Strength of LDP and main opposition party for prefectural legislatures	59
3.2	Frequency of articles reporting on written opinions passed by prefectural legislatures	63
3.3	Frequency of written opinions passed by prefectural legislatures	64
5.1	Career backgrounds of governors	101
5.2	Changing frequency of meetings between PM and governors	104
5.3	Frequency of meetings between PM and governors by location	105
5.4	Proportion of meetings between PM and governors by category	105
5.5	Proportion of meetings between PM and governors by category II	107
5.6	Media reporting on governors criticizing cabinet/PM and vice versa	108
5.7	Actions listed on NGA homepage by fiscal year	110

Tables

1.1	Types of multi-level conflict, their features, and examples	29
3.1	Channels of upward influence over national policy for local legislators	60
3.2	List of multi-level policy conflicts over national policy, by frequency of reporting and WOs	66
3.3	Number and frequency of WOs passed by types of prefectures under LDP administrations, between 1987 and 2015	68
4.1	Average number of WOs submitted per prefecture (by strength of LDP in legislature) under DPJ administrations, 2009–2012	86
4.2	DPJ local branch support for key national policies as revealed by WOs	87
5.1	Challenges made by governors against national policy	114

Acknowledgements

This book would not have been possible without generous help and advice from many people.

I am extremely grateful to Steven Reed, Masahiko Tatebayashi, Satoshi Machidori, Kengo Soga, Naofumi Fujimura, Akira Tsuji, and Yosuke Sunahara for providing immensely useful and thorough reviews of my manuscript drafts.

The book also benefitted from presentations at the Association of Asian Studies, Japanese Society for Public Administration, and Kansai Gyosei Kenkyu-kai. I thank panelists and audience for their feedback.

I would like to thank Kiyosada Somae, Haruya Sakamoto, and Sato Manabu for introducing me to various interview contacts in Okinawa and other regions at early stages of fieldwork. I am also grateful to various journalists at *Ryukyu Shimpo*, *Okinawa Times*, and *Hokkaido Shimbun*, the research department at LDP headquarters, as well as the research department at the National Association of Chairpersons of Prefectural Assemblies for help in providing data. Thanks also to Daniel Smith for sharing his data set on candidate backgrounds. The book, in particular the comparative chapter, benefitted from two grants from the Japanese Society for the Promotion of Sciences (JSPS) which allowed me to conduct research within Japan and make research trips to the UK and Canada. I would also like to thank my two assistants at Kyoto University, Shuzo Tani and Takuma Ogawa, who provided outstanding support for data input and other research work.

In terms of logistics, I would like to thank our *hoikuen* in Tokyo and the Tokaido Shinkansen, where much of this book was written, allowing me to live a slightly crazy life of shuttling weekly between Tokyo and Kyoto in the past year.

Finally, I want to thank my family for their continued support during this project. Shigeki for his generous comments and encouragements. Gerd and Emi for their motherly and sisterly love from France and Sweden. Teruko and Kimaki for sharing their wonderful house in Tokyo. Karin and Hugo for bringing so much joy. And Kaoru, for always keeping what's central and peripheral in fine balance.

Introduction

There is an unresolved tension in the general perception of local politics in modern representative democracies.

On the one hand, there is the vague, but repeated truism that 'all politics is local'. The slogan implies that the success of national candidates and parties depends on how well they address local demands and constituency needs. It has now become a phrase used whenever local issues shape the direction of national politics. Indeed, evidence of the impact of local politics in the national arena can be found everywhere: state legislatures in the US shaping national policy initiatives in vital areas like health care, gun control, and voter registration; new European political parties – green, regional, and extreme right parties – have emerged into the national legislature after first cutting their teeth at local level; specific regions such as Scotland, Catalonia, and Quebec are threatening the unity of their states through demands for greater autonomy.

Local politics is also seen as vital in and of itself for the health of democracy. Not only are local governments 'schools of democracy', but they act as 'bulwarks of liberty' against the supposedly centralizing, tyrannical tendency of the state. Local politics, with its potential for greater voter participation, deliberation, and scrutiny of elected politicians, is seen as a vital battleground to roll back the general crisis of representative democracy. Parties on the left and right, international development agencies, and business organizations have promoted decentralization as a good thing. Empowering local governments, they argue, is seen as the surest path to more accountable, responsive, and streamlined democracy. Struggles for local autonomy have stoked strong political passions. The local referendum for independence in Scotland, for example, generated record turnout after weeks of intense political engagement among voters. It was, for one observer, 'the biggest surge of creative democratic energy the country had seen'.[1]

On the other hand, local politics has generally not attracted as much enthusiasm from voters, or researchers, compared to the national arena. Local government has been deemed the domain of 'low politics' – areas not vital for the survival of a state – in centralized states like the UK. Even in a federal country such as the US, where state governments have considerable autonomy, local politics has been characterized a 'backwater' of research until recently (Haider-Markel 2014).

2 Introduction

Indeed, local governments are overshadowed by more powerful central or federal governments that control the vital state functions of setting monetary, fiscal, and trade policy as well as engaging in war and diplomacy. Scholars have pointed out that local governments are fundamentally constrained. Since provinces and cities do not control the movement of people and capital across sub-state borders, they are unable to effectively redistribute and regulate within their 'city limits' (Peterson 1981). National governments, if they wish to avoid fiscal indiscipline and runaway debt, are compelled to place hard budget constraints on local governments, thereby limiting their ability to raise and spend money (Rodden 2002). These are but two of many serious constraints on local governments. These limitations lower the stakes of local elections and politics, which in turn lead to voter indifference. Indeed, turnout for local elections tends to be consistently lower in local than national elections across most democracies, although Japan is a rare exception (Horiuchi 2005). Moreover, in many states, those who do vote locally often treat local elections as less important, so-called 'second order' referendums on the performance of parties and governments at national level (Reif and Schmidt 1980; Jeffery and Hough 2003).

In Japan, which this book makes its case, the conflicted relationship towards local politics is also evident. Voters and media have periodically frothed with excitement whenever outspoken and popular governors have pursued new initiatives or challenged the capital. Even relatively minor local elections are reported as either ringing endorsement or damaging indictments of the ruling party in Tokyo. Local innovations in policy are widely reported, sometimes leading to their diffusion across the country. Decentralization has been promoted breathlessly as a cure-all for some time in Japan as well. Many advocates have pinned hopes on expanded local autonomy to combat Japan's 'lost decades' of economic stagnation, depopulation, and democratic disengagement.

Yet turnout in Japanese local elections is historically low, and dissatisfaction towards local politics considerable, with increasing calls for local legislatures to be shrunk (or even abolished). Local politicians are ridiculed in the media for scandals involving expenses, sexual harassment, or corruption (Hijino 2015). When local governments hit headlines in vital policy areas, they come across as both powerful and powerless. High-profile governors such as those from Tokyo and Osaka have been able to command the ear of prime ministers, seemingly able to pressure national legislation and projects in their interest. Local governments have dragged their feet against national policies for years (such as two decades of Okinawa prefecture successfully blocking relocation of a US base to Henoko). In other instances (such as the Tokyo metropolitan government's grumbling about paying for the Tokyo Olympic stadium facilities), local governments have been strong-armed into cooperation by the capital. Moments of exciting local revolt against unpopular national policies emerge, but then are over-ridden by government pressures and legislation.

Considering these unresolved tensions, the book departs from a very simple and straightforward question: how can local politics matter? We seek to know if local elections and governments, politicians and party branches can make a difference, particularly in relation to significant political decisions. Specifically, when and how can local politics have the power to shape or resist significant national policy initiatives?

The question of local power in Japan

In post-war Japan, these questions of local power have been posed in two ways. First, scholars have asked to what extent Japanese local governments possess local autonomy, and hence are able to pursue policies at local level independent of central government interference. Second, observers have investigated ways in which local politics shape national-level politics and policy.

In terms of local autonomy, different historical periods have highlighted either the elements of centralized control or of local discretion of Japanese local governments. In the early post-war period, the dominant interpretation among observers was that the Japanese state was highly centralized and that local governments were mainly agents of the centre. Though responsible for an increasingly large share of the expanding welfare state in the post-war period, local governments were unable to exercise policy initiative or diverge substantially from centralized standards set in the centre. In this view, local governments were limited in their autonomy by a web of national laws, central ministerial oversight and regulations, as well as critical dependence on the centre for financial resources (Steiner 1965; Tsuji 1976).

This characterization of Japanese local government being helplessly constrained agents of the centre was undermined by an unexpected period of local activity during the late 1960s and 1970s. During this period, local governments under control of opposition parties pursued innovative policy-making in environmental regulation and welfare provision. The measures at times exceeded their legal authority, diverged from national standards, and challenged central ministry guidelines (Muramatsu 1975; Reed 1982). Local governments not only were able to prevail against the central government in defending their actions, but their policies spread beyond their locality to other local governments and were co-opted by the central government in a process of 'policy diffusion' (Ito 2002, 2006). Furthermore, local government policy and budget spending were found to be affected by the partisan composition and interactions of local legislatures and executives throughout the post-war period (Soga and Machidori 2007; Sunahara 2012).

In terms of the second question, scholars have tried to capture how local politics (its elections, local politicians, and territorial interests) shaped national policy. Their analytical focus naturally fell on the Liberal Democratic Party (LDP), which was dominant locally and nationally throughout the post-war period. Revisionist analyses emerged from the mid-1970s countering the view of local politics as being irrelevant under a highly centralized legal framework. Muramatsu (1975, 1988) indicated how local conservatives (prefectural and municipal legislators as well as directly elected mayors and governors) were able to draw out benefits from the centre by participating in a bottom-up and

4   Introduction

inclusive policy-making process. This bottom-up dynamic involved a 'rugby scrum' linking local politicians, local governments, local Diet members, and national-level bureaucrats (Muramatsu 2010). Policy demands were channelled upward to the ruling party and coordinated among ministries and various sectional interest groups. Local governments (and local politicians representing these areas) competed among each other in 'horizontal political competition' to capture a greater share of expanding governmental spending to various regions. Local governments were thus not passive recipients of national subsidies, but active players shaping policy and capturing benefits in their favour (Muramatsu 1975, 1988).

Local politics influenced national policy not only through such vertical linkages within the LDP but also in providing an arena for opposition parties to challenge the centre. During the mid-1960s and 1970s, local governments controlled by leftist governors and mayors challenged local and national conservatives on a platform questioning unregulated high growth (Flanagan *et al.* 1980). These Socialist and/or Communist-backed governors implemented local bylaws expanding welfare services and enforcing pollution regulations which superseded or even contravened national laws and regulations. Many of these initiatives were copied by other local governments or were co-opted into national standards. Local opposition thus served to alter national policy by representing policy preferences which could not emerge nationally and by counterbalancing one-party dominance at national level, making Japanese democracy more responsive to voter demands (Soga and Machidori 2007, p. 202).

The historical experience by and large suggests Japan's regions achieved their territorial interests not so much through exercising local discretion and autonomy (which was largely constricted throughout the period, albeit with some leeway for manoeuvre) but primarily through its political influence on the centre to draw out preferred policies. Local government power in the post-war period thus depended on contextual factors: the nature of intra-party integration, local opposition strength, and the availability of redistributive resources. As such, Japanese local power has been highly contingent; such contingency is probably also the reason why interest in local government has ebbed and flowed over time.

A new disequilibrium between centre and regions

These past evaluations and descriptive models of Japanese local power, however, have become inadequate since the 1990s. Three broad processes have transpired which have transformed the dynamics between national and local levels of politics in the past quarter century. These trends have been observed and analysed separately, but not comprehensively understood in terms of its impact on the local influence over national politics.

First, the links between national and local politics have weakened as the interests and preferences of national and local politicians have become less aligned. Electoral reforms in 1994 have contributed to greater programmatic competition between two major parties targeting floating voters under strong executive

Introduction 5

leadership. But local elections remain under the old electoral rules, which have hindered the emergence of two-party programmatic competition locally. Reapportionment has also meant the national party's centre of gravity has shifted towards urban districts, while its local branches (especially its numerous rural ones) remain beholden to a narrower set of local interest groups and organized voters. Municipal mergers have also drastically reduced the number of local politicians, reducing channels of communication between centre and localities.

Second, the Japanese state has undergone a steady, albeit gradual, process of administrative and fiscal decentralization with the central government less and less committed to maintaining inter-regional equality. The ruling LDP undertook a number of wholescale administrative and fiscal decentralization reforms, begun in 1995 and accelerated under the Koizumi administration (2001–2006). As described earlier, these administrative decentralization measures reduced central government intervention and expanded local government discretion. A set of local government fiscal reforms (2002–2006) resulted in a sharp decline in grants and earmarked subsidies (including public works spending) to the regions. Periodic interventions of 'compensation' to shore up support in economically disadvantaged rural areas continue to occur (usually during election years, particularly prior to major local elections and the Upper House elections) (Kitamura 2014). But the central government has continued to encourage deregulation and self-sufficiency among regions, emphasizing regional diversity and competition between localities rather than pursue balanced growth.

Third, the stability of inter-governmental relations has been disrupted by LDP electoral volatility in the national arena which has occurred together with the emergence of non-partisan governors and mayors and regional parties at the local level. The formation of a Democratic Party of Japan (DPJ) government in 2009 created a historically unprecedented situation in Japan whereby the party in government at national level faced a majority of prefectural legislatures controlled by another party (the LDP). Such partisan incongruence across levels of government has generated a new dynamic and strains in inter-governmental relations. Since the late 1990s non-partisan governors – maintaining equal distance to all parties – have emerged with increasing frequency. These governors, many of them high-profile figures attracting considerable media attention, focused on cost-cutting and administrative reform at local level. Some, such as those in Osaka, Shiga, and Aichi, invented their own regional parties to consolidate power locally, resulting in complex strains with incumbent parties nationally and locally.

The three trends reflect an overall unravelling of the symbiotic ties linking local and national governments through the ruling party's vertically integrated organization. As these centre-local ties weakened, successive LDP and DPJ administrations pursued structural reforms including decentralization, privatization of public services such as the postal network and highways, as well as overall reduction in spending on public works and redistribution to local governments. Though opposed by local governments and partisans as measures which 'abandoned the regions' (*chihō kirisute*), these measures have, by and large, been

6 *Introduction*

implemented. Since the 1990s, then, Japan has become a far less 'peripherally oriented' political economy (Calder 1988) as regional inequalities increase. Demographic and economic crises in the regions during this period have not resulted in the kind of redistributive political compensation seen in the past.

The argument about Japan and in a broader context

Since the 1990s then, the equilibrium generated by the traditional symbiotic relations between the centre and regions under a dominant party have been replaced by disequilibrium and strains between the two levels in Japan.

What remains unanswered is how Japanese local politics can still matter under these new circumstances. What powers do Japanese local politicians both in legislature and executive have to influence national policy if traditional partisan channels of bottom-up policy-making have been severed? If we look at key conflicts between central and local governments, how have the various national and local political actors engaged in them? If there is a shift to more conflictual relations, what are the consequences of such a shift? What sort of new equilibrium are both centre and localities seeking to create out of this state of flux? These dynamics must be examined in order to be able to understand whether and how local governments matter in the new environment of the post-1990s Japan. This is the goal of this book.

To foretell our findings, the book argues that changes in the national political arena, fiscal and administrative decentralization, together with broader socio-economic trends, have led to a decoupling of once closely integrated national and local party systems in Japan. This process of 'decoupling' refers to the process of national and local party organizations becoming de-aligned in terms of electoral incentives and interests. These trends have had, and will continue to have, significant consequences for elections and policy-making in Japanese politics. These consequences include: greater externalized intra-party conflict; more conflictual inter-governmental relations between central and local governments controlled by different parties; and the rise of chief executives with agendas and resources increasingly autonomous of the national ruling party.

Although being a book primarily about Japan, the study seeks to contribute to a broader understanding of how local partisans shape national policy-making. Existing literature, mostly on federal systems, has theorized and investigated how the degree of state centralization, vertical integration for party organizations, and partisan congruence in different levels of government affect inter-governmental relations. Although these claims will be explored in greater depth in the succeeding chapters, we set out the key arguments that relate to the book's concerns.

First, an important literature on federal systems and party organizations has argued that nation-wide parties with integrated organizations create a balance between national and local interests, prevent one level from acting against the interest of the other, and stabilize inter-governmental relations to sustain the federal system (Riker 1964; Filippov *et al.* 2004). Hence, vertical integration of parties ensures damaging conflicts over policy between levels of government are contained and defused.

Second, following this logic of party integration, when different parties control different levels of government, these channels of vertical integration are lost and inter-governmental relations are expected to be more conflictual and strained (McEwen *et al.* 2012).

Third, local executives play an important role in inter-governmental negotiations and conflicts, particularly in states where partisan channels are weakened and local governments have considerable policy autonomy from the central government. (Chandler and Chandler 1987; Watts 1989). Moreover, directly elected executives generally tend to be weakly loyal agents to parties (Samuels and Shugart 2010). Thus governors or mayors – who are local presidents – who gain greater autonomy and resources through state decentralization are likely to challenge national policy programmes.

These theoretical expectations will be tested in our investigation of Japan's experience of multi-level conflict. First, we ascertain if inter-governmental relations have become more conflictual as the vertical integration of the LDP weakened over time since the mid-1990s. Second, we ascertain if periods of widespread partisan incongruence (during the DPJ administrations between 2009 and 2012) led to similarly or even more conflictual interactions between the central and local government than compared to periods of partisan congruence. Finally, as Japan combines both a parliamentary system at national level and a presidential system at local level (a relatively rare combination found in few of the older democracies), Japan provides a useful case of examining how partisan affiliation of local directly elected executives (governors and mayors) affect interactions with the national government over policy. Japanese local executives in theory gained greater powers as a result of decentralization reforms since 2000. We can thus ascertain if the expanded autonomy of prefectural governors generated more frequently conflictual relations with the central government. Close investigation of cases in which local executives challenged the centre should reveal if the expansion of local powers actually played a role in strengthening their position against the central government.

We thus test these existing expectations about the role of vertical integration, partisan congruence across levels, and partisan affiliation/autonomy of local chief executives on multi-level policy conflict through the case of Japan. Figure 1.1 provides an overview of the structure of the main arguments and their corresponding empirical chapters through the book.

The book also seeks to go beyond these claims and make some observations in a yet underdeveloped area: the question of how effective different types of multi-level channels are for securing local interests in national policy formation. Existing studies do not systematically analyse how such conflicts occur (the channels and resources used by both sides). Nor does existing theory provide guidance about which side tends to prevail when national and local preferences diverge.

The book's comparative ambition is, through its investigation of Japan and other cases, to model how local governments impact national policy-making

8 *Introduction*

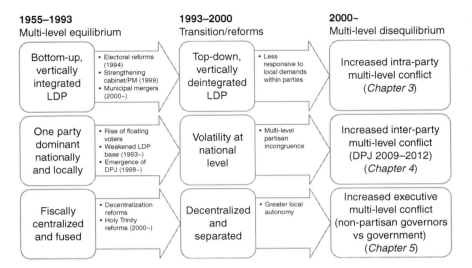

Figure I.1 Structure and overview of book.
Source: compiled by author.

through different types of multi-level conflict. To better generalize and put Japan in context, we investigate a few select comparative cases (Canada, Germany, and the UK) which exhibit different types of multi-level interaction and conflict.

The research strategy and outline

The book begins by clarifying the concept of multi-level conflict between national and local governments. The first chapter asks under what circumstances local preferences fail to be reflected in national policy, leading to confrontations and overt conflict between central and local governments. Two dimensions are theorized to be most important in determining whether inter-governmental relations will tend to cooperation or conflict. The first factor is the degree of local autonomy (state decentralization) that provides local actors with resources independent of the centre, reducing incentives to cooperate with central governments when preferences diverge. The second factor is the degree of partisan linkages between levels of government: where party organizations are vertically integrated and congruent parties control different levels of government, multi-level relations should tend to greater cooperation.

The next chapter provides an empirical description of how these two dimensions in post-war Japan were transformed by various institutional reforms and socio-economic trends in the mid-1990s. Japan's local governments gained greater autonomy, particularly fiscal autonomy, as a result of a series of decentralization reforms, while electoral reforms and the ensuing centralization of the

Introduction 9

party organization have resulted in less vertical integration within the major parties. Finally, national-level electoral volatility has increased, generating greater partisan incongruence across legislatures as well as chief executives less beholden to the national ruling party.

Chapter 3 will focus on how local partisans of the LDP sought upward influence even as the party's vertical integration weakened and interests across levels became de-aligned. Under this new context, local branches of the ruling party engaged in externalized instances of resistance to major national policy initiatives. It will demonstrate how such multi-level intra-party policy conflicts have increased, the resources both levels possessed and used in pushing their preferences, and outcomes of such conflicts.

Chapter 4 demonstrates how local partisans have sought upward influence in the national arena when facing a national government of an opposition party – i.e. under conditions of multi-level incongruence. Investigation will focus on a crucial and unprecedented period of incongruence in Japan which occurred between 2009 and 2012 when the DPJ in national government faced a majority of prefectural legislatures controlled by the LDP.

Chapter 5 analyses how directly elected chief executives (governors) impact national policy processes. It investigates how the partisan affiliation of local executives affects their willingness to cooperate or confront the national government over policy. The chapter also analyses to what extent decentralization reforms since 2000 have strengthened the local executives' ability and willingness to challenge national policy.

Finally, the last chapter seeks to broaden and deepen these arguments about the importance of local autonomy and partisan channels in inter-governmental relations. We do this by looking at central-local government dynamics in other developed and established democracies beyond Japan. We select the three comparative case countries (Canada, Germany, and the UK) that manifest very strong features on the two dimensions of importance: the degree of local autonomy and the degree of partisan inter-linkages between levels of government. The three countries not only represent the most likely cases to confirm our model, but also provide a variety of institutional configurations and features which affect multi-level dynamics that can be usefully compared to Japan.

We conclude with a discussion of the difficulties for the central government facing increasing territorial interests and how the centre has been trying to establish a new kind of equilibrium with local governments.

Why such a book now?

Since the mid-1980s or so, Japanese local politics has largely fallen off the radar of the active research programme in English language literature. There have been few book-length treatments in English recently. Scheiner (2006) is a major exception. The work explains how the LDP's strength at local level and the opposition's failure to build local organizations was the basis for the conservatives' dominance of national electoral politics in the post-war period. According

10 *Introduction*

to this model, the LDP was able to dominate local politics by providing particularistic benefits to dependent local communities in a fiscally centralized state. Policy processes were bottom-up, with local interests channelled through vertically integrated party organizations, creating a stabilizing bargain between regions and the centre under the LDP's dominant period.

As I have already indicated, this model seems increasingly less applicable now. Since 2000, Japan has undergone a degree of fiscal decentralization, the LDP has reduced 'pork barrel' spending to regions and the LDP fell out of power, if briefly, between 2009 and 2012. The centralization of candidate selection-procedures as well as policy-making initiative in the party leadership has meant a less vertically integrated party organization for the LDP. This book will fill in our understanding of how the breakdown of this traditionally symbiotic relationship between regions and centre has altered the role of local politics.

There are other excellent studies in the English literature tangential to my themes which I draw from, but these do not consider multi-level interactions over policy. One major study (Krauss and Pekkanen 2011) traces the changes in the LDP's parties' internal institutions (such as factions and *kōenkai* – personal campaign machines) in the post-war period. Although describing the weakening links between national and local legislators, their work does not really deal with, as I do, how local actors with their own particular interests and resources affect national policy processes. Other studies analyse the effects of municipal mergers on the LDP's electoral performance (Shimizu 2012; Horiuchi *et al.* 2015), the emergence of local parties and their entry into the national arena (Reed 2013), or how decentralization has led to the emergence of more autonomous chief executives and regional parties (Hijino 2013, 2014). Once again, these studies do not directly confront the question of how local influence on national policy is changing as a result of these trends.

There has been a growing and much richer body of research on local elections, party organizations, and party systems in the Japanese language literature since the 1990s. These include highly comprehensive studies investigating how the partisan composition of local legislatures and their interactions with the local executive affect local policy output (e.g. Soga and Machodori 2007; Sunahara 2011; Tsuji 2015). Others have looked variously at how party organizations, *kōenkai* structures, and local campaigning have changed as a result of electoral system reforms at national level.[2] Uekami (2013) theorizes how Japan's 'asymmetrical' multi-level electoral environments separate Japan's national and local party system, demonstrating how preferences for policy and leadership selection of national and local LDP actors have diverged. These above studies, though expanding our knowledge of local political processes and changing organizational dynamics, do not explore how these trends affect actual national policy outcomes through multi-level coordination and conflict.

Muramatsu's latest work (2010) has shown more broadly the breakdown of the traditional symbiotic links between the ruling party and bureaucracy since the 1990s, but also specifically its vital central-local linkages. The analysis draws from various survey data to show how interactions between national and local actors have broken down. His thesis largely overlaps with the book's assessment about what has changed, but leaves unanswered questions about how local political actors have engaged in this new disequilibrium to defend territorial interests.

Finally, an edited volume on multi-level dynamics within parties (Tatebayashi 2013) provides a useful theoretical framework to understand the LDP and DPJ in terms of levels of autonomy and degree of vertical integration. It is also a rich quarry of case studies investigating LDP and DPJ local branch interactions with the centre. The chapters in this volume, though, do not explicitly theorize and address how these multi-level dynamics affect policy conflicts between the regions and the centre. Moreover, the book leaves out the vital role chief executives play in this mix of interactions between national and local partisans.

Analysing the capacity of local governments and politicians to affect national policy initiatives is also an important addition to our understanding of Japanese domestic politics. First, it serves to refine the growing literature analysing how institutional changes have created conditions allowing more decisive, top-down leadership in Japan (Takenaka 2006). Although most of this literature recognizes some institutional features – primarily its strong bicameralism – which restrain leadership and dilute 'Westminsterization' (e.g. Mulgan 2000; Estévez-Abe 2006) in Japan, none have squarely assessed the constraints of local party organizations and local governments on top-down leadership.

My book thus will draw from advances made in comparative research on multi-level party politics and inter-governmental relations to Japan. It departs from preceding work, however, in that it seeks to understand the broader sources and extent of local power under this new, unsettled environment. It follows in the tradition of a body of work coming out of analyses of the 1970s and 1980s on political channels of influence in central-local government relations (Reed 1982; Muramatsu 1986) and partisan opposition in progressive local governments (Steiner *et al.* 1980). I hope to extend this frame of analysis to the past quarter century of Japanese local politics since the 1990s.

Notes

1 Neal Ascherson, 'Scottish independence: The biggest surge of creative democratic energy the country has ever seen must not go to waste', *Guardian*, 21 September 2015. Available at www.theguardian.com/commentisfree/2014/sep/21/scotland-independence-creative-energy-must-not-be-wasted [accessed 20 October 2016].
2 See special issue of *Leviathan*, vol. 51, Autumn 2012.

References

Calder, K.E. 1988, *Crisis and compensation: Public policy and political stability in Japan, 1949–1986*, Princeton University Press.
Chandler, W.M. and Chandler, M.A. 1987, 'Federalism and political parties', *European Journal of Political Economy*, vol. 3, no. 1, pp. 87–109.
Estévez-Abe, M. 2006, 'Japan's shift toward a Westminster system: A structural analysis of the 2005 lower house election and its aftermath', *Asian Survey*, vol. 46, no. 4, pp. 632–651.

12 *Introduction*

Filippov, M., Ordeshook, P.C., and Shvetsova, O. 2004, *Designing federalism: A theory of self-sustainable federal institutions*, Cambridge University Press.

Flanagan, S.C., Krauss, E.S., and Steiner, K. (eds) 1980, *Political opposition and local politics in Japan*, Princeton University Press.

Haider-Markel, D.P. 2014, 'Introduction: The study of state and local politics and policy', in D.P. Haider-Markel (ed.), *Oxford handbook of state and local government*, Oxford University Press.

Hijino, K.V.L. 2013, 'Liabilities of partisan labels: Independents in Japanese local elections', *Social Science Japan Journal*, vol. 16, no. 1, pp. 63–85.

Hijino, K.V.L. 2014, 'Intra-party conflicts over gubernatorial campaigns in Japan: Delegation or franchise?', *Party Politics*, vol. 20, no. 1, pp. 78–88.

Hijino, K.V.L. 2015, 'Regional inequality in 2014: Urgent issue, tepid election', in R. Pekkanen, S.R. Reed, and E. Scheiner (eds), *Japan decides 2014: The Japanese general election*, Palgrave Macmillan.

Horiuchi, Y. 2005, *Institutions, incentives and electoral participation in Japan: Cross-level and cross-national perspectives*, Routledge.

Horiuchi, Y., Saito, J., and Yamada, K. 2015, 'Removing boundaries, losing connections: Electoral consequences of local government reform in Japan', *Journal of East Asian Studies*, vol. 15, no. 1, pp. 99–125.

Ito, S. 2002, *Jichitai seisaku katei no dōtai: Seisaku inobeishon to hakyū*, Keio daigaku shuppankai.

Ito, S. 2006, *Jichitaihatsu no seisaku kakushin: Keikan jōrei kara keikan hō he*, Bokutakusha.

Jeffery, C. and Hough, D. 2003, 'Regional elections in multi-level systems', *European Urban and Regional Studies*, vol. 10, no. 3, pp. 199–212.

Kitamura, W. 2014, '*Chikishuken*' kaikaku, in M. Ito and T. Miyamoto (eds), *Minshutō Seiken no chosen to zasetsu: Sono keikenkara naniwo manabuka*, Nihon Keizai hyoronsha.

Krauss, E.S. and Pekkanen, R.J. 2011, *The rise and fall of Japan's LDP: Political party organizations as historical institutions*, Cornell University Press.

McEwen, N., Swenden, W., and Bolleyer, N. 2012, 'Intergovernmental relations in the UK: Continuity in a time of change?', *The British Journal of Politics & International Relations*, vol. 14, no. 2, pp. 323–343.

Mulgan, A.G. 2000, 'Japan's political leadership deficit', *Australian Journal of Political Science*, vol. 35, no. 2, pp. 183–202.

Muramatsu, M. 1975, 'The impact of economic growth policies on local politics in Japan', *Asian Survey*, vol. 15, no. 9, pp. 799–816.

Muramatsu, M. 1986, 'Center-local political relations in Japan: A lateral competition model', *Journal of Japanese Studies*, vol. 12, no. 2, pp. 303–327.

Muramatsu, M. 1988, *Chihōjichi*, Tokyo daigaku shuppankai.

Muramatsu, M. 2010, *Seikansukuramugata riidāshippu no hōkai*, Toyo keizai shimposha.

Peterson, P.E. 1981, *City limits*, University of Chicago Press.

Reed, S.R. 1982, 'Is Japanese government really centralized?', *Journal of Japanese Studies*, vol. 8, no. 1, pp. 133–164.

Reed, S.R. 2013, 'The survival of "third parties" in Japan's mixed-member electoral system', in K.E. Kushida and P.Y. Lipscy (eds), *Japan under the DPJ: The politics of transition and governance*, Walter H. Shorenstein Asia-Pacific Research Center.

Reif, K. and Schmitt, H. 1980, 'Nine second-order national elections: A conceptual framework for the analysis of European election results', *European Journal of Political Research*, vol. 8, no. 1, pp. 3–44.

Riker, W.H. 1964, *Federalism: Origin, operation, significance*, Little, Brown.

Introduction 13

Rodden, J. 2002, 'The dilemma of fiscal federalism: Grants and fiscal performance around the world', *American Journal of Political Science*, vol. 46, no. 3, pp. 670–687.

Samuels, D.J. and Shugart, M.S. 2010, *Presidents, parties, and prime ministers: How the separation of powers affects party organization and behavior*, Cambridge University Press.

Scheiner, E. 2006, *Democracy without competition in Japan: Opposition failure in a one-party dominant state*, Cambridge University Press.

Shimizu, K. 2012, 'Electoral consequences of municipal mergers', *Journal of East Asian Studies*, vol. 12, no. 3, pp. 381–408.

Soga, K. and Machidori, S. 2007, *Nihon no chihō seiji: Nigen daihyōsei seifu no seisaku sentaku*, Nagoya Daigaku Shuppan.

Steiner, K. 1965, *Local government in Japan*, Stanford University Press.

Steiner, K., Krauss, E.S., and Flanagan, S.E. (eds) 1980, *Political opposition and local politics in Japan*, Princeton University Press.

Sunahara, Y. 2011, *Chihō seifu no minshushugi: Zaisei shigen no seiyaku to chihō seifu no seisaku sentaku*, Yuhikaku.

Sunahara, Y. 2012, 'Seiken kōtai to reiki yūdō seiji', in T. Mikuriya (ed.), *'Seiji shudō' no kyōkun: Seiken kōtai wa nani wo motarasitaka*, Keiso shobo.

Takenaka, H. 2006, *Shushō shihai: Nihon seiji no henbō*, Chuko shinsho.

Tatebayashi, M. (ed.) 2013, *Seitōsoshiki no seijigaku*, Toyo Keizai shimpo.

Tsuji, A. 2015, *Sengo nihon chihō seijishiron: Nigen daihyōsei no rittaiteki bunseki*, Bokutakusha.

Tsuji, K. 1976, *Gyōsei no riron: Gyōseigaku kōza* (Vol. 1), Tokyo daigaku shuppankai.

Uekami, T. 2013, *Seitō seiji to fukinitsuna senkyo seido: Kokusei, chihō seiji, tōshu dōshutsu katei*, Tokyo daigaku shuppankai.

Watts, R.L. 1989, *Executive federalism: A comparative analysis* (vol. 26), IIGR, Queen's University.

1 Theories of local power and multi-level conflict

Why do territorial conflicts occur between the centre and periphery of a state? What determines the extent to which relations between the central government and local (regional) governments are cooperative or conflictual? More broadly, what are the sources of local power and influence on the centre, both during cooperative periods and moments of open conflict? These are some of the main theoretical questions which will be unpacked in this first chapter before exploring these issues for the local politics of Japan in the rest of the book.[1]

Two dimensions are theorized to be most important in determining whether inter-governmental relations will tend to cooperation or conflict. The first factor is the degree of local autonomy which provides local actors with resources independent of the centre, reducing incentives to cooperate with central governments when preferences diverge. The second factor is the degree of partisan linkages between the levels of government: where party organizations are vertically integrated and congruent parties control different levels of government, policy differences can be internally adjusted and multi-level relations should tend to greater cooperation.

When these two channels linking national and local levels of governments are weak, conflicts are more likely to emerge. These externalized conflicts will then be manifested in three areas: (1) within the same party organizations; (2) across legislatures at both levels of government controlled by different partisan forces; (3) across executives at both levels of government controlled by different partisan forces.

Based on these above theoretical discussions, the chapter will provide a set of hypotheses about multi-level conflict in Japan since the 1990s which will be tested in the following chapters.

What are multi-level policy conflicts?

Conflict, in general, begins when two or more actors in some type of relationship diverge in their interests. When these actors perceive that the overall benefits from maintaining cooperative (or indifferent) relations have become less than the potential gains to be made from opposing or challenging the other, the likelihood of conflict increases. And if, furthermore, there is an uncertainty

Local power and multi-level conflict 15

about outcomes in the event of conflict – i.e. one side is not dominant in the relationship[2] – conflict would further likely occur.

Applying this to the question of national and local relations in a state, conflicts occur when policy preferences diverge in one or more areas, the incentives to maintain overall cooperative relations weaken, and one or both sides believe it has the resources and capacity to challenge the other successfully. Moreover, there are conflicts which arise not just from divergence in policy area, but when one level of government seeks to expand its policy scope or arrogate more resources for itself from the other level. This is a recurring theme in the federalism literature (e.g. Filippov *et al.* 2004) where the federal party encroaches on subnational state powers and resources, or the reverse.

Interactions between national and local governments are described widely as inter-governmental relations (IGR). IGR constitutes 'the working connections that tie central governments to those constituent units that enjoy measures of independent and inter-dependent political power, governmental control and decision-making' (Agranoff 2004, p. 26). IGR occurs over various policy fields and differ in terms of intensity of inter-governmental interaction and the degree of cooperation, conflict, and compromise. IGR can be shaped by the design of the constitution, institutional framework for interaction, socio-economic and political factors, as well as personal qualities of involved actors (Bolleyer 2009).

Undertaking a comparative survey of IGR, Reed points to a number of consistent and important findings about the interdependence of local and national government (1986, pp. 6–11). In most countries, different levels of government share powers and jurisdictions and, as a result, cooperation is the dominant mode of relations. This interdependence also coexists with inevitable differences across levels in terms of priorities and goals as well as determining who will pay for and be politically responsible for shared policies. These disagreements, however, are resolved mainly through bargaining, rather than confrontation, since neither side can 'opt out' of their relationship (at least through normal procedures). Breakdown of the relationship may occur, in terms of non-cooperation and unilateral actions on either side, but as these are costly for both levels, participants over time learn to avoid confrontation. Japanese IGR is no exception to this pattern (Reed 1986).

Nevertheless, underlying tensions periodically erupt into publicized conflicts between levels of government. Why then should we care about these rare instances of multi-level conflict, apart from the drama and media interest generated by such confrontations? These externalized conflicts are of interest because they are empirically very useful in assessing local and national power. The regular exercise of local autonomy cannot tell us whether central governments are opposed to, but unable to prevent, these local decisions or are simply happy to have delegated these decisions to its local units. In other words, the delegation of power and the transfer of powers to local governments (or from national party HQ to its local branches) are 'observationally equivalent' (Van Houten 2009, p. 148).

16 *Local power and multi-level conflict*

It is only through observing the outcomes of conflict where both sides are in clear disagreement over policy preferences that we can assess which side has power over the other in determining outcomes. In such circumstances, both sides would resort to usually dormant resources (sanctions and threats) not used in regular bargaining to prevail. The efficacy of these resources becomes evident through the resolution of conflict. Thus multi-level conflicts and their outcomes can help reveal the substantial interests and powers held by both national and local levels of government as well as within parties.

How do such intra-level conflicts manifest themselves? First, confrontations across levels of government occur in many forms. They could be disagreements/ conflicts between levels over the implementation of either national initiatives or local policy. They can involve confrontations between the national government and a single local government, a cluster of local governments in a particular geographic region, or many, perhaps the majority, of local governments. They may involve single or several ministries, local bureaucrats, national and local politicians, or a combination of these various actors. They may involve situations where both levels of government are controlled by the same party or coalition of parties (congruent) or by different parties (incongruent). Furthermore, when local governments have both directly elected executives and legislatures, the local level could be united or divided across these two branches in their position vis-à-vis the national level.

The word 'conflict' is ambiguous and covers a range of intensity in confrontations between national and local governments. A conflict could be relatively localized and contained (e.g. disagreement over local interpretations of national programmes, local politicians merely voicing protest over national party programmes). But they could also be more full-blown non-cooperation of local governments (e.g. local executives refusing to provide permits for significant national projects such as the building of military bases) and full-scale revolts by local politicians to the national party leadership (e.g. local politicians refusing to support co-partisans in national elections or backing opposition parties nationally). In the gravest instances, breakdown of relations between national and local governments may lead to use of unilateral action, even use of force (such as Eisenhower federalizing the National Guard and dispatching it to Arkansas to defend the federal desegregation resolution).

It is also important to note the risks of extrapolating too much from the outcome of a single multi-level conflict. Central governments may prevail in some battles and not in others, depending on the context and the issue at hand. Either side may prioritize the particular policy outcome of a conflict more than the other, leading to greater commitment and willingness to fight for its preference. A study of a single conflict between governments will therefore not indicate the overall, cumulative power of either side. A series of conflicts across different policy areas and their outcomes may give us a better indication of the overall dynamics in IGR.

Perhaps more important than who wins what particular conflict is what the frequency of externalized conflict reveals. If one side is fully in control of the other in a relationship, conflicts would be unlikely to emerge as the dominated side would perceive any resistance as futile and costly. When there is uncertainty about outcomes, that is, either side believes in the possibility of prevailing, local (or national) governments would be more willing to challenge the other in open conflict. Thus, frequency of such conflicts, a state of disequilibrium, would indicate not only a breakdown in interdependent relations, but that neither side is dominant in the relationship.

Defining local politics and power

What determines this balance of power in an inter-governmental relationship? To answer this, we must first define the scope of local politics and then also define power.

Local politics refers to a wide range of actors and processes, but primarily we are referring to politicians, legislatures, executives, branches of national parties, regional parties, local government officials, as well as elections and policy-making at the subnational level (either in regions or municipalities). National politics, in turn, refers to a wide range of actors and processes, but primarily we are referring to national politicians, legislatures, national parties, headquarters and leadership (the party executive), central ministries and bureaucracies as well as national elections and policy-making. Some actors hold both national and local roles, and are hard to characterize as being either purely local or national. For example, national legislators, local party branches, and party members may represent local concerns and identify with local interest, but they are also, oftentimes, agents of the party at national level. Thus 'centre-local relations' connote various relationships of the multiple actors between national and local levels of government, some of whom are not clearly identifiable in either camp.

The concept of power is highly contested and multi-faceted, and its definitional debates need not trouble us here. The book applies Robert Dahl's standard definition of power where power is understood as influence over other actors in shaping outcomes: X has power over Y in so far as: (i) X is able, in one way or another,[3] to get Y to do something (ii) that is more to X's liking, and (iii) which Y would not otherwise have done (Goodin 1998, p. 7).

If this standard of power is applied to the relationship between central and local governments, then the following should be true: local governments have power over the central government in so far as they are able, in one way or another, to get the central government to do something which is in the local governments' interests and which the central government would not otherwise have done. More broadly speaking, local governments have relationships with other actors (local residents, local businesses, other local governments, non-governmental organizations, even foreign states). In general, then, local governments will be said to be powerful if their interests can prevail over the interests of other actors.

18 *Local power and multi-level conflict*

Local autonomy vs dependent inter-governmental relations

More commonly, local power is understood in terms of the extent of local government autonomy. Autonomy has been defined as the condition in which 'local governments themselves manage the collective affairs of the local citizens ... using their own political and administrative mechanisms, localities define their own interests'[4] (Muramatsu 1988, p. 126). Local autonomy thus focuses on the extent to which local governments have discretion to make decisions in local matters, free from intervention of the central government.

Local autonomy depends on the extent to which local governments have both legal authority as well as the necessary resources for policy-making. In federal states, local governments have final constitutional authority to act independently of the national government in at least one policy realm. In unitary states, local governments are granted authority over policy areas through national legislation, but such authority is not guaranteed constitutionally and can be rescinded by changes of legislation. In both federal and unitary states, the extent of policy areas granted to local governments varies. The greater the extent to which actual policy-making power resides in local governments, the more decentralized a state is said to be.

In practice, it is very difficult to measure overall levels of decentralization in a state. Local governments tend to possess sole policy discretion in some areas, not in others, and often share authority with the national level (or even supranational) over large areas of policy. Simply tallying up the different policy areas in which local governments have sole or shared administrative authority will not allow for effective comparisons of decentralization across states. To enable comparisons of the level of decentralization across states, political scientists have looked at how much of the public expenditure and revenues are generated by the local government as opposed to the national one. The assumption is thus: the larger the total expenditures of local governments, the larger the scope of their policy-making activity; and the larger the share of locally raised fiscal revenues for local governments, the greater the discretion they possess in spending this resource.

These simple indicators of 'expenditure decentralization' and 'fiscal decentralization', however, are considered problematic in that they do not account for the degree of central government controls and interference in how local governments choose to spend or raise their own revenues (Rodden 2006, p. 26). As mentioned earlier, in most states, local governments share policy-making authority and jointly fund major policy areas. Thus, simple figures of fiscal revenues or expenditures cannot provide a clear picture of local government autonomy in different policy domains.

However measured, one could argue that the more discretion and resources local governments possess to achieve their own policy goals, the less they need to fear in terms of intervention and retaliatory actions from the central government. This should mean that when local autonomy is high (where their discretion is guaranteed constitutionally in federal states or legislation provides for

Local power and multi-level conflict 19

strong local policy and fiscal discretion in unitary states), we should expect local governments to be more willing to challenge central government actions which they disagree with. Contrariwise, where local governments have limited or low autonomy, local actors would fear central government anger or retaliation and desist from challenging national policy decisions.

If both levels of government are separated from the other and only responsible for their respective policy areas, there appears to be little reason for multi-level policy conflict. Each level of government should simply mind its own business and go its own way. This is true in so far as governments at either level are unaffected by the autonomous policy decisions taken at the other level. Such complete isolation from the effects of policy at other levels of government is unlikely in modern states, however. Decisions at both local and national levels of government – however funded or decided within the remit of one level – often have spillover effects to other levels of government. Put another way, responsibilities and resources for a policy area could be constitutionally (or legally) allocated solely to either the national or local level of government. But the political and economic effects of these policy areas cannot be contained at one level. This, then, is a source of conflict across levels of government, even if they have clearly separated roles and power in 'layer cake' fashion.

An additional point should be made here from the perspective of central government 'autonomy'. Central governments may also be more or less dependent on (or autonomous from) local governments to legislate and implement national policy. Such conditions arise when central and local governments share legislating powers over national policy (such as through the German Bundesrat) and more commonly share the funding/implementation of local-national policies. In such a situation where the national government must rely on local governments for delivery of services, inter-governmental relations are expected to be cooperative.

Ultimately, the question of cooperation centres on how dependent – one could say fused – national and local governments are to each other. The more jurisdictions and functions are shared by levels of government, the more reluctant will either side be in engaging in conflicts which could damage cooperative relations necessary to achieve national and local policy goals. Such a state has been described as a 'fused' local government system where central and local governments share 'overlapping authority' (Muramatsu 1997, pp. 137–141). Under such conditions where both local and national governments lack autonomy, multi-level conflicts should be less likely.

Influence over national policy

Another important feature of local government power besides local autonomy is its capacity to influence national-level decisions. Local governments and political actors seek and exert influence over national policy areas – from inter-governmental fiscal transfers, developmental projects, environmental regulation, to immigration policy – which are vital to their interests. Without explaining

20 *Local power and multi-level conflict*

how and to what extent local political actors engage with and influence national policy direction, we will not have an accurate description of how 'powerful' local governments are.

Local governments may have formal channels of influencing national policy. One of the more direct and powerful channels would be the existence of second chambers in national legislatures that provide weight to territorial interests (such as the US Senate or more directly the German Bundesrat). Other channels would include various institutionalized fora for negotiation and bargaining between governments (such as the proliferation of committees and conferences attended by executives from federal and provincial governments in Canada). Other formal mechanisms include dispute resolution institutions that seek to resolve differences between national and local governments (such as the UK Joint Ministerial Committee founded to resolve differences between Westminster and the devolved regional governments). Though this is not an exclusive list, where these formal administrative channels function effectively, one would expect multi-level conflict to be less disruptive, or at least manifested through these more institutionalized frameworks.

In addition to these administrative channels, local actors possess partisan channels to influence national policy. These can be divided primarily into three channels, which, when frustrated or weakened, are expected lead to multi-level conflict.

The first are intra-party multi-level interactions (between the national headquarters and local branches within a party organization). The second are multi-level interactions between legislatures in different levels of government. The third are the dynamics between national and local executives at different levels of government.

These three main channels are affected by (1) whether party organizations are vertically integrated or de-integrated; (2) whether partisan composition of legislatures across levels of government are congruent or incongruent; and (3) whether local executives are more or less dependent on the political executive and/or ruling party at national level to achieve their preferences. When these channels of local influence over national policy are weakened by lack of vertical integration, lack of partisan congruence, and strong autonomy of local executives, we expect greater multi-level conflict.

We provide a discussion of how each of these variables potentially affects the frequency and intensity of multi-level policy conflict in turn.

Intra-party multi-level dynamics

A rich and influential body of research into federal systems (e.g. Riker 1964; Dyck 1996; Detterbeck and Renzsch 2003; Filippov *et al.* 2004) has highlighted how relations between central and local governments are vitally shaped by the degree of party integration, i.e. the extent of organizational linkages, interdependence, and cooperation between the central and regional branches of a state-wide party. Vertical integration within a party is seen to 'offer

Local power and multi-level conflict   21

mechanisms for brokering disagreements among constituent units' (Thorlakson 2009, p. 161).[5] Integrated parties have 'basic ideological similarity [at national and local levels] and few policy disputes' (Dyck 1996, p. 162).

Integrated parties emerge from electoral and institutional environments in which both national and local branches are equally incentivized to maintain the party's reputation, label, and overall strength.[6] Thus, an integrated party can be defined as

> one in which, for national politicians, the long-term strategy of preserving the party's overall electoral coalition takes precedence over the short-term tactic of seeking immediate gains from challenging local and regional autonomy ... Conversely, local and regional politicians will not seek to disrupt unduly the functions of the federal government for fear of damaging the electoral standing of national politicians for their party, and thereby, their own subsequent electoral chances.
>
> (Filippov *et al.* 2004, p. 194)

Integration occurs when national and local politicians are mutually dependent for their re-election and policy implementation. Both sides of an integrated party thus 'mutually delegate' decision-making power to better achieve mutually beneficial goals (Filippov *et al.* 2004, p. 195). Open disputes which may damage the party label are avoided and both sides seek 'to negotiate internal differences out of public view and, in a self-regulating way, to otherwise repress disruptive issues'[7] (Filippov *et al.* 2004, p. 186). A lack of integration thus tends to greater intra-party conflicts across levels of government, even when both levels are controlled by the same party.

Existing literature has investigated how the degree of vertical party integration is shaped by electoral contexts, central-local government relations, as well as the ideology and historical origins of the parties themselves. When parties compete in national and local electoral contexts that are similar (similar or identical electoral systems, district magnitudes, electoral cycle), these conditions generate electoral incentives for national and local politicians to maintain party unity and policy cohesion. This in turn facilitates party integration (Filippov *et al.* 2004; Tatebayashi 2013). On the other hand, parties that compete in differing electoral environments at national and local levels (for example under different electoral systems or electoral cycles) will tend towards weaker vertical integration.

Others have argued that the degree of state centralization shapes the structure of the party organization (and vice versa). Where the state is highly decentralized and central governments weak, there is less incentive for local politicians to cooperate in order to capture the national levers of power. This could lead to centrifugal effects in the party organization, weakening the party's vertical integration (e.g. Riker 1964; Chhibber and Kollman 2009). Similarly, where national and local governments do not share responsibility for the funding and implementing of various administrative functions, there is less need for cooperation among levels of the same party. This separation of functions

22   *Local power and multi-level conflict*

(referred to as 'jurisdictional' division of labour between levels of government) compared to a sharing of functions (referred to as 'functional' division of labour) is seen to contribute to a bifurcation of national and local levels of the party (Chandler and Chandler 1987). In states where local governments possess a greater share of exclusive policy functions, there is less incentive for local party organizations to cooperate with the national level. Local elites face less risk in challenging the centre over policy direction and the distribution of resources, resulting in more conflictual multi-level relations.

Finally, others have argued that it is not just the external environment but also factors endogenous to the party which shape the degree of vertical integration within parties. These factors include the genetic origins and ideology of parties as well as the strategic choices of party leaders in shaping the levels of vertical integration and centralization of party organizations. For example, socialist parties have tended towards more centralized and hierarchical multi-level organizations, whereas green parties have emphasized greater local autonomy within party organizations (Panebianco 1988; Detterbeck 2012). Party leaders facing increasingly diverging local electoral environments, e.g. in the face of regional parties and separatist demands, have also been seen to choose to relax top-down control and delegate greater autonomy to local party organizations (Van Biezen and Hopkin 2006). This in turn could lead to less integration within the party organization as local branches pursue strategies and goals divergent from the national HQ. Thus strategic agency also plays a role in shaping party organizations.

Whatever the complex combination of causes, where parties are weakly integrated, there will be fewer opportunities for internally resolving differences between national and local interests represented by the party HQ and local branches. Less integration thus spells greater multi-level conflict.

Inter-party multi-level dynamics

Multi-level interactions occur not just within parties, but across different parties that compete and hold public offices in national and local legislatures. Whether the same or different parties control governments at different levels – i.e. the degree of multi-level partisan congruence – is another key variable identified as shaping the nature of inter-governmental relations (Chandler and Chandler 1987; Renzsch 1999; Burgess 2006). Party congruence refers to a situation when governments at different levels are controlled by the same political parties, while party incongruence refers to situations when different levels of government are controlled by different parties (McEwen *et al.* 2012, p. 190).

What, then, causes multi-level incongruence? Three different types of factors can be highlighted briefly. The first cause is the existence of institutional differences in the electoral environments of both levels (where electoral systems and cycles differ) resulting in different parties being represented at national and local level. The second cause is the existence of voter logics/strategies which vary between elections at different levels of government. For example, if voters perceive of local elections as referenda for the performance of national parties and seek to 'balance' or 'punish' national ruling parties by voting for opposition parties at local level, national and local partisan incongruence emerges. The third cause is the existence of heterogeneous socio-political conditions across a state. These territorial differences in interests and identities lead to the emergence of representation at local level that diverges from the national average. In areas where certain interests or groups are highly concentrated, certain parties may be more represented locally than in the national average: e.g. regional parties with concentrated support in certain regions or the prevalence of socialist parties in urban or manufacturing areas. Territorial concentrations locally can result in national-local incongruence in party systems.

Under congruent conditions state-wide parties can provide organizational linkages and integrative functions across jurisdictional divides in coordinating policy, information exchange, and conflict resolution. Without these links, greater differences in policy preferences between levels of government may emerge. Such a situation would make policy coordination difficult, especially when authority over policy implementation and funding is shared across national and local levels of government (McEwen *et al.* 2012, p. 190). Partisan congruence and incongruence become less important, however, if parties are not integrated. When parties at both levels do not have strong vertical linkages, they are unlikely to resolve intra-party differences or to engage in opposition across levels of government regardless of whether both levels of government are controlled by the same or different parties.

In political systems which have presidential systems of separately elected executives at national and/or local level, partisan dynamics across levels of government are more complicated than in systems where both levels are parliamentary with only a directly elected legislature. In these cases, the executive and legislature at national level can be controlled by the same party (united government) or different parties (divided government), facing local government divided or united across their legislature and executive. In some very rare cases (e.g. Japan, Italy, and some councils in the UK), a parliamentary government at national level (single or coalition government) exists alongside local presidential systems with an elected governor/mayor and elected local legislature.

Multi-level incongruence also refers to a complex situation of different parties singly or in coalition controlling different branches of government to different degrees. For example, 'full incongruence' occurs when both levels are controlled by completely different partisan forces, as opposed to 'partial incongruence' where, through coalition governments, at least one party is in coalition governments at both national and local levels. Full incongruence is expected to lead to more pronounced effects on multi-level relations (McEwen *et al.* 2012, p. 191). An additional consideration in local politics is the frequent appearance of nonpartisan chief executives and legislators that are affiliated to no party (or perhaps only to a regional party with no presence nationally).

In general, certain combinations of electoral and executive systems can be said to make multi-level partisan incongruence and conflict more likely. When

24   *Local power and multi-level conflict*

both national and local executives are chosen by majoritarian systems (under single-member district electoral rules), relations are likely to be more conflictual than when executives are selected from more proportional electoral systems.[8] Bolleyer (2006) argues that where power is shared in coalition governments at both levels there is a higher likelihood of partisan congruence (overlap) in the ruling governments at national and local level, compared to those under power-concentrating majoritarian systems. Where power is divided (bicameral or presidential systems), the likelihood of partisan players using their veto powers is higher and likely to limit the creation of stable/institutionalized IGR (Bolleyer 2006). For all the possible combinations, where legislative and executive power is under united partisan control, that level of government would be able to better unify policy positions and act against the other level of government. Following the logic of veto-player theory (Tsebelis 2002), less partisan divisions in either national or local government should generally result in more unified and stronger negotiating positions against the other level of government.

In sum, partisan in/congruence, like the vertical integration of parties, is caused by a variety of factors including electoral and executive system design, voter strategies, and heterogeneous socio-economic condition across a state. Whatever its source, the expectations are that the greater the degree of partisan congruence across levels of government controlled by vertically integrated parties, the more likely multi-level relations would be cooperative. Contrariwise, where partisan incongruence is widespread and parties competing at both levels are integrated, we should expect greater multi-level conflicts and tensions.

Inter-executive multi-level dynamics

Multi-level interactions occur within parties, between legislatures, and also between the executives of both national and local levels of government. In this third and final channel, the local political executive (leader of the ruling party in the local legislature or a directly elected governor) interacts with the national political executive (the prime minister and ministers) in different ways. In one extreme, the local executive may basically act as an agent of the national government, possessing little autonomy and loyally implementing national policies. On the other extreme, the local executive may be a highly autonomous actor who consistently represents territorial interests against the state, challenging national authority and policy whenever necessary. These types of interactions will determine the nature of upward influence local executives will have on national policy as well as how cooperative/conflictual relations will be.

Whether a local executive is more an agent or an autonomous actor will depend on many variables, but these factors can be subsumed into two variables, namely: (1) extent of the local executive's formal policy-making powers (local autonomy); (2) the degree to which the local executive depends on the national ruling party to achieve his/her policy and electoral goals (party-dependence). The expectation is that, where the local executive possesses formal discretion and political resources independent of the national government and/or ruling

Local power and multi-level conflict 25

party, the local executive will be more willing to challenge national decisions without fear of losing vital resources held by the national executive.

If local executives lack policy autonomy, they would be compelled to cooperate with the national level to achieve local goals. Under such conditions, local governments and executives would be less willing to challenge the national government more openly. On the other hand, when local government autonomy is considerable and central government interference in local decision-making limited (such as occurs under highly decentralized states with separated jurisdictions), we should expect local executives to be more willing to confront the national government. Thus greater policy autonomy at local level should contribute to more frequent multi-level conflicts.[9]

Local executives may also depend on partisan support in the local legislature to pass their budgets and policies. The more a governor or local premier depends on the local branch of a national ruling party for local legislative support, the less he/she will be prepared to challenge the national executive on various national policy positions. This is particularly the case if this ruling party is well integrated and both levels united in responding to a challenge from the local executive as a threat to the party as a whole. On the other hand, if a local executive does not rely on the ruling party at local level, but on the legislative backing of other parties (opposition or regional parties) in legislature, it would have less to fear in challenging the national executive over policy. A similar dynamic exists in terms of the local chief executives' dependency on the ruling party at national level for his or her re-election. If local executives depend on national partisan affiliation, party nomination, campaign mobilization, and other support such as funding for their own elections, their willingness to challenge the national ruling party over policy will be constrained.

Finally, in local government systems with directly elected chief executives (governors and mayors), the local executive will have a more complex relationship to the national and local party organizations than local executives from local government systems that are parliamentary. Directly elected executives (presidents) tend to be less loyal and less dependent on legislative parties, than executives elected and given confidence by a legislature (prime ministers) (Samuels and Shugart 2010). In the same way, governors and mayors who are local presidents often tend to be partisan 'outsiders', and appeal to the general electorate as non-partisans. Unlike legislators with narrower constituencies, they view themselves as representatives of the whole local government, rather than representatives of a party, constituency, or particular social/interest groups (Soga and Machidori 2007). Thus for directly elected chief executives, we expect party backing in elections to be less important than the extent of their administrative powers and financial resource to achieve their goals.

In sum, where decentralization expands local powers, independent financial resources are available, and the ruling party at local level does not control the local legislature, the local executive is likely to be more willing to put up a fight against national policy.

The two dimensions shaping multi-level conflict

To recap, local governments and actors have varying degrees of power over local matters and influence over national matters. The extent of this power is shaped by the structure and administrative features of the local government system but also from the party organizations and partisan configuration of both levels of government. From this discussion two dimensions were theorized to be most important in determining whether inter-governmental relations will tend to cooperation or conflict: the degree of local autonomy (how closely fused central and local governments are administratively) and the degree of partisan congruence and vertical integration between the levels of government. Expressed formally, we predict that:

1 Where local governments possess limited local autonomy and are more fused with the central government (share delivery and funding of administrative functions), multi-level interactions would tend to greater cooperation.

1a Where local governments possess greater local autonomy and are less fused administratively with central government (possesses exclusive jurisdiction over various functions), multi-level interactions would tend to greater conflict.

2 Where local governments possess partisan channels to influence national policy (through vertically integrated party organizations and congruent partisan control of both levels of government), multi-level interactions would tend to greater cooperation.

2a Where local governments lack partisan channels to influence national policy (due to incongruent partisan control of both levels of government), multi-level interactions would tend to greater conflict.

Combining these two dimensions, the following four categories emerge as indicated in Figure 1.1.

In the figure there are four outcomes: a quadrant characterized by multi-level cooperation and stability and three other quadrants characterized by differing types of inter-governmental conflict. The respective quadrants include the different periods for Japan and three other countries (Canada, Germany, and the UK) which will be analysed in Chapter 6.[10]

The top-right quadrant (1) reflects conditions of low local autonomy and high partisan congruence, in which interactions between national and local governments tend to greatest stability and cooperation. Conflicts, though they may arise, will be internally resolved through the mutual incentives to cooperate over shared responsibilities as well as through partisan linkages and congruence. It should be a stable bargain, where both sides mutually gain and seek to maintain the reciprocal relationship, and avoid measures that may damage relations in the long term. Japan (1955–1993) under LDP dominance with its highly congruent national and local governments and a highly fused system of low local autonomy would fall in this category. Germany will also be found here as it has

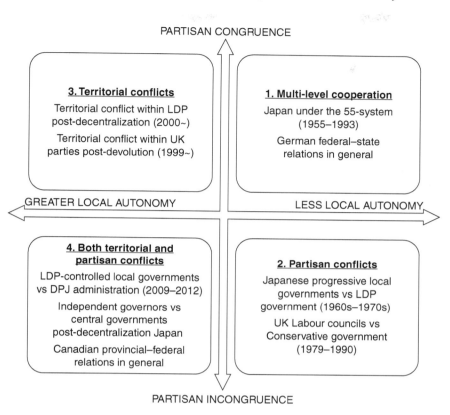

Figure 1.1 Local autonomy and partisan congruence shaping multi-level conflict.
Source: compiled by author.

highly integrated parties and party systems at national and local level as well as closely fused federal-state relations, resulting in cooperative IGR.

The bottom-right quadrant (2) would involve a situation when different parties control different levels of government under a centralized system of limited local autonomy. Despite low local autonomy, local governments under control of opposition parties may challenge national governments as a partisan strategy. These challenges would involve local governments opposing national policy regardless of territory-specific interests. That is, local partisans would use whatever local governments they control as a platform to attack national policies. Conflict would therefore take place primarily over universal, programmatic issues, and ideological matters that divide the parties. National-level opposition parties (or regional parties) may also come to power locally by opposing ruling party positions on policy issues which affect specific regions. In this case, the multi-level conflict under partisan incongruence would be more territory-specific. But under conditions of lower local autonomy, we would expect party competition to be nationalized and local partisans to primarily mount challenges to nation-wide policies affecting the whole state, not just specific territories. The period of opposition party control of urban areas in Japan (circa 1965–1975) and the resistance of opposition-controlled UK local councils to national policies under the Thatcher administration (1979–1990) are examples of partisan incongruence under centralized (fused) local government conditions.

The top-left quadrant (3) captures decentralized conditions where local actors possess strong local autonomy, but national and local governments are congruently controlled. In this context, greater local autonomy will incentivize voters and partisans to focus on local policy solutions and this may lead them to diverge from national party positions, even if they are supporters (members) of the same party at both levels. Thus, despite partisan congruence, high local autonomy will result in multi-level conflicts emerging within the party, between its national and local organizations. These tensions and conflicts under conditions of higher local autonomy will be primarily based on territory-specific issues. Here we can place the intra-party tensions emerging under conditions of partisan congruence within the national ruling party and their local branches in post-decentralization Japan as well as the conflicts between UK national ruling parties and their branches in the devolved regions (e.g. Scotland and Wales).

Finally, in the bottom-left quadrant (4) when local governments possess high levels of local autonomy and partisan incongruence exists, multi-level conflicts will likely become prevalent and unrestrained. In this combination of features, both national and local governments would be prepared to challenge the other if their respective interests are threatened, making this condition the most conflictual of all quadrants in the figure. Local executives would be less dependent on national governments administratively and national ruling parties for their own elections or local policy goals, resulting in territorial-based challenges against national policy. In addition, partisan incongruence may trigger local partisan challenges against the central government (although in highly decentralized systems, such a situation would be less likely as national and local party systems tend to be separated arenas). Both partisan and territorial conflicts are possible in this quadrant. Japan post-decentralization and under conditions of partisan incongruence (DPJ administration 2009–2012) evinces these features. Canada has a highly separated local government system with divergent party systems at national and local level generating prevalent multi-level conflict. It can thus also be placed in this quadrant.

These two dimensions of local autonomy and partisan congruence generate multi-level conflict in three areas: those that occur within parties, between different parties, and between executives at different levels of government. In Table 1.1, the three types of multi-level conflict are summarized in terms of their causes and features. Below these descriptions are examples of such conflict that will be investigated in the rest of the book.

Local power and multi-level conflict 29

Table 1.1 Types of multi-level conflict, their features, and examples

Type of multi-level conflict	Intra-party conflict	Inter-party conflict	Inter-executive conflict
Proximate causes	Vertical integration within party organization weakens	Partisan incongruence occurs	Local autonomy expands
Underlying causes	Diverging electoral systems, electoral cycles and/or executive systems, decentralization	Diverging electoral systems, electoral cycles, and/or executive systems	Decentralization
	National and local partisans less (or unequally) committed to maintain party label and policy unity	Voters see local election as 'second order' referendums/ local government as arena to challenge national ruling party	Local executives less dependent on national ruling party executive for local electoral and policy goals
Manifestation	Territory-specific conflicts	Territory-specific conflicts/nation-wide ideological partisan conflicts	Territory-specific conflicts
Resolution	Intra-party compromises or local partisans continue to resist/defect	Policy cooptation by centre or continued conflict	Inter-government compromises or continued conflict
Examples from Japan covered in the book	Territorial policy conflicts – primarily between rural branches of LDP and national party executive (postal privatization, TPPs) or NIMBY issues (nuclear power, public work project)	Territorial policy conflicts (TPP, petition system) and NIMBY issues (dams, nuclear power) + ideological partisan conflicts across all regions (foreigner voting rights, security issues, welfare, and environmental regulations in the 1970s, e.g.)	Conflicts over Okinawa bases, shared funding, and public works projects between central government and governors
Examples from casc countries covered in the book	Tensions with branches in devolved regions for UK parties/tensions over fiscal equalization between German provinces	Conflicts with Labour-held local councils under UK Conservative government	Fiscal equalization conflicts between federal and provincial executives in Canada

Source: Compiled by author.

Hypotheses for Japan

These theoretical expectations lead to a number of hypotheses for multi-level relations in Japan since the 1990s, which will be investigated empirically in the relevant chapters.

First, during the LDP's predominant period (1955–1993), the state was fiscally and administratively centralized, but central and local governments shared in the funding and implementation of large areas of policy creating a 'fused-type' local government system. The Japanese state was also characterized by strong partisan multi-level linkages: a party (LDP) with strong vertical linkages between mutually dependent local and national politicians was in power at the national level and most local governments. Under these conditions, the LDP's dominant period was characterized by cooperative and stable multi-level relations. The one source of overt multi-level conflict came under conditions of partisan incongruence, when opposition-party-backed governors and mayors captured offices in urban areas during the progressive local government era (1960s–1970s) (Chapter 2).

Second, electoral and decentralization reform since the mid-1990s reduced the fusion of national and local governments as well as weakened partisan linkages between the two levels. In the context of less fused central-local government relations, we expect increased frequency of multi-level conflicts and tensions within parties (Chapter 3). We also expect these conflicts within parties to be primarily territory-specific, focusing on local actions seeking to defend local interests. In contrast, the multi-level conflicts under partisan incongruence of the DPJ administration would also include programmatic and ideological, rather than just territorial, challenges to the central government (Chapter 4).

Third, prefectural governors in Japan have gained more discretionary powers and face less central government intervention as a result of decentralization since the mid-1990s. There has also been a trend of governors distancing themselves from the national parties, standing as non-partisan candidates in the same period. We expect that under these conditions of increased autonomy, the frequency of local executives involved in multi-level conflicts have increased generally. Moreover, we expect these challenges by independent local executives to be based on territorial interests, rather than on partisan, ideological divisions between national and local governments (Chapter 5).

Comparative case countries besides Japan will also be investigated on these two dimensions (Chapter 6). Germany will be investigated as a case with low local autonomy (a high integration of national and local policy-making processes) and comparatively low levels of partisan incongruence. The UK will be investigated as an example of a highly centralized state, that has undergone increased local autonomy, where partisan incongruence is common. Canada is a prime example of a highly decentralized state where party systems are separated at both levels and party congruence limited. We expect the three countries to evince high levels of multi-level cooperation (Germany), multi-level partisan

Local power and multi-level conflict   31

conflicts (UK before devolution), multi-level territorial conflicts (UK after devolution), and multi-level territorial and partisan conflicts (Canada).

Existing literature thus provides us with expectations as to whether we should expect national and local politics to interact in a cooperative or conflictual manner. We emphasize here that our theoretical predictions are primarily about the frequency and type of such multi-level conflicts. We argue that the three types of conflicts within parties, between parties, and executives at national and local levels should increase or decrease depending on the conditions of local autonomy and partisan incongruence. Moreover, under conditions of partisan incongruence, multi-level conflicts will not only emerge over region-specific differences in policy with the national executive, but also over more programmatic/nation-wide partisan challenges to policy.

Our theories therefore do not predict in any way how these multi-level conflicts will play out and through what channels they will take place. For this understanding, each of the chapters provides descriptions and analysis of case examples of these conflicts. First, these case studies are used to confirm the causal mechanism that greater local autonomy and/or partisan incongruence is actually causing these conflicts. Second, these representative case studies are compared to generate inferences about how such conflicts actually develop and resolve themselves.

Multi-level interactions in Japan – which have been transformed from a cooperative to a more strained and conflictual one in recent years – should provide instances in exploring these questions. We turn first to understanding how a multi-level equilibrium emerged in the post-war period in Japan and has been gradually dismantled since the 1990s.

Notes

1 For those readers primarily interested in the Japanese case, this theoretical chapter can be skimmed or skipped without impeding ability to follow arguments and descriptions put forward in the more empirical chapters on Japan (Chapters 2–5).

2 There are many instances of conflict between two groups where one side is clearly dominant and the other side unlikely to prevail. In such cases, the subordinate side perhaps perceives of a chance, however slim, of altering the relationship through conflict. More likely, they may perceive the costs of the current arrangement to be so great (or benefits so little) that the risks/costs of engaging in conflict are deemed negligible and the symbolic/normative benefits of engaging in externalized resistance to be worthwhile. Consider resistance movements under occupation or revolts by oppressed minority groups against dominant states as examples.

3 This influence could be exerted explicitly through open coercion or implicitly, through control of agendas and ideas – the second and third 'faces' of power delineated by Lukes (1986), or in whatever shape or form. What is important is that one side has these various levers/resources of power and uses them to influence others in their own interest.

4 Autonomy can also be understood as the product of two functions: 'self-steering and self-control'. Autonomy is the power of government to take action based on their own judgement (self-steering) and, using the information they obtain about the

32 *Local power and multi-level conflict*

results, to correct any mistakes in judgement (self-control). This self-steering and self-control is often called independence (Muramatsu 1988, p. 127).

5 Thorlakson (2009) finds variation within integrated parties in terms of local autonomy and 'upward influence' on national party matters. In a survey of federal parties, she finds that some are highly integrated, yet authority over key local decisions – discipline, policy campaigning, internal organization, and candidate and leader selection – are held tightly by the party headquarters. Others are integrated while providing greater local autonomy and channels of upward influence on the national party matters.

6 According to Filippov *et al.* (2004, p. 192), the seven criteria for an integrated party are:

1 The party's organization exists and fields candidates at all levels of government.
2 The party's electoral success at the national level facilitates the electoral success of its candidates at the local and regional level.
3 The regional and local organizations and candidates of the party retain sufficient autonomy, to direct their own campaigns.
4 National platforms are acceptable in local terms and are interpreted in local terms by local politicians campaigning on behalf of national parties in national elections.
5 Every component of the party contributes to the party's overall success.
6 Winning nationally requires that the party and its candidates campaign locally.
7 The offices the party seeks to fill through election at local levels control valuable resources and those who fill them can implement policy that can either aid or thwart the policies implemented at the national level.

These conditions result through, among others, decentralized system of intra-party candidate selection, simultaneous elections at different political levels, and representation of the state level in second chambers nationally.

7 From the perspective of integration as a form of 'mutual delegation', it may be misleading to speak of one level of the party having 'power over' another level. If both sides depend on each other and are committed to maintaining a relationship, the relationship cannot be understood in terms of one side dominating another with directions of influence going only in one way. Since an integrated party is based on mutual dependence and delegation, influence can occur both upwards and downwards.

In a similar vein, recent models of party organizations in unitary states also suggest more fluid and bargained relations between national and local elements, challenging the traditional emphasis on the hierarchical nature of their organizations.

Classical party models – primarily from Western European democracies – such as the mass membership party (Michels), the cadre party (Duverger), the catch-all party (Kirchheimer), the electoral professional party (Pannebianco), and the cartel party (Katz and Mair) – were based on the concept of a party as a single identifiable organization with a single locus of control (Carty 2004). These classical conceptions have been challenged by authors who emphasize how party organizations compete in different electoral environments and territories, which necessitates a territorial response. This 'stratarchical imperative' has led, in some conceptions, to the party leadership delegating autonomy to its local branches in a delegation model (Van Houten 2009) or for national and local levels to strike mutually beneficial bargains across levels in a franchise model (Carty 2004).

8 Personal communication with Sunahara Yosuke, 6 November 2016.

9 One caveat would be that the decentralization of administrative authority does not necessarily guarantee local governments the financial resources to achieve their goals. It is only when the local government possesses both financial resources and administrative discretion that their local executive would be more willing to challenge the centre than local governments which do not have these resources.

10 Naturally, in any given state, the national government and ruling party face a number of different local governments controlled by either their own or opposition parties, led by executives with different degrees of dependence on the national party. These characterizations of cooperative or conflictual multi-level relations reflect the most prevalent type of interactions between national and local governments at any period of time.

References

Agranoff, R. 2004, 'Autonomy, devolution and intergovernmental relations', *Regional & Federal Studies*, vol. 14, no. 1, pp. 26–65.

Bolleyer, N. 2006, 'Federal dynamics in Canada, the United States, and Switzerland: How substates' internal organization affects intergovernmental relations', *Publius: The Journal of Federalism*, vol. 36, no. 4, pp. 471–502.

Bolleyer, N. 2009, *Intergovernmental cooperation: Rational choices in federal systems and beyond*, Oxford University Press.

Burgess, M. 2006, *Comparative federalism: Theory and practice*, Routledge.

Carty, R.K. 2004, 'Parties as franchise systems: The stratarchical organizational imperative', *Party Politics*, vol. 10, no. 1, pp. 5–24.

Chandler, W.M. and Chandler, M.A. 1987, 'Federalism and political parties', *European Journal of Political Economy*, vol. 3, no. 1, pp. 87–109.

Chhibber, P. and Kollman, K. 2009, *The formation of national party systems: Federalism and party competition in Canada, Great Britain, India, and the United States*, Princeton University Press.

Detterbeck, K. 2012, *Multi-level party politics in Western Europe* (Vol. 2), Basingstoke: Palgrave Macmillan.

Detterbeck, K. and Renzsch, W. 2003, 'Multi-level electoral competition: The German case', *European Urban and Regional Studies*, vol. 10, no. 3, pp. 257–269.

Dyck, R. 1996, 'Relations between federal and provincial parties', in B. Tanguay and A.G. Gagnon (eds), *Canadian parties in transition*, Nelson, pp. 160–189.

Filippov, M., Ordeshook, P.C., and Shvetsova, O. 2004, *Designing federalism: A theory of self-sustainable federal institutions*, Cambridge University Press.

Goodin, R.E. 1998, *A new handbook of political science*, Oxford University Press on Demand.

Lukes, S. 1986. *Power*, New York University Press.

McEwen, N., Swenden, W., and Bolleyer, N. 2012, 'Introduction: Political opposition in a multi-level context', *The British Journal of Politics & International Relations*, vol. 14, no. 2, pp. 187–197.

Muramatsu, M. 1988, *Chihōjichi*, Tokyo daigaku shuppankai.

Muramatsu, M. 1997 [Scheiner and White translation], *Local power in the Japanese state*, University of California Press.

Panebianco, A. 1988, *Political parties: Organization and power*, Cambridge University Press.

Reed, S.R. 1986, *Japanese prefectures and policymaking*, University of Pittsburgh Press.

Renzsch, W. 1999, 'Party competition in the German federal state: New variations on an old theme', *Regional & Federal Studies*, vol. 9, no. 3, pp. 180–192.

Riker, W.H. 1964, *Federalism: Origin, operation, significance*, Little, Brown.

Rodden, J. 2006, *Hamilton's paradox: The promise and peril of fiscal federalism*, Cambridge University Press.

34 Local power and multi-level conflict

Samuels, D.J. and Shugart, M.S. 2010, *Presidents, parties, and prime ministers: How the separation of powers affects party organization and behavior*, Cambridge University Press.

Soga, K. and Machidori, S. 2007, *Nihon no chihō seiji: Nigen daihyōsei seifu no seisaku sentaku*, Nagoya Daigaku Shuppan.

Tatebayashi, M. (ed.) 2013, *Seitōsoshiki no seijigaku*, Toyo Keizai shimpo.

Thorlakson, L. 2009, 'Patterns of party integration, influence and autonomy in seven federations', *Party Politics*, vol. 15, no. 2, pp. 157–177.

Tsebelis, G. 2002, *Veto players: How political institutions work*, Princeton University Press.

Van Biezen, I. and Hopkin, J. 2006. 'Party organization in multi-level contexts', in D. Hough and C. Jeffery (eds), *Devolution and electoral politics*, Manchester University Press, pp. 14–36.

Van Houten, P. 2009, 'Multi-level relations in political parties: A delegation approach', *Party Politics*, vol. 15, no. 2, pp. 137–156.

2 Local autonomy and partisan linkages in post-war Japan

Strengthening local government and improving local democracy has been a recurring theme in post-war Japan. US occupation authorities believed that decentralization and democratization of local government were vital in preventing a return to pre-war militarism and authoritarianism. During the early post-war years, scholars and activists argued for greater civic participation and civic-mindedness at local level as a key step to realizing popular sovereignty in Japan's fledgling democracy (Narumi 1994). In the 1960s and 1970s, directly elected governors and mayors backed by socialist and communist parties emerged across Japan, successfully challenging the national agenda of unbridled economic growth. This 'progressive government period' was followed by 'a period of localism' (*chihō no jidai*) and then a 'period of local revolt' (*chihō hanran no jidai*). These slogans embodied hopes that the regions could act as a counterweight and stimulus against an increasingly complacent centre dominated by the conservatives. High-profile local politicians – such as Kumamoto governor Hosokawa Morihiro – criticized excessive centralization of the state with surprising venom and praised the possibilities of localism uncritically (Hosokawa and Iwakuni 1991).

By the 1980s, with the influx of neo-liberal ideas about smaller government from abroad, growing voices within the ruling party and business community were arguing that Japan needed to streamline the state through decentralization. These reformers claimed that local economies were constrained by excessive regulations and oversight from central ministries. Deregulation and decentralization, they argued, would trigger virtuous competition within regions. Local innovation and initiatives would halt the depopulation and hollowing out of economies in rural areas. A major set of decentralization laws were passed in 2000 and successive administrations of the LDP and DPJ have called and implemented further transfers of powers from central to local government (Hijino 2016).

Though the trajectory of the past few decades has been towards an expansion of local autonomy and reducing central government interference, it has not, paradoxically, made Japan's regions more capable of dealing with its problems. After nearly two decades of administrative and fiscal decentralization (1995–2015) Japan's regions are facing deepening social, economic, and demographic crises. Over-concentration of the population and business resources in Tokyo has continued unabated. The majority of areas beyond the capital have suffered depopulation, loss of jobs, and crises in local government finances and governance. The general crisis of Japan's regions was given new urgency when in 2014, a high-profile report (the so-called 'Masuda report') claimed that as many as 800 (nearly half) of Japan's municipalities were at risk of becoming extinct by 2040.

Successive administrations since 2000 reduced fiscal support of local governments and allowed greater regional inequalities to emerge. Income differences between prefectures have begun to moderately increase since 2000 after having fallen sharply throughout the post-war period (Figure 2.1). When comparing difference in average salaries for those in Tokyo and the poorest regions, the gap has approached historical levels (Hijino 2015).

These developments, accelerating under the Koizumi administration (2001–2006) triggered widespread resistance from local governments and politicians. The refrain that the 'voice of the regions was not heard' became a common one. The perception of worsening regional inequality surged and remained at elevated levels from around this time (Figure 2.2). In the meantime, voters did not demonstrate enthusiasm or support for local governments: voting turnout in all types of local elections has fallen to record post-war lows since decentralization reforms began in 2000.[1]

How can we explain this combination of expanding local autonomy and worsening socio-economic conditions for Japan's local governments? What role did local politics – its elections, politicians, and local party organizations – play in this process?

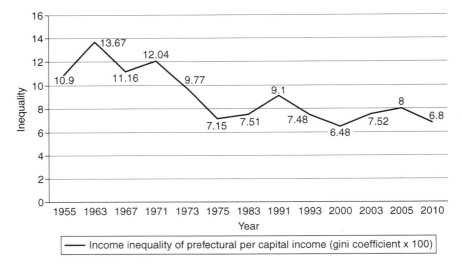

Figure 2.1 Regional inequality as measured by per capita prefectural income.

Sources: Kaji (2006) and for 2005 and 2010, Ministry of Land, Infrastructure, and Transport: www.mlit.go.jp/common/001020274.pdf.

Local autonomy and partisan linkages 37

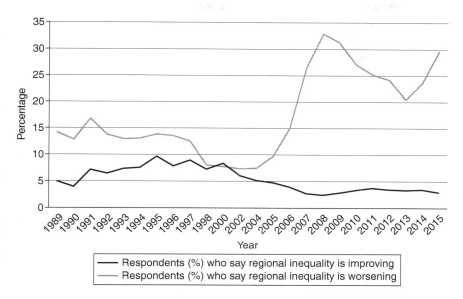

Figure 2.2 Perceived expansion of regional inequalities in Japan.
Source: compiled by author from Cabinet Office survey: *Shakai ishiki ni kansuru seron chōsa*, 1989–2015.

This chapter provides an overview of the changing context of local power in post-war Japan in two stages. It first investigates changes in levels of formal local autonomy as established constitutionally and through laws regulating the local government system. It then expands in greater detail about changes in the partisan channels of local influence on national matters, which we hold to be the more important basis of local power. This overview will allow us to understand the changing context which has led to more strained and conflictual relations between national and local governments since the 1990s.

Administratively centralized, but highly 'fused' local government system

After Japan's surrender in 1945, the Allied Occupation decentralized Japan's pre-war political institutions in the belief that the establishment of more autonomous local governments would serve to demilitarize and democratize Japan. These measures included a constitutional guarantee of local government autonomy (Article 92), abolishing the internal affairs ministry, decentralization of police and education boards, instituting direct elections for prefectural governors, and strengthening the locally elected legislature vis-à-vis the local executive (Steiner 1965, chapters 5 and 6).

But with escalating Cold War tensions in the region and fear that local governments would fall under communist and socialist influence, many

38 *Local autonomy and partisan linkages*

decentralizing measures were reversed. Early recommendations by an advisory commission led by the economist Carl Shoup in 1950 to separate and clarify the functions of national and local governments and provide greater financial resources to local governments were rejected. Local education boards and police services were recentralized in 1954 and 1956 respectively. Even under the occupation period, newly expanded welfare programmes were centralized and standardized nationally, and then delegated to local governments under close ministry supervision (Ichikawa 2012).

The post-war local government system in Japan thus emerged as a strongly centralized one, with various features allowing centralized control and limiting local administrative autonomy. These include a system of delegated functions mandating local executives to carry out a wide range of programmes and public services based on national law or government ordinance, limited revenue-raising powers of local governments in terms of local taxation and debt-issuance, and the dispatch of national bureaucrats to local governments for supervision, among other mechanisms (Steiner 1965; Tsuji 1976). These features formed a so-called 'vertical administrative control' model of local government which has been challenged over time (Muramatsu 1975, 1988, 1997). Scholars have demonstrated how local governments possessed leeway for local policy discretion and strategies to use these mechanisms of centralization to their advantage (Reed 1982, 1986). Despite such revisionist analyses, formal local government autonomy has been constrained, particularly by a fiscal centralization that regulates local expenditures and revenues, limiting financial flexibility and preventing the initiation of policies requiring their own funding (Reed 1986, pp. 31–32, 149; De Wit 2002; Sunahara 2011, p. 25).

At the same time as being highly centralized, particularly fiscally, the Japanese local government system was a highly fused one where the central government depended on local governments to implement and administer a wide range of national policy programmes. The concept of a 'fused' local government system refers to the sharing between national and local governments of a policy area, either in terms of legal authority, funding, or implementation. In Japan, central, prefectural, and municipal governments have been 'bound closely together and share authority over a given policy area' (Muramatsu 1997, p. 139). Such fusion of national and local functions resulted from a system of delegated functions (*kikan innin jimu*) and local government tax transfers (*chihō kōfuzei*) in the post-war period which expanded local expenditures and administrative capacity of local governments under central ministry oversight.

The central government mandated a wide range of functions to be delivered by local governments through a system of delegated functions. In this system, local governments implemented and delivered administrative services in the jurisdiction of the national government, in effect acting as local branches of the national government. Although criticized as an undesirable legacy of pre-war centralization which limited local government autonomy, these delegated functions ensured uniformity for the wide range of public services delivered by local governments. These delegated functions increased over time as the welfare state expanded and governmental functions increased (Steiner 1965, p. 236). Although local governments were at the front lines of public service delivery in major areas such as health, education, and welfare, the central government retained control of standards and levels (Mochida 2001), thereby ensuring uniformity of public services.

The state also established a system of fiscal transfers early in the post-war period so that all local governments, regardless of the strength of their tax base, could actually finance their growing range of mandated functions. The key mechanism of fiscal equalization among local governments was the local allocation tax grant system enacted in 1952. The system emerged after a prior system of fiscal equalization established under the Occupation period generated fluctuations in the size of local grants, causing revenue shortages for local governments (Steiner 1965, pp. 288–289). These local grants, funded by a given percentage of major national taxes, were allocations given to local governments to correct inequalities in their fiscal resources and ensure that residents receive a consistent standard of public services regardless of where they live. The Local Allocation Tax (*chihō kōfuzei* or LAT) is raised centrally and redistributed to local governments based on a prescribed formula which calculates local revenue needs. These large-scale transfers through the LAT system have succeeded in reducing territorial inequalities in fiscal resources extensively (Mochida 2001).

The combined effect of these two features – large fiscal transfers and delegated functions – has been a local government system that Amakawa Akira (1983) characterized as administratively centralized and highly 'fused'. By the time decentralization reforms commenced in 2000, Japanese local government expenditures comprised over 60 per cent of total state expenditures, while self-raised tax revenues for local governments were around 40 per cent (Nishio 2007, p. 14). Comparatively speaking, both levels of local self-raised revenues and local expenditures are much higher than most unitary states, notably even those of decentralized states in Scandinavia (Tatebayashi *et al.* 2008, p. 304). Though fiscally and administratively centralized, Japanese prefectures and municipalities were large and active in the implementation of many public services jointly with the central government.

Challenges to centralization and gradual decoupling since 1990s

Focusing on the more visible elements of centralized administrative control, a wide range of actors within Japan called for decentralization. The centralization of the Japanese state, they argued, suppressed local democratic process, stifled local policy innovation, weakened local economic development, and generated administrative inefficiencies, among other problems.[2] By the late 1970s, the slowdown of the Japanese economy and fiscal pressures stemming from growing public service costs combined with neo-liberal policy ideas from outside Japan. The mixture triggered a process of administrative reforms led by the Ad hoc Commission for Administrative Reform (*Rinchō*) during the 1980s. In 1990, the commission recommended decentralization, along with an overall streamlining

40 *Local autonomy and partisan linkages*

of local government, to combat administrative inefficiency. These recommendations led to a bipartisan resolution to promote decentralization by both houses of the Japanese Diet in June 1993. In the following year, the Diet passed a Decentralization Promotion Law, which eventually led to a series of decentralization measures beginning in 2000.

The decentralization omnibus law in 2000 resulted in many of the formal administrative features of centralized control over local government to be reduced. Local and national governments were placed on equal footing, with their respective roles and discretionary powers clarified. The system of agency delegated functions was abolished and the responsibility for a majority of these functions was transferred to local governments. Rules and process for central intervention in local matters were clarified, and in event of inter-governmental conflict, a central-local dispute resolving mechanism was put in place. In connection to these decentralization measures, smaller municipalities were encouraged to merge with the goal of expanding the capabilities of local governments that were to receive newly devolved powers. As a result, between 1999 and 2006, the number of municipalities declined from 3,223 to 1,820. Finally, a set of fiscal decentralization reforms (2002–2006) were implemented under the Koizumi administration. These so-called 'Holy Trinity reforms' involved the reform of local government subsidies, general grants, and the transferring of tax revenue sources to local governments.

These reforms have frequently been characterized as 'incomplete', not only by proponents of decentralization and local governments themselves, but by successive LDP and DPJ administrations. Nishio (2007, 2013), scholar and key participant in the decentralization committees, has indicated the various limitations to these reforms and remaining constraints on local autonomy.

Although acknowledging that discretion of local governments to pass local bylaws has expanded 'formally', Nishio points to a web of pre-existing laws and ordinances which continue to limit room for local policy discretion. After the reforms, local governments were now allowed to disregard ministerial guidance (*tūtatsu*, *tsūchi*) when interpreting national laws for local implementation. Yet Nishio points out that there have been very few cases in which local governments interpreted laws differently from ministerial guidance. Nor have local governments actively challenged national governments through the newly established central-local government dispute resolution committee (Nishio 2013, pp. 72–77). Surveys also indicate that a majority of mayors, especially of smaller fiscally weaker cities, have a relatively low estimation of decentralization reforms and find little has effectively changed in their discretionary powers (Muramatsu 2009, p. 11). Overall, administrative decentralization appears not to have led to local governments actively using their expanded autonomy.

A similar lack of substantial diversity continues to characterize local government tax policy. Reforms to local tax laws in 1998 and 2000 expanded the discretion of local governments to change local tax rates and implement new local taxes (non-statutory general tax = *hōteigai futsūzei*). These changes have led to a handful of new taxes, albeit which represent very small revenues for local governments, with specific purpose use in areas such as tourism, environmental protection, and industrial waste (Sunahara 2011, pp. 172–174). Aside from these special-purpose taxes and a few publicized cases of changes to local tax rates (such as lowering local residence taxes in Nagoya city), decentralization reforms have not brought about great divergence in local tax rates.[3]

Fiscal decentralization measures during the Koizumi administration had a more direct and negative impact on local government resources. Between 2002 and 2006, the central government reduced national subsidies tied to specific expenditures, increased general discretionary grants, and transferred some tax revenue sources to local governments. The outcome, however, was highly unsatisfactory as local governments experienced a sharp drop in their total revenues, while expenditure obligations remained. Local governor and mayor associations publically criticized fiscal decentralization under the Koizumi administration.[4] They claimed that the sharp cuts to local government subsidies and grants, together with limited transfers of tax revenue sources, were 'far removed from the original intentions of decentralization reform' and 'resulting in growing local distrust of the reform itself'.[5]

Broader data confirm these criticisms. During this period, local governments have only moderately gained greater financial self-sufficiency, but have less room for manoeuvre as the ratio of obligatory expenditures has increased. In particular, local government debt levels have surged since 1990, tying more expenditures to debt servicing and constraining discretionary spending (Figure 2.3).

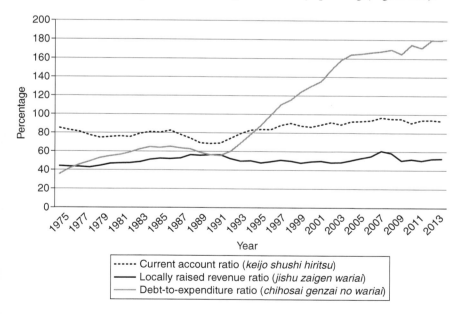

Figure 2.3 Ratio of locally raised revenues, current account to expenditure, and debt-to-expenditure for prefectural governments.

Source: *Sōmushō* E-stat database: www.e-stat.go.jp/SG1/estat/eStatTopPortal.do.

42 *Local autonomy and partisan linkages*

The decentralization measures undertaken in the first half of 2000 were thus incomplete, in terms of providing substantial autonomy and resources to local governments. A reflection of this is how decentralization has remained on the agenda with scholars, media, government commissions, and parties all calling for further decentralization in the latter half of the 2000s (Hijino 2015). In December of 2006, the Abe administration (2006–2007) passed a Decentralization Reform Promotion Law and established the Decentralization Reform Promotion Committee. The committee recommended, among other things: further transfer of tax revenue sources to local governments; localization of consumption tax and creation of a lateral fiscal adjustment system; abolishing of central government regional branches; and reforms to improve the democratic functions of local legislatures. Proposals to abolish and merge prefectures into regions to create a new region-based local government system (henceforth *dōshusei*) also re-emerged during this time (Nishio 2007, pp. 203–212). Decentralization reforms were also pushed by the DPJ administrations (2009–2012), including the creation of an official advisory council to promote 'regional sovereignty'.[6] Since 2012, however, both the DPJ and LDP have toned down their emphasis on decentralization reform in electoral campaigns (Hijino 2016).

The broader assessment is that though decentralization reforms in Japan since 2000 have been inadequate and are ongoing, the overall relationship between central and local governments has shifted, particularly through fiscal decentralization and the abolishing of delegated functions, to a more 'separated' rather than 'fused' local government system (Tatebayashi *et al.* 2008, pp. 324–325).

Finally, it is important to note that despite the separation of policy responsibilities and greater autonomy granted to local governments in Japan, ultimate control remains in the capital. In unitary states like Japan, the central government, if it so desires, can introduce laws which retract, over-ride, or countermand local decision-making powers. As unitary states have no constitutional provisions protecting local authority from central government encroachment, even the very existence of individual local governments is not guaranteed.

These unitary powers were painfully evident when the Okinawa governor refused to aid the national government in renewing land leases used for US bases in Okinawa. Tokyo pressured the Okinawan governor to comply through the courts and then revised the laws the following year (*chūryūgun yōchi tokusohō*) so that similar local non-compliance would not occur in the future. Although instances of central government passing legislation to over-ride local resistance are rare, national politicians have threatened to use such legislation. In an illustrative recent example, the Minister of Education threatened to pass a special measure law to force cooperation after the Tokyo governor indicated he may refuse to pay for construction of a controversial Olympic stadium in Tokyo.[7]

These examples show how Japanese local governments are always in the 'shadow' of the central government and that local autonomy is permitted ultimately at the pleasure of the central government. Although guarantees protect local governments from 'illegal' central government intervention, the point is

Local autonomy and partisan linkages 43

that laws can be changed. Local actors then must find other channels to persuade or threaten national political actors from legislating against their interest. This is where partisan channels of influence on the national government become essential for local power.

Vertical integration in the LDP and local influence

Despite limits to their autonomy, Japanese local governments, and more broadly local politics, have strongly influenced national politics and policy-making in the post-war period. The conditions which allowed local political actors to engage in and shape national policy changed substantially in the past 25 years, both in terms of multi-level party congruence and vertical integration. Tracing this transformation will allow us to understand the new context in which local politics is engaging with the centre.

Muramatsu (1975, 1988) highlighted the channels by which local actors (prefectural and municipal legislators as well as directly elected mayors and governors) were able to draw out benefits from the centre by participating in a bottom-up and inclusive policy-making process. Such dynamics emerged early on. In a famous example, when the central government proposed to designate a few sites for intensive public investments under the New Industrial Cities Construction Act of 1962, local Diet members in tandem with local governments and politicians demanded the investments be widely dispersed. 'LDP Diet members from rural areas organized an association to block the original proposal, to insert a new objective (correcting regional differences in income redistribution), and simultaneously to extend the number of sites for investment' (Muramatsu 1986, p. 324). Prefectures seeking regional designation mobilized local politicians and unleashed 'the greatest petition war in history' against the national government. Original plans by the ministry and business organizations to concentrate development in economically 'rational' fashion within the Pacific Sea belt area was transformed by such bottom-up political pressures and the number of designated sites increased.

This bottom-up dynamic has been characterized as a 'rugby scrum' linking local politicians, local governments, local Diet members, and national-level bureaucrats (Muramatsu 2010). Local governments (and local politicians representing these areas) competed among each other in 'lateral political competition' to capture a greater share of expanding governmental spending to various regions. Local governments were thus not passive recipients of national subsidies, but active players shaping policy and capturing benefits in their favour (Muramatsu 1975, 1988). Numerous examples have demonstrated this dynamic of lateral competition shaping national policy: governors lobbying the national government to pass a law to provide support for depopulating areas; local politicians and officials lobbying for rural development programmes; governors and mayors lobbying central ministries and local Diet members for various grants; innovation in local policies such as welfare and environmental regulation leading to lateral competition and diffusion across local governments, and their eventual

44 *Local autonomy and partisan linkages*

adoption by the central government as a new national standard (Muramatsu 1975, 1988; Reed 1982).

Such local lobbying was necessary because of Japan's highly centralized fiscal structure, which meant local governments, particularly those in poorer rural areas, needed to attract centrally funded projects and resources for development and jobs (Scheiner 2006). It was successful because individual local Diet members were strongly dependent on local actors for their elections, while being able to offer influence over law making and budget allocation at the centre. During the LDP's dominant period (1955–1993), candidates from the ruling party competed with co-partisans in multi-member district which elevated the importance of personal reputation and votes over party reputation or programmes. Candidates thus were incentivized to build up personal campaign machines (*kōenkai*) and differentiate themselves by targeted policies to specific areas and occupational interests within their district. In this context of intra-party competition, local conservatives joined a particular local LDP Diet member in a pyramidal network (*keiretsu*) of mutual exchange. These municipal and prefectural politicians served as vital hands and feet for Diet members during and between elections, maintaining links and mobilizing local interest groups and voters. Diet members were thus heavily dependent on their local support network, with local prefectural and municipal politicians at its core, for re-election (Fukui and Fukai 1996; Scheiner 2006).

Moreover, the reliance of Diet members on these personal networks meant they were less susceptible to top-down control. Party organization and policy-making process at national level were accordingly decentralized. This meant that backbenchers could influence the direction of national policy and budgeting at an early stage. National policy was thus formed primarily by adjusting at the centre policy preferences (mainly demands for pork and redistribution to specific areas) emanating from networks of local interests found across the country. This is in contrast to a model of more top-down policy-making driven by party leadership, universalistic policy programmes, or technocratic concerns of overall economic efficiency.

Among local interests, those of rural areas played a particularly strong influence on national policy direction. Malapportionment of electoral districts meant rural areas were disproportionally represented in the national legislature. As these regions formed the traditional base for the LDP, rural demands for redistribution and market protection were heeded more closely than those of urban areas (Rosenbluth and Thies 2010). Last, but not least, local branches provided an important pool of national-level candidates for the ruling party. Through the 1970s to mid-1990s, nearly a quarter to a third of national LDP politicians in the Lower House had experience as local legislators, who in turn held important executive posts in the party (Mawatari 2010, chapter 5). A regionally oriented outlook was arguably built into the party at national level as a result of the stream of local politicians entering the Diet.

In sum, local politics shaped national policy in the LDP's dominant period because the ruling party organization was responsive, and beholden, to bottom-up

Local autonomy and partisan linkages 45

demands. The LDP was integrated, as per Filippov's definition (see Chapter 1), in the sense of both national and local levels of the party acting in mutual support to maintain their electoral coalition. The party organized and competed across all levels of government, with success in one aiding the other. National LDP politicians and leadership needed local politicians to win elections and maintain a local network of interest groups. Local politicians, on the other hand, needed legislative majorities at national level to ensure continued benefits to flow to their regions (which in turn helped them win local elections). Policy influence flowed upwards through local actors lobbying for national policies and downwards through centralized redistribution and regulation. The relationship could thus be considered one of mutual dependence and delegation, benefitting the party as a whole.[8]

Weakening vertical integration within the LDP since the 1990s

Yet this symbiotic relationship between the national and local levels of the ruling party has gradually weakened since the 1990s. Three vectors of change can be identified: first, electoral and administrative reforms led to more majoritarian competition under centralized leadership at national level; second, in consequence, the ruling party has shifted its policy emphasis in favour of its traditional support base in rural areas towards median voters in more urban districts; and finally, these changes in electoral competition did not occur at local level, leading to a disjuncture between the two levels of the party.

Electoral system reforms in the mid-1990s shifted Japan's national electoral environment to a more majoritarian one characterized by two-party competition, universal rather than particularistic policies, and stronger party leadership. These electoral reforms pushed Japan from its traditional emphasis on policies targeting particular districts and organized voters, to one focused on more programmatic policies targeting the unorganized median voter (Rosenbluth and Thies 2010). Electoral and campaign finance reforms in 1994 also strengthened the LDP's party leadership, enabling it to enforce greater discipline (primarily through control over candidate nominations and party subventions) over backbenchers in the Diet (Asano 2006). Administrative reforms have also expanded cabinet influence over the ministries, further strengthening the party executive in office (Estévez-Abe 2006). In tandem with these developments, a rise in 'floating' voters with weaker party loyalties and the 'presidentialization' of elections has heightened the role of the prime minister and his image/leadership in electoral contests (Krauss and Nyblade 2005).

Electoral reforms in 1994 also resulted in sharply reducing district malapportionment which had traditionally given a disproportionate advantage to rural voters and their interests over urban ones (McElwain 2013). Reapportionment has meant the LDP could no longer focus simply on courting and relying on rural areas to provide legislative majorities as in the past. Although the LDP's core support and organizational strength continued to be in rural areas, the

46 *Local autonomy and partisan linkages*

centre of gravity in electoral competition has shifted towards urban areas and the unaffiliated median voter. This is not to say that rural areas and their traditional interests have become insignificant: malapportionment continues to give greater weight to rural votes (especially for the Upper House) and recent elections demonstrate the importance of rural/semi-rural districts and their interest groups, such as farmers, with strong links to local LDP politicians (Mulgan 2013). The new electoral environment, however, has meant the party leadership must court both urban and rural interests which may not always be compatible.

Under these conditions of increased majoritarian competition focused on the swing voter, administrations since the mid-1990s promoted and implemented a host of top-down reform packages. These initiatives were aimed at courting unaffiliated voters, but harmed vested interests linked to the rural LDP and its local representatives. Guided by the goal of fiscal discipline and ideological pressures for smaller government, the policy programmes pursued in the period were largely those which reduced government spending to and protection of organized voters, while deregulating and opening up markets. Key measures included privatization of the national highway corporation and postal services, reforms to the local government system including municipal mergers and fiscal decentralization, cuts to public works spending including road construction, and trade liberalization, including agricultural trade.

These changes were painful for many of Japan's rural regions dependent on services and jobs generated by the public sector and protected by market regulations. Despite periodic interventions of 'compensation' to shore up support in the regions usually during election years, particularly for major local elections and the Upper House), the central government has continued to encourage deregulation and self-sufficiency among regions. An earlier norm and discourse of 'balanced growth across the nation' was replaced by an emphasis on regional diversity and 'virtuous competition' between localities.

Unlike these developments at national level, local elections continue to be conducted under the single non-transferable vote (SNTV) system.[9] Candidates in local elections thus continue to seek out narrow bands of support through particularistic promises targeting specific areas and local interest groups within the district. Unlike national-level competition, they depend less on the party label or universal programmes. Exit polls corroborate this point. From 2000 to 2014, respondents polled for HoR elections stating that they voted based on party rather than candidate qualities have increased (from about 44 to 50–60 per cent), while the number of those who stated they voted focusing on candidate characteristics has fallen (from 44 to 30 per cent).[10] In contrast, the number of voters in prefectural legislative elections who stated that they voted based on party considerations remained lower (albeit rising from 15 to 37 per cent between 1999 and 2011), while those voting on candidate characteristics remained higher (albeit falling from 75 to 50 per cent in the same period), than for national elections.[11] Although party competition appears to be strengthening at prefectural level, the personal vote remains relatively important compared to national Lower House elections.

Local autonomy and partisan linkages 47

Survey data from 2010 suggest that prefectural legislators of the LDP continue to maintain the same kind of bases of support targeting specific occupational interest groups (business groups, agriculture, and construction) and geographic areas, as when the national electoral system took place under SNTV (Shinada 2012). Uekami (2013) has indicated how Japan's 'asymmetrical' multi-level electoral environments bifurcate Japan's national and local party system, demonstrating how preferences for policy and leadership selection of national and local LDP actors have diverged. The widening difference in voter turnout (prefectural assembly elections turnout has on average been 10–15 per cent lower than national elections) and the different timing of national and local elections have also presumably added to national and local representation diverging.

These differences in the local and national electoral environments have eroded incentives for both national and local conservatives to align and adjust interests, that is, to maintain vertical integration. From the perspective of local legislators, the reduction of flow of pork to regions and fiscal decentralization has meant they have less reason to affiliate and support the ruling party at the national level. Increased volatility of national party competition – demonstrated by the ousting of the LDP from the reins of national power once in 1993 and then again between 2009 and 2012 – has meant local politicians could not be certain of securing influence at the centre by binding themselves to only the LDP. With greater powers accruing to local chief executives through decentralization, local legislators have greater incentives to affiliate and support governors and mayors not backed by the LDP, even to the lengths of leaving the LDP to join new regional parties started by chief executives (Hijino 2014).

From the perspective of individual Diet members, receiving campaign support from local legislators and backing of local interest groups remain important (Krauss and Pekkanen 2011), but not enough to win elections in larger single-member districts. The proportion of floating voters not affiliated to any party or organized interests has surged from around 20 per cent in the 1980s to hovering around 40–60 per cent since the mid-1990s (Tanaka *et al.* 2009, p. 8). As these unaffiliated voters chose among parties largely based on party reputation, programmes, and the image of party leadership, politicians must avoid actions which may hurt these party assets. In this context, individual Diet members have been forced to choose between loyalty to their local supporters or to national leadership – as was most dramatically illustrated during the postal privatization snap election in 2005.

Data over time also show how local actors of the LDP have become increasingly delinked from the national level, with traditional intra-party channels of communication becoming weaker. Surveys of national politicians indicate decreasing levels of interaction with local politicians as well as weakening influence of local politicians on national policy processes (Muramatsu 2010, pp. 200–209). Between 1987 and 2002, national politicians from both the LDP and opposition parties reported to have met less frequently with local chief executives and municipal and prefectural legislators (ibid., p. 201). During the same

48 *Local autonomy and partisan linkages*

periods, interactions between central ministry bureaucrats and local representatives have also fallen (ibid., p. 209). Municipal mergers which have reduced the number of municipal politicians by nearly 40 per cent have drastically reduced the links between national and local politicians and weakened the LDP's support base (Shimizu 2012).

The proportion of Diet members in the House of Representatives with experience in local politics fell moderately between 1996 and 2014, suggesting a less regionally oriented makeup of the Diet (Figure 2.4). Although still far higher than international levels and a significant source of national candidates, the career path from local to national has become one less travelled. Particularly noticeable is how the LDP has been sourcing fewer and fewer of its new candidates from the local pool in the same period, with the proportion dropping below 30 per cent since 2000. In contrast, the DPJ, and new emerging third-pole parties, have increasingly relied on local politicians as a source of their candidates (see Smith 2013, 2015).

Even as national and local linkages weaken, the LDP national leadership has not acquired resources to effectively control its local base. Case studies have shown that in many prefectural branches, prefectural-level politicians control the selection of local-level candidates, including gubernatorial candidates, leadership

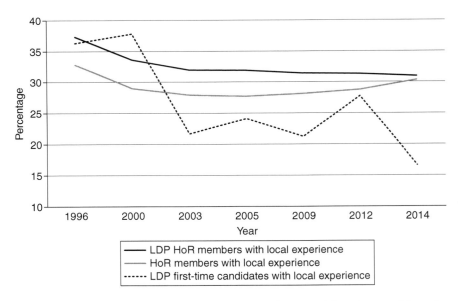

Figure 2.4 Proportion of all incumbents, LDP incumbents, and first-time candidates for the House Representative with experience in local politics (prefectural or municipal).

Source: Steven R. Reed and Daniel M. Smith, The Reed–Smith Japanese House of Representatives Elections Data Set.

Note
Version: 9 March 2016. https://sites.google.com/site/danielmarkhamsmith/data.

Local autonomy and partisan linkages 49

selection within the prefectural branch, as well as local-level campaign planning and policy formation (Tatebayashi 2013, pp. 300–303). And since the party label remains relatively unimportant locally,[12] threats to take party nominations from local legislators or exhortations not to damage party reputation and policy unity are not effective. Studies have found little evidence of the LDP leadership being successful in intervening in local party matters, including attempts to parachute in gubernatorial candidates (Hijino 2014).

Unlike other more centralized and hierarchical mass-parties, the LDP cannot integrate its party organization through top-down control. The party has thus become more de-integrated with local branches beyond control of the centre, with greater potential for multi-level conflict and disequilibrium.

Partisan incongruence across levels

Another important channel of local influence on the centre in Japan has been through opposition party control of governments at local level which resulted in changes in national policy and electoral strategy.

Although the ruling LDP has dominated most prefectural-level legislatures, their grip on local chief executive posts has been less secure. During the 'progressive local government' period from the latter half of the 1960s to the early 1970s, opposition parties on the left (Japan Socialist Party, Democratic Socialist Party of Japan, and Japan Communist Party) backed gubernatorial and mayoral candidates with increasing success. At its peak, 40 per cent of the Japanese population lived in areas with progressive local governments under nine governors (including Kyoto, Tokyo, and Osaka) as well as 130 out of 643 city mayors (including Yokohama, Nagoya, Kyoto City, Osaka City, and Kobe) (Steiner *et al.* 1980, p. 6).

These progressive local governments significantly impacted national politics and policies by local policy innovations in pollution control, environmental preservation, and expansion of social welfare services (such as free medical care to the elderly) which went beyond nationally mandated levels. These were criticized initially by central ministries as illegal ordinances, but eventually spread to other local governments and adopted into national legislation (Muramatsu 1975; Steiner *et al.* 1980, pp. 342–352; Reed 1982).

Local opposition succeeded by challenging the national consensus and agenda of growth, focusing on problems that the ruling party had not dealt with, such as industrial and urban pollution as well as welfare for urban workers and ageing population. Local opposition also succeeded by overcoming ideological divisions that had fragmented parties at national level. This allowed pragmatic coalitions, primarily between the Japan Communist Party (JCP) and Japan Socialist Party (JSP), but also variations involving the Komeito and DSP (Maeda 1995).

These progressive candidates emphasized their direct contacts with unorganized voters, rather than their links to the central government. They stressed grassroots participation, campaigning with slogans such as 'direct democracy'

50 *Local autonomy and partisan linkages*

and 'dialogue with the citizens' and the 'Conference of the 10,000 Representatives' (Steiner *et al.* 1980, pp. 328–330). While portraying themselves as broad left-leaning coalitions, progressive governors once in power expanded their support to more traditionally conservative supporters, such as small and medium enterprises. These progressive chief executives also linked across laterally – such as the National Association of Progressive Mayors (*Zenkoku Kakushin shichōkai*) – which formed effective coalitions in supporting challenges against the centre (Steiner *et al.* 1980, pp. 344, 347). Moreover, these progressives were not only confronting the central government with local issues, but consciously challenging the centre and its political agenda (Reed 1982, p. 163). Slogans for progressive local candidates, such as the 1971 Tokyo gubernatorial election slogan of 'Stop the Sato' (the LDP prime minister at the time), underscore how local challenge was sold to voters not merely as a localized issue.

For the ruling conservatives at the centre, the expanding strength of the opposition in the largest cities during this period posed a political 'crisis' (Calder 1988, pp. 103–109). In response, LDP administrations began to compensate by co-opting and extending popular local environmental and welfare ordinances from around 1970. They rapidly expanded their welfare programmes around this time, with the government conspicuously announcing 1973 to be the 'birth year of welfare' (*fukushi gannen*). During this period of local electoral crisis, local LDP politicians applied strong pressures on the central LDP to adopt and co-opt local opposition through national legislation (Muramatsu 1975, p. 814).

Thus we can understand the progressive local government period as one of widespread multi-level party incongruence, with numerous local government executives under control by opposition parties at national level (an important caveat is that the incongruence was limited to opposition control of the executive level, with most local legislatures remaining under LDP control during this period). The incongruence triggered conflicts over local by-laws against central ministries, which localities often won. More importantly these conflicts generated pressures against the central government to adopt and nationalize local demands.

As progressive policy programmes were co-opted by the centre and local finances suffered after the recession following the Oil Shock in 1973, local governments controlled by the opposition receded. Progressive governors in Tokyo, Osaka, and Kyoto were replaced by LDP-backed former bureaucrats who criticized overly expanded welfare programmes as fiscally profligate. By 1979, there were only two local governors backed by parties on the left or the centre who had won against LDP-backed candidates. Instead, the local chief executives became increasingly supported by a coalition involving the LDP and centrist parties (Komeito and DSP) during the 1970s and even broader coalitions involving both the LDP and the JSP during the 1980s. By the end of the 1980s, as many as 20 prefectures (out of 47) were held by governors backed by both conservative and progressive parties – so-called '*ainori*' (Soga and Machidori 2007, pp. 80–82).

Since the 1990s, four trends can be identified in local partisan composition of local legislatures and executive posts: multiparty-backed and non-partisan governors and mayors; weakness of opposition parties in capturing both local legislative and executive offices; the emergence of regional parties; and legislative incongruence during the LDP's period in national opposition.

First, the trend of multiparty coalitions in local governments continued and accelerated after the 1980s. At its peak level in 2000, 35 prefectures were held under governors that had been backed by coalitions involving the LDP and the main opposition party. During this period, however, a new trend of non-partisan governors (*mutōha chiji*) that received backing from none of the national parties emerged (Soga and Machidori 2007, pp. 83–84). Since 2000, the number of such independent governors[13] has surged, overtaking the number of governors backed by LDP headquarters in 2011. In the meantime, governors receiving backing from opposition parties and not the LDP remain at low levels. Despite a change of government at national level in 1994 and 2009, opposition-party (non-LDP) governors remain fewer than during the period of progressive local governments in the late 1960s and 1970s (Figure 2.5).

Second, the main opposition parties (the New Frontier Party (NFP) and DPJ) which emerged after the split of the LDP and implosion of the JSP in the mid-1990s were unable to expand in legislature or capture many gubernatorial posts, often failing to stand candidates or backing the same one as the LDP.

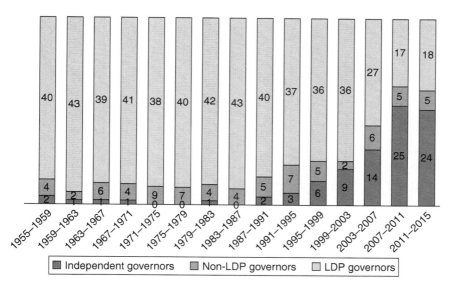

Figure 2.5 Partisan affiliation of governors (LDP, non-LDP, or Independent).

Source: Tsuji (2015) and for data after 2013 compiled by author from various newspapers.

Note

Independent governors are those that did not receive nominations from the headquarters of any national party (*honbu kōnin, suisen*), although they may have received support of local party organizations including that of the LDP (*kenren suisen*). LDP governors are those that received nomination from the national LDP (*honbu kōnin, suisen*). Non-LDP governors are those that received nomination from the headquarters of a national party beside the LDP.

52 Local autonomy and partisan linkages

The DPJ, despite gaining steadily throughout the 2000s on the national arena, were unable to expand into local legislatures, particularly those in rural areas. This failure to build a local network in legislatures meant continued weakness in contesting gubernatorial elections (Hijino 2013, 2014).

Third, during the brief period of 1993–1994 and later for three years during 2009–2012, Japan experienced widespread multi-level party incongruence involving a non-LDP government in the centre dealing with LDP-controlled legislatures at local level.

Finally, a handful of independent governors and mayors in Shiga, Osaka, Aichi, and Nagoya started regional parties in local legislatures, challenging the LDP and drawing defectors from national parties to them with considerable success. Although a notable development, aside from the case in Osaka, these regional parties and their leader chief executives have not succeeded in consolidating their strength locally. The rise of such non-partisan governors reflects candidate strategies to distance themselves from increasingly unpopular and volatile national parties at national level as well as fewer incentives to affiliate with national parties (particularly the LDP) that have reduced clientelistic spending to the regions and pushed for fiscal decentralization (Hijino 2014).

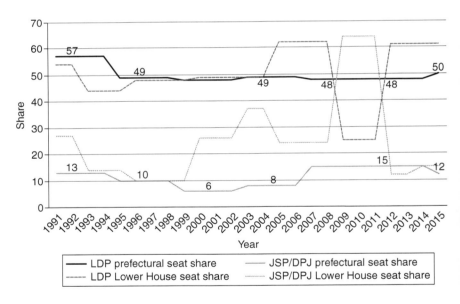

Figure 2.6 National volatility vs local stability in electoral outcomes for the LDP and main opposition party.

Source: compiled by author from Ministry of Internal Affairs and Communications election data (Prefectural seat share calculated from Unified Local Elections results; 44 prefectures excluding Tokyo, Ibaragi, and Okinawa. Lower House seat share for JSP until 1996, DPJ from 1996).

Conclusion

In this chapter we have demonstrated how Japanese local politics has mattered for local autonomy and its ability to shape national policies. The primary channels of upward influence have been the vertical integration of the LDP organization during its dominant period (1955–1993) and widespread multi-level party incongruence involving directly elected governors (and mayors) during the progressive local government period (1965–1972). Local autonomy over local matters has largely been constrained, albeit with some leeway for innovation and oftentimes requiring partisan pressures on the central government to achieve local initiatives. One would expect in a unitary state where local governments and their discretion ultimately exist at the pleasure of the centre, that partisan influence, not legal and administrative powers, is more vital for achieving territorial interests. Japan follows this logic.

The chapter has also indicated how these partisan channels of influence have weakened since the mid-1990s, even as formal local authority has expanded under decentralization reforms. The dominant party (LDP) is no longer vertically integrated; politicians at both levels have fewer incentives to commit to a reciprocally beneficial relationship and avoid disruptive conflicts. Fiscal constraints, ideological shifts, and electoral reforms have eroded the traditionally 'regionally oriented' nature of policy-making at the centre. In the meantime, opposition parties have not been able to capture local offices and local conservatives remained dominant in local legislatures. In light of these developments in party congruence and vertical integration, we expect Japan's multi-level relations to show greater strains and conflict since the mid-1990s. We begin to test these expectations by first turning our attention to the dynamic of conflict and cooperation within the LDP between national and local levels.

Notes

1 Turnout ranged from about 60–90 per cent for all types of local elections (prefectural and municipal legislative and executive elections) between 1955 and 1995, but these have all fallen below 60 per cent since 1999, reaching historical post-war lows below 50 per cent in 2015. (Data from Association for Promoting Fair Elections. Available at www.akaruisenkyo.or.jp/070various/073chihou/ [accessed 20 October 2016]).
2 See Narumi (1994) for a discussion of the decentralization debate between 1955 and 1993.
3 Insight gained through personal email correspondence with Professor Kitamura Wataru at the Faculty of Law, Osaka University in April 2016.
4 See the local government association's homepage for their statements during this period. Available at www.bunken.nga.gr.jp/trend/sanmi.html [accessed 22 February 2015].
5 *Sanmi ittai kaikaku ni kansuru kinkyū teigen*. 28 May 2006. Chihō roku dantai.
6 See Chapter 4, Sunahara (2012) and Kitamura (2014) for details on decentralization under the DPJ.
7 'Shin kokuritshu kyougijō no tohutan, monkashō "konkyo to naru hōseibi kentō"' *Asahi*, 9 June 2015.
8 An important caveat in the LDP's integration was that it was largely indifferent to the use and unity of the party label per se. Indeed, the prevalence of conservatives affiliated to the LDP but standing as 'independent' candidates, both at national and local

54   *Local autonomy and partisan linkages*

level, underscores this point. Mass parties such as the Communists or Komeito, with stronger ideological commitments and rooted in specific social groups or classes, were also vertically integrated but with more hierarchical organizations and a unified party programme. These parties placed greater emphasis on its party label in consequence, and did not permit local affiliates to stand as independents even in smallest municipal (village-level) elections.

9 Local assembly elections in Japan operate under SNTV rules in both single- and multi-member districts. Prefectural assemblies are divided into districts of 1 to as many as 19 seats, while larger municipalities are also split into districts of between 1 and a dozen seats or so.

10 Poll data from *Akarui Senkyo Suishinkyōkai 47th shūgiingiin sōsenkyo zenkoku ishikichōsa 2015* (p. 59). Available at www.akaruisenkyo.or.jp/wp/wp-content/uploa ds/2011/10/47syuishikicyosa-1.pdf [accessed 20 October 2016].

11 Poll data from *Akarui Senkyo Suishinkyōkai 17th tōitsu chihō senkyo zenkoku ishikichōsa 2012* (p. 38) Available at www.akaruisenkyo.or.jp/wp/wp-content/uploads/2012/ 07/17toituagiyo.pdf [accessed 20 October 2016].

12 The relative unimportance of party voting and party labels also explains the high prevalence of independent politicians in prefectural (22 per cent) and municipal (72 per cent) legislatures (as of 2015).

13 Independent governors are those that did not receive nominations from the headquarters of any national party (*hombu kōnin, suisen*), although they may have received support of local party organizations including that of the LDP (*kenren suisen*).

References

Amakawa, A. 1983, *Kōikigyōsei to chihōbunken*, Jurist (special edition).

Asano, M. 2006, *Shimin shakai ni okeru seido kaiakaku: Senkyo seido to kohosha rikuruto*, Keio gijuku daigaku shuppankai.

Calder, K.E. 1988, *Crisis and compensation: Public policy and political stability in Japan, 1949–1986*, Princeton University Press.

DeWit, A. 2002, 'Dry rot: The corruption of general subsidies in Japan', *Journal of the Asia Pacific Economy*, vol. 7, no. 3, pp. 355–378.

Estévez-Abe, M. 2006, 'Japan's shift toward a Westminster system: A structural analysis of the 2005 Lower House election and its aftermath', *Asian Survey*, vol. 46, no. 4, pp. 632–651.

Fukui, H. and Fukai, S.N. 1996, 'Pork barrel politics, networks, and local economic development in contemporary Japan', *Asian Survey*, vol. 36, no. 3, pp. 268–286.

Hijino, K.V.L. 2013, 'Liabilities of partisan labels: Independents in Japanese local elections', *Social Science Japan Journal*, vol. 16, no. 1, pp. 63–85.

Hijino, K.V.L. 2014, 'Intra-party conflicts over gubernatorial campaigns in Japan Delegation or franchise?', *Party Politics*, vol. 20, no. 1, pp. 78–88.

Hijino, K.V.L. 2015, 'Regional inequality in 2014: Urgent issue, tepid election', in R. Pekkanen, S.R. Reed, and E. Scheiner (eds), *Japan decides 2014: The Japanese general election*, Palgrave Macmillan.

Hijino, K.V.L. 2016, 'Selling the idea of local power: Decentralization reforms since the 1990s', in G. Steel (ed.), *Power in contemporary Japan*, Palgrave Macmillan, pp. 219–237.

Hosokawa, M. and Iwakuni, T. 1991, *Hina no ronri*, Kobunsha.

Ichikawa, Y. 2012, *Nihon no chūō chihō kankei: Gendaigata shūkentaisei no kigen to fukushikokka*, Horitsu bunkasha.

Kaji, Y. 2006, 'Chiiki kan kakusa to sono haikei', *National Diet Library Reference*, vol. 56, no. 4, pp. 83–104.

Local autonomy and partisan linkages   55

Kitamura, W. 2014, ' "Chikishuken" kaikaku', in M. Ito and T. Miyamoto (eds), *Minshutō Seiken no chosen to zasetsu: Sono keikenkara naniwo manabuka*, Nihon Keizai hyoronsh.

Krauss, E.S. and Nyblade, B. 2005, ' "Presidentialization" in Japan? The prime minister, media and elections in Japan', *British Journal of Political Science*, vol. 35, no. 2, pp. 357–368.

Krauss, E.S. and Pekkanen, R.J. 2011, *The rise and fall of Japan's LDP: Political party organizations as historical institutions*, Cornell University Press.

Maeda, Y. 1995, 'Rengō seiken kōsō to chiji senkyo: Kakushin jichitai kara sōyotokae', *Kokka gakkai zasshi*, vol. 108, no. 11, pp. 1329–1390.

Mawatari, T. 2010, *Sengo nihon no chihōgikai: 1955–2008*, Minerva shobo.

McElwain, K. 2013, 'The nationalization of Japanese elections', in K.E. Kushida and P.Y. Lipscy (eds), *Japan under the DPJ: The politics of transition and governance*, Walter H. Shorenstein Asia-Pacific Research Center.

Mochida, N. 2001, 'Taxes and transfers in Japan's local finance', (in Japanese) in M. Muramatsu, F. Iqbal, and I. Kume (eds), *Local government development in post-war Japan*, Oxford University Press, chapter 4.

Mulgan, A.G. 2013, 'Farmers and agricultural policies', in R. Pekkanen, S.R. Reed, and E. Scheiner (eds), *Japan decides 2012: The Japanese general election*, Palgrave Macmillan.

Muramatsu, M. 1975, 'The impact of economic growth policies on local politics in Japan', *Asian Survey*, vol. 15, no. 9, pp. 799–816.

Muramatsu, M. 1986, 'Central-local political relations in Japan: A lateral competition model', *The Journal of Japanese Studies*, vol. 12, no. 2, pp. 303–327.

Muramatsu, M. 1988, *Chihōjichi*, Tokyo daigaku shuppankai.

Muramatsu, M. 1997 [Scheiner and White translation], *Local power in the Japanese state*, University of California Press.

Muramatsu, M. 2009, *Bunken wa toshi gyōsei kikō wo kaetaka?* Daiichi hoki kabushikigaisha.

Muramatsu, M. 2010, *Seikansukuramugata riidāshippu no hōkai*, Toyo keizai shimposha.

Narumi, M. 1994, *Chihō bunken no shisō: Jichitaikaikaku no kiseki to tembō*, Gakuyo Shobo.

Nishio, M. 2007, *Chihō bunken kaikaku*, Tokyo Daigaku Shuppankai.

Nishio, M. 2013, *Jichi, bunken saikō: Chihōjichi wo kokorozasu hitatachie*, Gyosei.

Reed, S.R. 1982, 'Is Japanese government really centralized?', *Journal of Japanese Studies*, vol. 8, no. 1, pp. 133–164.

Reed, S.R. 1986, *Japanese prefectures and policymaking*, University of Pittsburgh Press.

Rosenbluth, F.M. and Thies, M.F. 2010, *Japan transformed: Political change and economic restructuring*, Princeton University Press.

Scheiner, E. 2006, *Democracy without competition in Japan: Opposition failure in a one-party dominant state*, Cambridge University Press.

Shimizu, K. 2012, 'Electoral consequences of municipal mergers', *Journal of East Asian Studies*, vol. 12, no. 3, pp. 381–408.

Shinada Y. 2012, 'Todōfuken gikaigiin no shijikiban', *Levaiathan*, vol. 51, pp. 10–32.

Smith, D.M. 2013, 'Candidate recruitment for the 2012 election: New parties, new methods … same old pool of candidates?', in R. Pekkanen, S.R. Reed, and E. Scheiner (eds), *Japan decides 2012: The Japanese general election*, Palgrave Macmillan, pp. 101–122.

Smith, D.M. 2015, 'Candidates in the 2014 election: Better coordination and higher candidate quality', in R. Pekkanen, S.R. Reed, and E. Scheiner (eds), *Japan decides 2014: The Japanese general election*, Palgrave Macmillan, pp. 118–133.

56 Local autonomy and partisan linkages

Soga, K. and Machidori, S. 2007, *Nihon no chihō seiji: Nigen daihyōsei seifu no seisaku sentaku*, Nagoya Daigaku Shuppan.

Steiner, K. 1965, *Local government in Japan*, Stanford University Press.

Steiner, K., Krauss, E.S., and Flanagan, S.E. (eds) 1980, *Political opposition and local politics in Japan*, Princeton University Press.

Sunahara, Y. 2011, *Chihō seifu no minshushugi: Zaisei shigen no seiyaku to chihō seifu no seisaku sentaku*, Yuhikaku.

Sunahara, Y. 2012, 'Seiken kōtai to reiki yūdō seiji', in T. Mikuriya (eds), *'Seiji shudō' no kyōkun: Seiken kōtai wa nani wo motarasitaka*, Keiso shobo.

Tanaka, A., Kono, M., Hino, A., Iida, T., and Yomiuri Shimbun Yoronchosabu 2009, *2009 nen, naze Seiken kōtai dattanoka: Yomiuri/Waseda no kyodōchōsa de yomitoku nihon seiji no tankan*, Keiso shobo.

Tatebayashi, M. (ed.) 2013, *Seitōsoshiki no seijigaku*, Toyo Keizai shimpo.

Tatebayashi, M., Soga, K., and Machidori, S. 2008, *Hikaku seiji seidoron*, Yuhikaku Alma.

Tsuji, A. 2015, *Sengo nihon chihō seijishiron: Nigen daihyōsei no rittaiteki bunseki*, Bokutakusha.

Tsuji, K. 1976, *Gyōsei no riron (Gyōseigaku kōza Vol. 1)*, Tokyo daigaku shuppankai.

Uekami, T. 2013, *Seitō seiji to fukinitsuna senkyo seido: Kokusei, chihō seiji, tōshu dōshutsu katei*, Tokyo daigaku shuppankai.

3 Campaigning against the capital
Multi-level conflicts within the LDP

In the 2012 and 2013 elections in Japan, media reported widely on the divergence of campaign promises between national and local branches of the ruling party.[1] Media lambasted inconsistencies in the national and local electoral promises of the party as 'double-tongued' and 'duplicitous'. Some observers went so far to call such policy inconsistency within the LDP 'a crisis of party politics'.[2]

A local LDP branch poster for the 2012 Lower House elections embodied these criticisms. The poster, printed and distributed by an official LDP candidate in a Hokkaido district, clearly promised that the LDP was opposing Japan's entry into negotiations for the Trans-Pacific Partnership (TPP) free trade agreement. The poster's categorical claims reassuring local Hokkaido farmers – 'Not lying, adamantly opposed to the TPP, and won't flip-flop: Cultivate Japan. LDP'[3] – were in contrast to the ambiguous position of the LDP national manifesto towards the TPP. When, only months after the election, the Abe administration announced Japan's formal entry, opposition parties and media attacked the ruling party with the problematic poster as proof of their supposed duplicity.[4]

Such 'twists' (*nejire*) in policy positions and campaigning have emerged between the party leadership and local prefectural organizations over various policies of the governing LDP in earlier periods, but they appear to have become graver, more public and consequential from around 2000. Since then, local LDP branches have diverged from the national party line and 'campaigned against Tokyo' on salient issues such as postal service privatization, nuclear energy, US military bases, and farm trade liberalization in dramatic fashion.

In all of these issues, local LDP politicians in dozens of prefectural assemblies have supported resolutions opposing the policy direction taken by the party at national level. In some instances, local LDP branches have supported parliamentary candidates that campaign explicitly against specific national-level policies. At times, prefectural branches have distributed region-specific manifestos in Lower and Upper House elections that diverge from the national one. Local LDP branches have split over whether they should back a gubernatorial candidate parachuted in from the party headquarters or support their own candidate opposing national policy.

58   *Campaigning against the capital*

Such multi-level intra-party conflicts over policy programmes have potentially grave effects on the LDP's party reputation, organizational unity, and electoral success. Following elections, successful candidates who have campaigned against their party's programmes have been unable to prevent party headquarters from moving forward with national policy. This has led voters to view their local LDP representatives as having 'betrayed' them, triggering a backlash in subsequent elections. In some cases, intra-party policy conflicts have triggered internal splits, resulting in official LDP candidates losing against rogue LDP candidates backed by the local LDP branch. Although rare, some of these splits have led to wholesale defections of local LDP legislators following national rebels out of the party.

The previous chapters argued that less vertical integration within parties and greater partisan incongruence across national and local levels of government contribute to greater potential for conflict between different levels of government. In this chapter, we test the first of these hypotheses: less integration within a party triggers more conflictual relations between national and local governments. We also seek to investigate how and when such conflicts impact national policy.

The various multi-level conflicts that have taken place in Japan since the 1990s open up room for testing this claim and investigating the processes and effects of local resistance to national policy. We consider the multi-level dynamics within the LDP at national and local level as this particular party has been in power at the national level for most of this period, aside from several months in 1993–1994 and between 2009 and 2012.

The rest of the chapter proceeds by first identifying the channels by which local LDP partisans oppose policy initiatives as well as the resources available to party HQ to control such resistance. It provides data of the types and changing frequency of local LDP opposition to national policy initiatives since the mid-1980s. After providing brief descriptions of the nature of these multi-level confrontations, it considers potential factors shaping the outcomes of each of these significant conflicts. In the latter half, we look in-depth at some specific cases of multi-level policy conflict within the LDP and compare their process and outcomes.

LDP organization and channels of intra-party interaction

Despite the volatility it has faced in national elections since the early 1990s, the conservatives have maintained a very strong presence in prefectural legislatures (see Figure 3.1). Together with its coalition partner Komeito, the LDP has maintained a majority in most prefectural legislatures during this period (with exceptions in Iwate, Tokyo, Osaka, Mie, and Okinawa). The LDP has been dominant in most prefectural legislatures throughout the post-war period, either holding a majority of seats alone or together with its coalition partner. As of 2015, the LDP was the largest party in all but two legislatures of Japan's 47 prefectures (Osaka, Okinawa) and 2 of the 20 largest designated cities (Osaka,

Campaigning against the capital 59

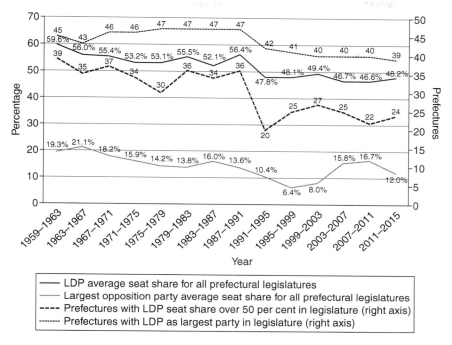

Figure 3.1 Strength of LDP and main opposition party for prefectural legislatures.
Source: compiled by author from *Asahi nenkan* data and newspaper reports.

Sakai). The LDP has a single-party majority in 32 prefectures and a majority together with the Komeito in 10 prefectures. Only in 5 prefectures does it not control the legislative majority, alone or with its coalition partner.

The LDP local network is organized across Japan in a largely standardized fashion in each of Japan's 47 prefectures. The 'local LDP' is composed of its local party members, district-level branches for each of the Lower House and Upper House districts (*senkyoku shibu*) led by incumbent parliamentarians and candidates, prefectural and municipal legislators, the LDP groups in these local legislatures (*kaiha* or *kengidan/shigidan*), municipal and occupational branches, along with their respective back-office staff and personal organization of supporters.

Among these various party branches and affiliates, the prefectural branch office (*todōfuken sōshibu rengōkai* = *kenren*, *toren*, *furen*, or *dōren*) serves as a vital over-arching umbrella organization. The *kenren* serve to aggregate various demands and concerns within the prefecture through their policy council (*kenren seimu chōsakai*) and relay this towards the national level (Sunahara 2013, p. 59). The *kenren* are also primarily responsible for the selection of candidates for prefectural (and at times municipal) legislatures as well as conducting searches and selection, including through open primaries, of national-level

60 *Campaigning against the capital*

candidates. Although the nominations of the prefectural branches are usually accepted by the party headquarters, there are rare instances in which party leadership rejects the nomination of parliamentary and gubernatorial candidates (Sunahara 2013, pp. 60–61).

Under this organizational structure, local LDP partisans have used both intra-party and extra-party channels to express their concerns to party leadership and influence national policy. There are roughly two internal and four external channels described in Table 3.1 below:

In terms of formal intra-party channels, the national conference of prefectural policy research council chairmen (*zenkoku seichō kaichō kaigi*) and national conference of prefectural branch chairmen (*zenkoku kanjichō kaigi*) allows prefectural branch executives to meet with national party executives to discuss party policy and strategy at regular intervals. These conferences, however, are arenas of discussion rather than decision-making – and it is unclear how much influence this plays on national policy formation (Tatebayashi 2013, pp. 59, 305). Moreover, much of the discussions within these conferences remain internal, although some of the content is disclosed to the public and media, making it difficult to determine their overall importance.

Local branches are also expected to state their concerns to the party at national level directly through the parliamentarians elected in their district.[5] These parliamentarians represent local interests in various policy divisions (*bukai*) and research committees (*chōsakai*) of the LDP organization at national level.[6] Case studies suggest that the existence of veteran and influential parliamentarians who pull their weight in the national-level arena provide channels of influence for local branches. Where such veterans do not exist, or if there are no local incumbents, local influence on national matters becomes limited (Tatebayashi 2013, p. 304). As the previous chapter indicated, recent electoral system reforms have resulted in the party executive gaining greater control over national-candidate selection. Combined with trends towards top-down executive leadership and the weakening of backbenchers in national policy-making, local branches' influence on national policy through their local Diet members is expected to have generally weakened.

Local LDP legislators express their preferences towards national policy directions through a number of extra-party channels as well. First, article 99 of the

Table 3.1 Channels of upward influence over national policy for local legislators

	Intra-party	*Extra-party*
Formal	Engage in multi-level party conferences	Pass written opinions Defect from party
Informal	Pressure local Diet members	Deviate from national campaign content Oppose official party candidates

Source: compiled by author.

Campaigning against the capital 61

Local Government Law grants Japanese local legislatures to pass 'written opinions' (*ikensho*) directed towards the national government about policy issues relating to the public good of the local government. Oftentimes these written opinions (henceforth WOs) pertain to matters of national policy, and express local support or opposition to national decisions that are being planned or have been legislated. These WOs are passed by prefectural and municipal legislatures, and are addressed and submitted to the Diet (usually to the Lower House and/ or Upper House chairman) and/or the executive (usually to specific ministries and ministers). Although not legally binding, these WOs signal to local voters and general public the reservations (or less often, the support) a local legislature may have for national policy.

Most WOs would not pass without local LDP legislators' support as most local prefectural legislatures are controlled by the local LDP (alone or in coalition with the local Komeito).

As such, WOs opposing national policy decisions by an LDP government should be interpreted as an expression of intra-party policy conflict. The national-level LDP organization is concerned about local resolutions which can generate 'informal political influence'.[7] The LDP HQ organizational office provided data on the number of WOs passed by prefectural legislatures in 2014, categorized depending on whether they were consistent with national policy. The data show that 1,010 WOs were passed in 2014, of which 91 per cent were consistent (or not directly relevant) to national party policy. The remaining 9 per cent of the WOs were deemed by party HQ officials to be problematic and not consistent with national policy.

The LDP HQ data indicate a divergence among prefectures in terms of the proportion of WOs passed which were not consistent with LDP national policy. In 2014, the five prefectures (Iwate, Kanagawa, Mie, Osaka, and Okinawa) where the LDP does not control a majority alone or with its coalition partner passed higher proportions of WOs that challenged or opposed national policy. Yet even in some prefectures, such as Wakayama, Fukuoka, and Tochigi where the LDP had majority control in the local legislature, between 10 and 15 per cent of the WOs passed were perceived as being inconsistent with national party policy.

LDP HQ generally does not intervene directly against these local resolutions nor sanction local legislators who back resolutions critical of national policy. The back office staff in the LDP generally receive informal clearance requests from local branches over the wording of a local resolution, but can only advise (not compel) local legislators to change the content of these WOs.[8] There are media reports of the LDP HQ requesting local branches to abstain from supporting problematic resolutions for key initiatives, although they do not seem to necessarily be heeded.

Second, local branches could act against national policy by campaigning on a different message from national headquarters. Prefectural branches publish local-version manifestos separate from the manifesto published by HQ. These local manifestos could omit or alter in nuance the policies promised in the

62 *Campaigning against the capital*

national-version manifesto. Here too, however, the party HQ does not screen drafts or coerce local branches to change the content of their local manifestos. Although HQ has on occasion sent notices to local branches asking them not to diverge from the national platform, there are few sanctions to enforce these requests.

Third, local branches could support a candidate who opposes national policy and/or refuse to support a nationally selected candidate. Individual national candidates backed by local legislators may campaign on promises that diverge from the national party line. Although such 'split elections' (*bunretsu senkyo*) for national or gubernatorial campaigns have happened with some frequency in the past, they tend to be conflicts of personality or faction within the local legislature. However, split elections in which differences in policy have been a prominent feature do occur, as the case studies described later will demonstrate.

In past cases, local LDP legislators supporting a rogue gubernatorial or national candidate against an official LDP candidate have been sanctioned, usually lightly, by an official reprimand (*keikoku*) or losing executive positions (*yakushoku teishi*) within the prefectural branch. Less commonly invoked are the more severe sanctions of warning to leave the party (*ritō kankoku*), suspension of membership (*tōin shikaku teishi*), or permanent eviction from party (*jyomei*). Reflecting the decentralized nature of the party organization, the sanctions meted out against these rogue candidates and their supporters are taken in most instances by the prefectural branch executive, not by party headquarters.

Fourth, and most drastically, local legislators could leave the LDP in opposition to national policy decisions. Local-level defection has occurred during the break-up of the LDP and JSP in the period of re-alignment during the mid-1990s (see Milazzo and Scheiner 2011). Local-level legislators have also left the LDP to join new parties such as the People's New Party (*Kokumin Shintō*) and Your Party (*Minna no Tō*) from LDP defections well as regional parties established by chief executives in the latter period (Hijino 2013). It is difficult to determine how much of such local-level party switching is driven by policy considerations, loyalty to local parliamentarians leaving the party, or other electoral strategic considerations. It is likely to be a combination of these factors, but an element of dissatisfaction with the LDP leadership's policy positions (at least ostensibly) plays a role. Defections are the gravest of all actions and taken only rarely. Such defections tend to occur when national parliamentarians leave the LDP and bring local politicians with them. Once a legislator has left the party, the only sanction the party leadership can make is to refuse to let them return to the party in the future.

Frequency and content of local LDP resistance

It is not feasible to ascertain all cases in which local LDP branches have used all types of formal and informal channels to oppose national policy. The research strategy adopted here is to look at intra-party conflicts over major policy initiatives reported widely in the national media. To do so, we look at national media reporting on written opinions (WOs = *ikensho*) passed by local legislatures challenging or questioning a major national policy initiative. When many legislatures pass such resolutions in legislature, they tend to generate reporting which highlights local resistance (and occasionally support) for significant policy initiatives.

Not all of the hundreds of WOs passed in prefectural legislatures are reported by the major newspapers. Rather they tend to report WOs which concern major government initiatives and when multiple prefectures pass such WOs. National newspapers provide searchable databases which allow us to track the number of articles reporting on WOs. As such, the reporting frequency and content can be used as a rough proxy to ascertain the kinds of major national policies being opposed or questioned by local politicians and the frequency in which this occurs.

Figure 3.2 below illustrates how the frequency of reporting on prefectural WOs has gradually increased over the period. Although a rough proxy, the gradual increase of reporting on prefectural WOs over this time suggests that publicized cases of multi-level conflict (in most cases involving LDP intra-party policy conflict) have become increasingly more common in the last 20 years.

Although fluctuating over specific years,[9] Figure 3.2 shows how during 1986 and 1991 the number of articles on WOs ranges at between 0 and 30 articles per year. This range increases to between around 20 and 80 articles in latter periods. Linear approximations of the trends show a gradual increase in the

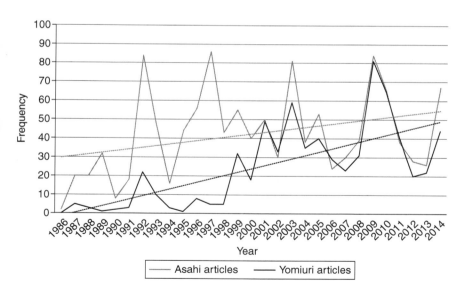

Figure 3.2 Frequency of articles reporting on written opinions (WOs) passed by prefectural legislatures.

Source: compiled by author from *Yomiuri Shimbun* database (*yomidasu*) and *Asahi Shimbun* database (Kikuzo II).

frequency of reporting on WOs during this period. The reporting increases during the Koizumi administration (2000–2006) as local legislatures across Japan criticize and oppose a series of top-down structural reforms. After falling during post-Koizumi LDP administrations, reporting on WOs surges as local legislatures pass various WOs criticizing the DPJ government during 2009–2012. Although dropping off with the return of the LDP to power in 2012, levels of WOs reporting remain at higher levels today compared to the pre-1995 period. In the post-2012 period, local legislatures have passed multiple WOs on major national policy initiatives by the second Abe administration in divisive issues relating to foreign security and constitutional reform, as well as nuclear power and foreign trade.

In fact, the media reporting on WOs largely follows the actual number of all WOs passed by all prefectural legislatures during the same period (Figure 3.3). It is important to note, however, that not all of these resolutions are opposing national policy. These figures include various requests, suggestions, and demands from national governments specific to the prefecture, which are not reported in the media. Nevertheless, if we assume that a certain portion of these WOs are those critical of national policy, the overall upward trend of WOs being passed supports the claim that local governments have become more critical of national policy.

Table 3.2 below lists major national policy initiatives which triggered WOs from local governments since the mid-1980s, where our database begins. The list includes policy areas which were reported widely by Japan's largest daily

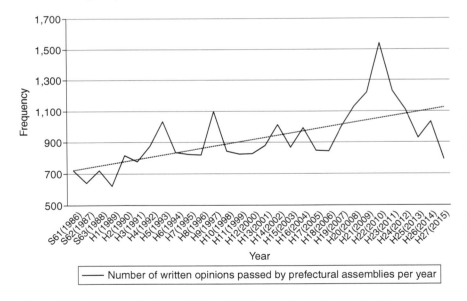

Figure 3.3 Frequency of written opinions (WOs) passed by prefectural legislatures.

Source: compiled by data provided by National Association of Chairpersons of Prefectural Assemblies (*zenkoku todōfukengikai gichōkai*).

newspapers in its national pages. All of these are policies which affect more than one local government, and multiple prefectural and municipal legislatures voiced their opposition or reluctance to the initiatives. They include the period in which WOs were passed concerning the policy area and the number of articles reporting on these actions. For select policy areas where data were available, the table includes the actual number of WOs passed and number of prefectures involved (some prefectures passed multiple resolutions on the same policy).

Table 3.2 shows that WOs were passed against policy issues concerning macro-level redistribution and fiscal policy (such as sales tax, road construction revenues, fiscal decentralization, and privatization), international trade (opening up of rice markets in the early 1990s, TPP – Trans-Pacific Partnership free trade agreement), foreign policy (US Japan defence cooperation guidelines and collective security), and reforms to political institutions (criticisms of political scandals in the early 1990s, electoral system and campaign reform, constitutional reform).

Many of these issues (postal privatization, fiscal decentralization, TPP, road construction revenues) in Table 3.2 were those that affect redistribution to Japan's rural regions directly. These are structural reforms that reduce the levels of government support for rural-area services and subsidies and/or reduce government protection of rural interests (such as farmers in TPP). Others, such as WOs opposing the introduction of single-member districts (1994) or unifying local petitioning to the national government through local DPJ branches (2009) relate to reforms that were perceived to reduce local channels of influence on national policy.

Many of these policy areas were also ones undertaken largely by top-down initiatives of the LDP leadership. During 2000–2006, the Koizumi administration proposed postal privatization, fiscal decentralization (particularly cuts to local subsidies), and reform of road construction revenues without gaining consensus from the party internally. The decision to enter into negotiations of TPP was initially announced by the DPJ Noda administration in 2011 without internal party consensus. It was inherited by the LDP Abe administration in 2013 without any substantial change of direction, followed by widespread internal protest from the party.

During the same period, newspapers have also frequently reported on recurring WOs involving questions of principle or ideology, rather than material interests. These are related to the role of Japan's military overseas, the right of foreign residents to vote, constitutional reform, and interpretations of history and content of history textbooks. In these cases, the WOs that are passed by LDP-controlled prefectural legislatures are those *supporting* the policy positions of the party at national level. For example, some prefectural and numerous municipal governments passed WOs demanding legislation to provide voting rights for foreign residents in Japan during 1993–2000. When the DPJ came to power promising to follow through on this reform, many local governments, led by local conservatives who were following the lead of the national LDP's position, passed WOs opposing such change in 2010. In another instance, during

Table 3.2 List of multi-level policy conflicts over national policy, by frequency of reporting and WOs

Period	Policy area	Search term [ikensho + kengikai + jiminto + tem]	Number of articles Asahi/Yomiuri		Number of prefectures passing WO	Type of policy
1987–1988	Sales tax*	*uriagezei*	31	6	34	redistributive
1987–2015	Consumption tax*	*shohizei*	67	9	9	redistributive
1992–1993	Political corruption – Kanemaru	*sagawa kyubin*	70	15	na	political institutions
1987–1992	Opening rice market*	*kome kaiho*	15	9	22	trade
1993–1994	Political reforms	*seiji kaikaku*	78	19	na	political institutions
1997, 2004–2005	Postal privatization*	*yusei*	45	25	41	redistributive
1999	Guidelines US-Japan treaty	*gaidolainn*	16	5	na	foreign policy
2001, 2008	Road revenue generalization*	*doro tokuteizaigen*	27	21	46	redistributive
2003–2004	Fiscal decentralization*	*sanmi ittai*	12	7	38	redistributive
2009	Reforming local petitioning*	*chinjo madoguchi*	9	15	34	political institutions
2009–2010	Foreign resident voting rights*	*gaikokujin sanseiken*	48	13	34	political institutions
2011–2016	Restarting nuclear plants*	*genpatsu saikado*	16	16	12	regulatory
2010–2014	TPP*	*TPP*	30	38	45	trade
2013–2014	Secrecy laws	*tokutei himitsu*	10	0	na	political institutions
2014–2015	Collective security*	*shudanteki jieiken*	52	11	12	foreign policy
2014	Constitutional reform	*kenpo kaisei*	13	12	na	political institutions
1984–2016	Total number of articles mentioning WO for the above issues		539	221		
1984–2016	Total number of all articles mentioning WO		1,289	728		
	Percentage share of selected issues in all reporting on WOs		42%	30%		

Source: compiled by author using *Yomiuri* and *Asahi* databases.

Note:
* = WOs used to generate analysis for Table 3.3.

Campaigning against the capital 67

the second Abe administration, local LDP groups initiated and passed resolutions in support of constitutional reform being advocated by the prime minister. It appears that on ideological matters that do not affect material interest, local conservatives are willing to support the positions of national party leadership. In general, however, the most frequently reported WOs tend to be those which oppose national initiatives that reduce redistribution and material support for regions.

Table 3.3 seeks to provide simple descriptive statistics of the types of prefectural legislatures which tended to pass resolutions critical of major national policies[10] between 1987 and 2015. The table divides prefectures into three types: those where the LDP is strong in the legislature and has only lost majority control once or zero times between 1986 and 2015 (35 prefectures); those where the LDP is weak, and has lost majority control 2–3 times during the same period (7 prefectures); and those where the LDP is weakest, losing legislative majority control 4 times or more during the same period (8 prefectures).[11] The total number of WOs passed on the 11 national policy issues with asterisks in Table 3.2 has been tallied. These totals are then divided by the number of prefectures by type to get comparable per prefecture averages of WOs being passed.

The results show that for all issues, the prefectural legislatures where the LDP has been most dominant have tended to submit WOs on the selected issues more often than where the LDP was not dominant. Cumulatively, 32 prefectures (or 68 per cent of all 47 prefectures) where the local LDP has been dominant, submitted 70 per cent of bills critical of the sampled national policies being driven by national LDP leadership. In other words, the main source of opposition to national policy for the LDP during this time came from prefectures controlled by its local co-partisans, rather than those from where it had lost majority control. These data indicate how partisan incongruence across levels contributed less to conflicts between central and local governments during LDP administrations between 1987 and 2015.

The tendency of LDP-dominant prefectures to be prone to opposing national policy may be explained in part by the fact that these are rural prefectures. Many of the issues that triggered multi-level conflicts (e.g. postal privatization, fiscal decentralization, agricultural trade liberalization) were those pitting national leadership against rural regions. LDP-dominant rural prefectures led the challenge against national policies, rather than the more urban prefectures (Tokyo, Aichi, Osaka, Kanagawa) where the LDP has been weaker, but less affected by these redistributive policies.

When focusing on the fewer instances of multi-level policy conflicts over non-redistributive issues (more ideological issues such as constitutional reform, foreign voting rights, national security matters), the pattern diverges. For these ideological policy issues which do not directly impinge on rural interests, partisan composition appears to affect the tendency of a local legislature to challenge national policy. For example, the prefectures which have submitted WOs opposing the LDP administration over changes to collective security laws in 2015 (20 WOs in total) were prefectures like Iwate and Mie in which the LDP does not

Table 3.3 Number and frequency of WOs passed by types of prefectures under LDP administrations, between 1987 and 2015

	LPD strong	LDP weak	LDP weakest	Urban prefectures	Rural prefectures	All
	32 other prefectures	*Hyogo, Fukuoka, Ishikawa, Shiga, Miyagi, Nagano, Kochi*	*Hokkaido, Kyoto, Iwate,Kansgawa, Mie, Osaka, Okinawa, Tokyo*	*Tokyo, Aichi, Osaka*	*44 others*	*47 prefectures*
Number of WOs for all policies	46	87	112	24	639	663
Percentage of total	70	13	17	4	96	100
Average per prefecture	14.5	12.4	14	8	14.5	14.2
By policy area						
TPP	105	29	18	1	151	152
Average per prefecture	3.3	4.1	2.3	0.3	3.4	4.8
Road revenues	158	0	24	5	207	212
Average per prefecture	4.9	0.0	3.0	1.7	4.7	6.6
Security bill	9	2	9	0	20	20
Average per prefecture	0.3	0.3	1.1	0.0	0.5	0.6
Restarting nuclear plants	8	0	1	0	9	9
Average per prefecture	0.3	0.0	0.1	0.0	0.2	0.3
Privatizing postal service	50	12	12	5	69	74
Average per prefecture	1.6	1.7	1.5	1.7	1.6	2.3

Source: compiled by author from data provided by National Association of Chairpersons of Prefectural Assemblies (*zenkoku todōfukengikai gichōkai*).

Note
LDP weakest = over 4 times of losing majorities, weak = 2–3 times of losing majorities, strong = 1–0 times of losing majorities, between 1986 and 2011 (Tsuji 2015, p. 393). N = 663.

Campaigning against the capital 69

have majorities. At the same time, prefectures such as Yamaguchi and Akita where the LDP is dominant have passed resolutions in support of the collective security measures.

Conditions and outcomes of multi-level conflicts

What impact, then, does the voicing of local opposition to national policy have on the eventual outcome of these initiatives? Voicing discontent through written opinions has no binding legal effect in stopping the ruling party leadership from passing policy into law. It may thus appear that voluble local opposition through passing these resolutions merely represents 'cheap talk' where local conservatives seek to distance themselves from unpopular or divisive national initiatives, without long-term commitment to resist policy change.

The behaviour of local conservatives during 1987 and 1988 over the introduction of the general sales tax and consumption tax is illustrative of such dynamics. The Nakasone administration submitted a bill introducing a general sales tax, despite mounting general opposition. Leading up to this period, local conservatives in prefectural legislatures across Japan, facing re-election in the joint unified elections later in March and April of the year, passed resolutions demanding to abolish or revise the sales tax. When the LDP suffered a severe defeat in an Upper House by-election in Iwate in early March of 1987 on the issue – which became known as the 'Iwate Shock' – even more local legislatures passed WOs against the policy.[12] Local LDP branches and gubernatorial candidates refused to invite party executives, including Prime Minister Nakasone, to come to their prefectures to campaign on their behalf.[13] Despite attempts to distance themselves from the party leadership, local conservatives suffered considerable losses in the local elections that year and the sales tax bill was abandoned.

In the following year, however, when the Takeshita administration submitted a bill introducing the consumption tax in place of the sales tax, local legislatures did not oppose it with the same ferocity. In part, this reflected changes in the content of the bill, which promised a proportion of the revenues to local governments, but also the fact that major local elections had passed, as the head of the National Association of Chairpersons of Prefectural Assemblies acknowledged in the media.[14] In this instance of multi-level opposition, local opposition may have added pressure on the national party leadership to shelve a national initiative. But their opposition was temporary and lasted only up to their own elections.

From the perspective of party leadership, the strategic decision to back down or push through on policy unpopular among local partisans depends on a whole array of factors. These include among other things: electoral calculations of the LDP leadership concerning implementation of policies that may be unpopular in certain regions but has support elsewhere; overall support for the cabinet; proximity to an election (be it national or local) and its expected impact; how widespread and intense local opposition has been; as well as the strength of opposition parties and their position on these specific initiatives.

70　*Campaigning against the capital*

As a general assumption, national party leadership would probably over-ride local resistance and implement a policy if it deemed the near-term electoral consequences from such an action to be acceptable. If local LDP resistance is limited to a few or several prefectures, popular support exists for a policy, and support ratings of the PM and cabinet are high, the party leadership may be willing to ignore or over-ride local revolts. On the other hand, when local branch opposition to a policy is extremely widespread and severe, popular support for the policy weak or divided, the party at national level unpopular, and opposition parties are also positioning themselves against the initiative, one would expect electoral consequences to be strongly negative.

For example, the Hashimoto administration stepped back from initial plans to fully privatize the postal services in 1997 after facing an uproar of protests from postal service masters, affiliated LDP parliamentarians, and local conservatives. At the time the Hashimoto cabinet had weak popular ratings (at 35 per cent) and poll numbers showed a majority of the public opposed to the policy (60 per cent) (Maclachlan 2011, p. 215). In contrast, the Koizumi administration persisted in fighting an equally intense surge of local opposition in 2005 and successfully pushed through postal privatization. At the peak of the conflict in the summer of 2005, Koizumi's support ratings in the public was higher (54 per cent) and public support in polls for the policy higher (62 per cent) than during Hashimoto's time.[15]

Thus resistance from local branches is only one of many factors impinging on national policy formation. The multi-level conflicts listed in Table 3.2 took place under a combination of varying conditions, each presenting a different calculus for leadership in terms of whether to persist or back down on the major initiatives. Without being able to control for these conditions, we do not have like-to-like comparisons where only the severity and extent of local LDP opposition differs. This makes it difficult to determine the general casual impact of local LDP resistance to national initiatives.

Rather than analyse all cases and their diverging contexts, three salient instances of intra-party conflict were selected to briefly trace the actions and effects of local insubordination. The policy areas are postal privatization, TPP, and US bases in Okinawa. These represent highly publicized intra-party conflicts in which LDP local branches went beyond 'cheap talk' of criticizing the initiatives and pursued various actions to resist national policy initiatives. Delving into these cases will help trace how local LDP branches sought to resist national initiatives and how party headquarters responded to these challenges.

Three cases of local LDP opposition

Postal privatization

Postal privatization reforms were pursued during two periods, under the Hashimoto administration in 1997 and the Koizumi administration in 2004–2005. Local conservatives resisted these changes in both instances, but we focus on the

Campaigning against the capital 71

Koizumi period as this particular conflict spilled over into national elections, as famously occurred in 2005, providing a test for local conservatives of their willingness to resist national policy.

The process of implementing the postal privatization policy epitomized Koizumi's top-down leadership as it bypassed traditional consensus making within the party (Maclachlan 2011). Postal reforms were resisted by postal office organizations in close cooperation with LDP parliamentarians dependent on their electoral support, particularly in rural areas.[16] Local conservatives joined this struggle against postal privatization primarily in two stages. First, starting in 2004, local LDP legislative groups at municipal and prefectural level passed WOs opposing privatization. Within a month of a cabinet decision of postal privatization taken in September 2004, 22 prefectures and nearly 1,600 municipalities had passed such WOs.[17] By the time the privatization bill was submitted, a total of 41 prefectural assemblies – most of them with local LDP holding majorities alone or together with its coalition partner – had submitted these WOs to the national government. There is no evidence of the national executive either trying to prevent or sanction the submission of these statements opposing national policy.

Local conservatives also used formal intra-party channels to express their concern about privatization in national meetings of prefectural branch chairmen,[18] calling for the party leadership to listen to local concerns. Both during this meeting and the party conference in January 2005, Koizumi repeated that the 'LDP is not a party that represents only certain interests or regions', refusing to listen to local opposition voices.

When these calls were rebuffed and Koizumi went on to submit the bill to Diet, local branches of the LDP backed Lower House LDP parliamentarians that had voted against the bill in July 2005. There were 26 LDP prefectural branches with incumbent parliamentarians who had voted against the bill. These branches faced two options leading up to the snap election in September which Koizumi called in response to this revolt: back the so-called 'postal rebels' or back the official LDP candidate nominated and parachuted in by party headquarters into their districts. Asano (2006, pp. 197–207) finds that of the 26 prefectures, 7 prefectures (Gifu, Okayama, Saga, Shizuoka, Tokushima, Yamanashi, and Oita) refused to accept the parachuted LDP candidates and persisted in supporting their local rebels up to the elections. These prefectural branches recommended (*kenren suisen*) the local rebel candidates against the LDP HQ nominated candidates. In the remaining 19 prefectures with postal rebels, the LDP branches decided to accept the official LDP candidates parachuted into their region by HQ or remained neutral towards either the official LDP or the local postal rebel candidate.

A simple comparison of the electoral results of the prefectures in which the local LDP branch was united against HQ and those which acceded to HQ pressure is suggestive. The 7 rebellious prefectural branches that persisted in opposing LDP HQ backed a total of 12 postal rebels. Of these, 9 were re-elected as independents and 3 lost their seats (a re-election rate of 75 per cent). For the

72 *Campaigning against the capital*

remaining 22 postal rebels in prefectures where the prefectural branches did not stand united behind them, only 5 were re-elected (a re-election rate of 23 per cent). These figures suggest that local LDP branches, if united behind their preferred candidate, could successfully back an independent candidate and defeat an official LDP candidate over differences in national policy.

Following this election, the LDP HQ demanded that local branches punish severely those responsible for supporting the postal rebels and carry out internal discipline. The party general secretary called the executives of eight prefectural branches to Tokyo to pressure them to take responsibility for campaigning against LDP candidates.[19] In the exceptional case of Gifu, where the postal rebels were most numerous, party HQ directly expelled two prefectural legislators who were executives in the local branch.[20] Elsewhere, most disciplinary actions were taken by prefectural branches. In these instances sanctions were light, such as official reprimands or demotion from executive positions in the party branch.[21]

Despite success among some prefectural branches in backing rebel candidates opposed to postal privatization, these were numerically too few to block legislation in Diet. The party leadership managed to ultimately pass the privatization bill, but widespread opposition, including those of local LDP branches, had resulted in various compromises (Machlaclan 2011, pp. 286–329). Moreover, successive LDP prime ministers after Koizumi waffled over the implementation of the reforms, re-admitting postal rebels as well as rebuilding ties with postal service interest groups. Under the DPJ government, the postal privatization law was revised and the process further delayed. The minister (Kamei Shizuka) in charge of postal affairs under the DPJ was a former LDP veteran who had left the party in 2005 to form a new party (Kokumin Shintō) and had secured a seat with the electoral support of local LDP politicians.[22]

Agricultural trade liberalization – TPP

Along with postal privatization, initiatives by the government to join the TPP triggered intense opposition from local governments in rural areas.[23] In November 2011, the DPJ Noda administration announced intentions to enter into the TPP, a multilateral trade agreement that was expected to substantially reduce tariff protection of Japanese farmers. The DPJ failed to formally enter into negotiations before losing power in 2012. During the 2012 election, the LDP campaigned on a vague promise not to join the TPP if it meant an indiscriminate abolition of tariffs. Numerous individual LDP Lower House candidates and local branches, however, stated their unconditional opposition to the TPP and actively campaigned against it. In March of 2013, Abe announced that Japan was entering into TPP negotiations. During the 2013 Upper House elections, rural LDP candidates faced the challenge of explaining the turnaround in LDP national policy and convincing local farmers of their commitment to protect agriculture.

Local branches of the LDP opposed TPP in a number of ways. First, they voiced their dissatisfaction towards the leadership in formal intra-party channels,

Such as the national meeting of prefectural branch chairmen.[24] Second, local legislators across multiple prefectures passed local resolutions opposing or calling for caution over TPP both under DPJ and LDP governments (Table 3.2). The LDP branches backed WOs categorically opposed to entering TPP negotiations prior to the 2012 elections. Twenty-eight prefectural legislators again passed similar WOs in the same month (March 2013) that Abe formally announced intentions to enter TPP negotiations. There have been no reports of local LDP branches being punished for supporting these WOs opposing TPP. Faced with this upsurge of criticism, the Abe government compromised in the following month to shield five 'sacred' agricultural items (rice, wheat, dairy, beef and pork, and sugar) from tariff cuts. Third, local branches campaigned against TPP by adjusting their local manifestos and policy programmes in national elections. Some prefectures avoided mentioning the TPP altogether in their local manifesto, despite it being in the national one.[25] In Hokkaido, Japan's largest agricultural region, the local LDP branch included the promise that the government will 'exit the TPP negotiations if key agricultural items are not protected' in its local manifesto, a promise not found in the national one.[26] This discrepancy in policy promises of national and local LDP was widely publicized in the media, leading HQ to call for local branches to abstain from diverging in campaign material.[27]

Local opposition to TPP also affected local elections, with the Saga gubernatorial elections in January 2015 a key instance. The LDP Saga branch initially nominated a gubernatorial candidate opposed to TPP and reforms of agricultural cooperatives. LDP headquarters, in a rare move, rejected the candidate and parachuted in another one who actively supported such measures (as well as restarting nuclear plants in Saga). The local LDP branch split over supporting the official LDP candidate against its original choice, a former bureaucrat who ran as an independent opposing these policies.[28] The non-LDP candidate won with support from the local Japan Agricultural cooperatives (JA) and a majority of local LDP legislators.

The results were reported as an instance of LDP headquarters failing to try to 'forcibly push national policy goals against local interests'.[29] Moreover, it highlighted the loyalty and dependence of local legislators to interest groups – in this case, JA – even at the cost of opposing Tokyo. None of the local legislators in the Saga LDP branch have been punished for these actions against HQ, although the Saga branch executive offered to resign as branch chairman. Following the Saga elections, however, the LDP leadership launched an attack on the JA aimed at weakening its political influence by passing legislation to reform the cooperative. This in turn has led to JA threats to not support local LDP legislators in future elections who do not oppose TPP or agricultural cooperative reform.[30]

Despite continued resistance from farmer groups working in tandem with national and local LDP politicians from rural prefectures, the LDP leadership announced a deal over TPP in October 2015. The agreement did not fully protect the five 'sacred' agricultural products, as had been promised by Abe in

74 *Campaigning against the capital*

2013, triggering criticism from farming representatives. In response, the Abe government promised various compensatory schemes to minimize the political fallout from the TPP agreement.[31] Here, as with the postal privatization, national initiatives were implemented with compromises and compensation to mollify opposition of interest groups working together with local LDP politicians.

Okinawa base relocation

The final case – intra-party conflict in the LDP over US base relocation policy in Okinawa prefecture – demonstrates dynamics which occur when an opposed policy is region-specific.

Until 2009, the LDP HQ and its local Okinawa branch were in agreement to relocate the US Marine Corps Airs Station Futenma in Okinawa to a new base to be constructed within the island. But in 2009, the newly elected DPJ administration promised to relocate the airbase outside of Okinawa. This raised the hopes of local voters, a majority in support of reducing the burden of hosting US military bases in the prefecture. The DPJ administration's promise led the prefectural LDP branch to switch its position and demand relocation of the base outside Okinawa, while the LDP national leadership maintained its original stance.

Numerous polls indicated that a majority of voters, both within and outside of Okinawa prefecture, opposed base relocation to Henoko Bay. The local LDP therefore was aware that they would face difficulty in the 2013 national elections without diverging from the LDP national line. The local LDP chairman negotiated extensively with the party HQ which 'grudgingly agreed' to allow this localized policy.[32] The Okinawa local LDP manifestos included promises to relocate the base outside of Okinawa, while the national manifesto did not contain such a promise. Although pressures from HQ emerged to fix this discrepancy, the local branch persisted and published its local manifestos unchanged.

Following the Upper House elections in 2013, the Abe administration sought to accelerate relocation plans. The party HQ stepped up pressures on parliamentarians elected from Okinawa districts, including reports of possible threats to withhold nominations in future elections for those continuing to oppose national policy. The Okinawa parliamentarians eventually announced their decision to accept relocation to Henoko. The local LDP branch also officially reversed its position soon after, followed by a similar agreement by the incumbent governor to accept relocation to Henoko and give his permission to begin construction of the new base facilities. This about-face by local LDP legislators, MPs, and governor who had campaigned and won national elections in opposition to Henoko was widely criticized as a 'betrayal' of Okinawan voters. In the subsequent 2014 election, all four Okinawa LDP Lower House incumbents lost their district seats.

These intra-party tensions spilled over into vital local chief executive elections. The Okinawa gubernatorial elections in January of 2014 became a divided election between the incumbent (Nakaima Hirokazu) who received official LDP nomination and a former LDP prefectural legislator and mayor of Naha city (Onaga Takeshi) opposing relocation to Henoko. The gubernatorial election centred upon the base issue and the challenger, who despite being a veteran LDP local legislator, secured the organizational support of other opposition parties, including the Japanese Communist Party, during the campaign. A number of local LDP legislators, primarily those in Naha city, including eight Naha municipal legislators, campaigned against the LDP official candidate. These legislators eventually left the party in opposition to national policy, although the local branch executive sought to stop them from leaving.[33]

After losing all district-level parliamentarians and a governor in Okinawa in 2014, the LDP HQ has tried to push forward with plans to relocate the Futenma base to Henoko. The Abe administration's attempt to accelerate the relocation process, however, has been blocked by Governor Onaga since March of 2015 after he called for a halt to construction work on the new base. Onaga later cancelled gubernatorial permission (based on local ordinance) to build a landfill for the base, and the central government has taken the matter to court to over-ride the governor's decision.[34] These local challenges by the Okinawa governor delayed national policy, while leaving LDP leadership with a highly publicized and damaging stand-off with local conservatives in Okinawa prefecture. A rogue LDP gubernatorial candidate supported by discontented elements within the local LDP branch has become a major hurdle for a critical national security policy.

Conclusion

As theory predicts, the chapter demonstrated that multi-level intra-party policy conflicts in the LDP have increased after the 1990s as party integration weakened and national and local electoral environments diverged. Resistance by the LDP local branches to national initiatives generated greater media attention, much of it critical of policy inconsistencies in the party. Despite signs of being more sensitive to such insubordination from below, the LDP national executive has been unable to do much about it. All of these reflect a decoupling of the two levels of the party over major policy areas and a readiness of the LDP leadership to carry out policies widely unpopular among local conservatives.

The intensity and outcomes of these conflicts vary considerably, but in the majority of the cases the party leadership eventually implemented policies which were initiated. Although not as powerful an institutional veto player as the Upper House, the LDP's disgruntled local LDP politicians have not only voiced opposition, but at times successfully backed non-LDP candidates opposed to national initiatives. Together with interest groups such as the postal service masters and agricultural cooperatives, local politicians have put pressures on their local Diet candidates electorally. At times, they have successfully backed gubernatorial candidates or defecting national LDP candidates opposed to the

76 *Campaigning against the capital*

LDP leadership's initiatives. These politicians have used their position to delay or challenge national programmes with some success. Certainly, the ruling party in control of the national legislature can ignore and over-ride such challenges. Yet it appears that in many instances, concerns of electoral backlash from its local branches have limited strong-arming by the centre. The LDP's old guard in the regions, though not always fully blocking change, thus slowed down the 're-invention' of LDP from a party beholden to local interests to a more unified, programmatic party.

How damaging, then, would it have been for the ruling party if local conservatives actually succeeded in halting major policy initiatives? The eventual electoral impact of local conservatives successfully blocking a major policy initiative is not necessarily clear; the LDP may lose some pro-reform swing voters, while gaining votes from its traditional base. Some of these measures command majority support albeit with significant levels of opposition among national voters (postal privatization, TPP), while others faced stronger public opposition (sales and consumption tax, collective security). Moreover, initiatives criticized by local conservatives (aside from postal privatization during the 2005 election) were not promoted as key electoral campaign themes.[35] Instead, precisely because of their divisive nature they were played down, illustrating how the ruling party is torn by the need/desire to pursue difficult reforms without alienating their rural base. Despite pushing through difficult reforms, past administrations have generally watered down, provided compensation, or even backtracked on these policies.

The greater costs to the LDP leadership of intractable local conservatives may rather be in how the resulting party disunity prevents the party from generating support for difficult policies from the public. Local conservatives, representing rural preferences, have acted as a countervailing voice against a party leadership seeking to carry out what were deemed as necessary, national-level reforms. As rural conservatives have an entrenched voice in local politics, when they 'campaign against Tokyo', the LDP leadership's ability to convince the Japanese public of difficult reforms is weakened. If local conservatives were more loyal agents of the centre, the LDP may have been better able to persuade hostile voters in rural regions to accept these policy changes.

In light of these concerns, the party HQ may want to re-negotiate this relationship with local branches and unify its position across levels. The LDP, however, appears to have few resources to do so. Following the postal privatization conflict, party leadership took measures to centralize party organization further. But these were limited to expanding controls over backbench parliamentarians, not local legislators. At the time, LDP chairman Tsutomu Takebe threatened to strip away discretionary power over local candidate nominations from local branches, but this never materialized.[36] In any case such a step may be futile, as local LDP legislators are largely not dependent on the party label or funding for their own elections.

In the meantime, most rural conservatives are likely to remain grudgingly affiliated to the LDP. In rural areas, there are no other viable opposition parties

Campaigning against the capital 77

championing alternative policies in the national political arena. New parties such as People's New Party (*Kokumin shintō*), People's Life Party (*Seikatsu no tō*), or New Party Daichi (*Shintō daichi*) formed by parliamentarians defecting from the LDP or DPJ to represent rural interests have fizzled out. These groups have also failed to generate strong local organizations or capture important gubernatorial or mayoral posts to attract local defectors and voters away from the LDP in the local electoral arena. Local conservatives will likely thus remain affiliated, but weakly integrated within the LDP, but resist initiatives by the central government through their dominance in local legislatures.

In terms of Japan's national-level party competition, the dominance of the LDP in local legislatures – particularly in its rural strongholds – has traditionally been perceived as one of its greatest advantages over rival parties. Scholars have demonstrated how the LDP's wide and entrenched network of local legislators have acted as the party's 'hands and feet' to mobilize voters as well as provided a vital pool of quality candidates for national elections (Scheiner 2006, pp. 132–145). In contrast, the opposition parties' lack of strong roots in local politics, particularly in rural areas, has hurt their ability to campaign and secure candidates across the country. The weakness of opposition parties locally was thus a key cause of endemic opposition failure nationally during the post-war period (Scheiner 2006). The chapter has shown how the LDP's local base is becoming a problem as much as an asset for carrying out policies favoured by the party executive and majority voters.

Historically, the current emergence of local opposition from within the LDP represents a significant counterpoint to another important period of local opposition to the centre in Japan during the 1960s and 1970s. During this period, policy change came from below. So-called 'progressive local governments' led by governors and mayors backed by parties on the left successfully challenged central government on welfare and environmental policies (Steiner *et al.* 1980). In comparison, the post-2000s have been a period where reforms have been pursued by the LDP party leadership at centre, but resisted by an entrenched and dominant local LDP. The conservatives in local legislatures have behaved as 'activists' within their party, dragging their foot and generally delaying policy change from above.

These intra-party conflicts within the LDP, although a key feature, are only one aspect of the changing national and local partisan dynamic in Japan since the 1990s. The next chapter investigates how multi-level conflicts occurred across party lines when different parties controlled national and local governments.

Notes

1 This chapter is a revised and expanded version of a previously published article: Hijino, Ken Victor Leonard, 'Local politics in Japan: The old guard strikes back', *Asian Survey*, vol. 56, no. 5, September/October 2016.
2 'Nimaijita zuruiyo', *Chunichi Shimbun*, 7 June 2013.
3 '*Uso tsukanai, TPP danko hantai, burenai; nihon wo tagayasu jimintō*'.

78 *Campaigning against the capital*

4 'Shushō wa "danko hantai to ittakotowa ichidomo nai" to ittaga kono senkyokōhō wa nannanoka', *Shimbun Akahata*, 9 April 2016. 'Kenshō TPP:1 kome he ikinari saigotūchō', *Asahi Shimbun*, 18 November 2015.

5 Interview with LDP HQ organization headquarters staff (*soshiki undō hombu*), 23 February 2015.

6 Interview ibid.

7 Interview with LDP HQ organization headquarters staff (*soshiki undō hombu*) in Tokyo, 23 February 2015.

8 Interview ibid.

9 An exceptional jump in WOs reporting in 1992–1993 is related to WOs passed across Japan denouncing political corruption concerning the Recruit scandal at the time. Asahi data show a spike in reporting on WOs in 1997–1998; many of these are WOs related to history textbook revisions concerning comfort women, which the Yomiuri largely did not report.

10 The policies used in these calculations are those where the author has complete data of the date and prefecture submitting the WOs (shared by the National Association of Chairpersons of Prefectural Assemblies). These are the ones in Table 3.2 with all columns of data filled. In addition, the data exclude WOs passed under non-LDP governments in 1993–1994 and 2009–2012 since we are seeking to assess frequency of intra-party conflicts between LDP administrations and local LDP-controlled legislatures.

11 The typology of prefectural legislatures in terms of LDP strength is calculated from data provided by Tsuji (2015, p. 216, pp. 391–393).

12 'Han uriagezei no ugki, chihōgikai de kakudai 31 todōfuken de jimin mo sanka', *Asahi Shimbun*, 16 March 1987.

13 'Shushō no ōen okotowari katamaranu yūzei nittei' (87 tōitsu chihōsen), *Asahi Shimbun*, 17 March 1987.

14 'Shōhizei hantai kaketsu ha zero chihōgikai samagawari no taiō', *Yomiuri Shimbun*, 17 July 1988.

15 'Shūinsen 30 nichi kōji "kanshin dai" jōshō 57% zenkaisen uwamawaru: Yomiuri Shimbun yoron chōsa', *Yomiuri Shimbun*, 27 August 2005.

16 Although polls indicate that about 42 per cent of the Japanese public supported the policy against 30 per cent opposition in May 2005, opposition towards postal privatization was stronger among rural residents concerned of a decline in postal services in remote areas. See poll in *Asahi Shimbun*, 31 May.

17 'Nijuni todofuken de ikensho saitaku', *Asahi Shimbun*, 10 October 2004.

18 ' "Jimin, ichibu dantai no daihyō de nai" Koizumi kaikaku he kyōryōku wo zenkoku kanjichō ni yōsei', *Asahi Shimbun*, 18 January 2005.

19 'Chiho mo kejime atsuryoku', *Asahi Shimbun*, 15 November 2005.

20 'Jimin Takebe kanjichō, Gifu kengi ni rito yokyu', *Asahi Shimbun*, 16 December 2005.

21 Moreover, 11 postal rebels who had been re-elected as independents were later re-admitted into the party under the Abe administration. As a result, most of the local legislators (such as those in Tottori prefecture) that had left the party on the postal issue were also eventually re-admitted into the LDP.

22 'Hiroshima rokku, mitsudomoe, kinpaku', *Asahi Shimbun*, 7 September 2005.

23 Popular support has increased over time for the TPP, but diverges across rural and urban areas. In one poll, 53 per cent supported TPP, but agricultural regions such as Hokkaido and Tohoku had a majority of voters opposing it. See *Sankei Shimbun*, 15 February 2013.

24 For example, media reports criticisms levelled against the party leadership over TPP in the LDP's national prefectural branch chairmen meeting in 2013 and 2015.

25 'Jimin kenren ga chiiki koyaku', *Yomiuri Shimbun*, 29 June 2013.

26 Interview with Hokkaido Shimbun reporters, 5 February 2015.

Campaigning against the capital 79

27 'Chiikiban koyaku, jimin ga kuryo', *Asahi Shimbun*, 11 May 2013.
28 'Chijisen jishitsu jishu tohyo he', *Asahi Shimbun*, 19 December 2014.
29 'Jimin haiboku, Saga no ran de mieta koto', *Asahi Shimbun*, 14 January 2015.
30 See Aurelia G. Mulgan, 'The Empire Strikes Back: Reforming Japan's agricultural co-ops and the local elections', *East Asia Forum*, 9 April 2015. Available at www.east-asiaforum.org/2015/04/09/the-empire-strikes-back-reforming-japans-agricultural-co-ops-and-the-local-elections/ [accessed 5 November 2015].
31 See Aurelia G. Mulgan, 'Abe looks to reassure farmers on TPP', *East Asia Forum*, 15 October 2015. Available at www.eastasiaforum.org/2015/10/15/abe-looks-to-reassure-farmers-on-tpp/ [accessed 5 November 2015].
32 Interview with Onaga Masatoshi, former chairman of Okinawa LDP prefectural branch, 13 February 2015.
33 Interview, ibid.
34 'Seifu, Okinawa chiji wo teiso', *Asahi Shimbun*, 17 November 2015.
35 This tactic of downplaying divisive policy areas (TPP, agricultural reform, energy policy, and Okinawa) in campaigning has been evident in the 2012 and 2014 elections. Pekannen *et al.* (2013, 2015).
36 'Chiho mo kejime atsuryoku', *Asahi Shimbun*, 15 November 2005.

References

Asano, M. 2006, *Shimin shakai ni okeru seido kaiakaku: Senkyo seido to kohosha rikuruto*, Keio gijuku daigaku shuppan.
Hijino, K.V.L. 2013, 'Liabilities of partisan labels: Independents in Japanese local elections', *Social Science Japan Journal*, vol. 16, no. 1, pp. 63–85.
Maclachlan, P.L. 2011, *The people's post office: The history and politics of the Japanese postal system, 1871–2010*, Harvard University Asia Center.
Milazzo, C. and Scheiner, E. 2011, 'When do you follow the (national) leader? Party switching by subnational legislators in Japan', *Electoral Studies*, vol. 30, no. 1, pp. 148–161.
Pekkanen, R., Reed, S.R., and Scheiner, E. (eds) 2013, *Japan decides 2012: The Japanese general election*, Palgrave Macmillan, pp. 101–122.
Pekkanen, R., Reed, S.R., and Scheiner, E. (eds) 2016, *Japan decides 2014: The Japanese general election*, Palgrave Macmillan, pp. 118–133.
Scheiner, E. 2006, *Democracy without competition in Japan: Opposition failure in a one-party dominant state*, Cambridge University Press.
Steiner, K., Krauss, E.S., and Flanagan, S.E. (eds) 1980, *Political opposition and local politics in Japan*, Princeton University Press.
Sunahara, Y. 2013, 'Seitō no chihōsoshiki to chihōgiin no bunsek', in M. Tatebayashi (ed.), *Seitōsoshiki no seijigaku*, Toyo Keizai shimpo.
Tatebayashi, M. (ed.) 2013, *Seitōsoshiki no seijigaku*, Toyo Keizai shimpo.
Tsuji, A. 2015, *Sengo nihon chihō seijishiron: Nigen daihyōsei no rittaiteki bunseki*, Bokutakusha.

4 The politics of local opposition
Multi-level conflicts under the DPJ

Barely a week had passed since the LDP suffered a historic loss of seats in the Lower House and was booted out of government in August 2009 before local conservatives began to assert themselves. In meetings of local prefectural branches across Japan, local LDP politicians blamed national party leadership and Diet members for the election results. Some argued that the past decade of party headquarters ignoring local demands resulted in the withering of the party's grassroots and catastrophic defeat at national elections. Local politicians called for a rebuilding of the party with demands for more open candidate selection procedures, greater communication and cooperation between local and national politicians, and more on-the-ground campaigning and mobilization efforts by Diet members.[1]

The national party leadership, at the head of a small surviving rump in the Lower House, was entering opposition for the first time in more than 15 years. Despite being wiped out at national level, the LDP continued to hold a majority alone or with its coalition partners in most prefectural assemblies. Though facing severe criticism from its local base, the party leadership was soon turning to the local branches for aid in returning to power nationally. The departing Prime Minister Aso Taro apologized to local branches for electoral defeat while claiming to rebuild the party on 'the prefectural branches that are our greatest asset'.[2]

In the meantime, the newly minted DPJ administration controlled comfortable majorities in both chambers of Diet and was, at least initially, firmly in charge of the reins of national power. Looking beyond the capital, however, the DPJ leadership faced LDP-controlled legislatures and few chief executives sympathetic to the party in most regions. With only 15 per cent of all prefectural assembly seats, compared to the LDP's 48 per cent, the DPJ was thin on the ground (see Figure 2.5 and Figure 3.1). Even in the handful of prefectures where the DPJ was relatively strong (e.g. in Iwate and Tokyo where it was the largest party, and its strongholds such as Hokkaido and Aichi), the party did not have majorities to control the local legislative agenda. It had an equally weak presence among the directly-elected local executive offices for governor and mayor. As of August 2009, only two governors (Iwate and Shizuoka) had been backed by the DPJ and won against an LDP-backed opponent.

The politics of local opposition 81

Not only was the DPJ facing an entrenched network of conservatives at local level, it came to power with an agenda that drastically reformed local-centre relations and challenged traditional rural interests. In its election manifesto, the party had prioritized decentralization reforms and a shift 'from concrete to people': reducing the dependence of regional economies to traditional public works and expanding universal welfare programmes. The party promised to cancel major dams, abolish highway tolls, reduce construction of new highways, as well as reset US military base arrangements in Okinawa. Many of these national policy programmes threatened region-specific interests and traditional clientelist groups with strong links to local conservatives. These DPJ programmes were thus an invitation to revolt from local conservatives, who, sharing no partisan affiliation to the DPJ, were less fettered than under LDP administrations to challenge programmes emanating from the new ruling party.

Hence during the length of the DPJ administration (2009–2012), Japan experienced an unprecedented degree of multi-level incongruence where different partisan forces controlled national and local levels of government. During its administration, the DPJ failed to transform its national power to advantage locally, remaining a weak presence in local politics. Even after a major local election in 2011, local conservatives maintained dominance in legislatures, albeit with some losses to newly emerging regional parties.

The landslide victory of the DPJ in 2009 thus represented an anomalous situation[3] for Japan's multi-level dynamics. It serves as a valuable natural experiment to investigate the impact of widespread partisan incongruence across levels of government. We can ask if these conditions generated greater conflict over policy between national and local levels of government than during periods of partisan congruence, as existing literature suggests. Or were these multi-level conflicts similar to those that occur within a de-integrated and decentralized party? What impact did widespread local opposition from the LDP base have on DPJ national policy-making, i.e. how does partisan incongruence affect national policy processes?

This chapter provides an analysis of how local partisans in public office challenge a national government under control of another party. It compares the frequency and types of conflicts over policy that occurred primarily within the national and local levels of one party (within the LDP or within the DPJ) with those that occurred across party lines (DPJ against the LDP). We investigate these questions in the rest of the chapter by first setting out what we should theoretically expect in terms of the behaviour of the LDP, DPJ, and regional parties under conditions of partisan incongruence.

The chapter then provides an overview of multi-level relations under the three years of the DPJ administration and descriptive quantitative data on local written opinions for national policies under the DPJ, comparing it with those under LDP administrations. We then focus on some key cases of multi-level conflict in three categories: those that involved redistributive matters to rural regions in general; region-specific issues such as public works and nuclear power

82 *The politics of local opposition*

plants; and other policy initiatives which do not directly affect territorial interests. These cases are investigated to observe what influence local partisans had in shaping national policy process under the DPJ.

Expectations for the local LDP and DPJ branches

There are two groups of local partisans and their interactions with the DPJ administration which we will investigate and compare: the LDP and the DPJ in prefectural legislatures. The characteristics of these respective party organizations are expected to affect the behaviour of local partisans to national politics and policy-making, so these are expounded briefly below.

First, as the previous chapters indicated, by 2009, the LDP became an increasingly de-integrated party with linkages of shared interests at national and local level weakening since the mid-1990s. The question which arises is whether these decoupled local LDP branches were willing to aid, and if so under what context, its national counterpart that had fallen into opposition. One would expect that with a weakened and chastened party leadership in opposition, the party at national level no longer could initiate legislation and push its policy agenda against local opposition. Instead, the power dynamic is expected to shift towards local LDP organizations. Using their considerable autonomy and resources (linkages to interest groups and members, mobilizing voters for national elections, and control over local legislatures), we expect the local LDP would take initiative and seek to reshape the party at national level under DPJ administrations.

Second, we expect local branches of the DPJ to be largely subordinate to the national leadership in government as a result of its relatively weak party organization. The DPJ has a much weaker local base than the LDP, as well as heterogeneous party organization of varying degrees of size and autonomy across Japan's prefectures.[4] For the majority of prefectures where the DPJ lacked a strong presence, there is evidence that local party organizations were not very active. These 'hollowed out' local branches were easily influenced by pressures from national party headquarters or Diet members in areas such as candidate selection and policy formation (Tatebayashi 2013, pp. 305–306). We expect these DPJ prefectures with feeble local branches to follow the lead of HQ and not challenge initiatives from the centre.

But where the DPJ had a stronger local party organization, there is evidence to suggest greater autonomy vis-à-vis party headquarters and locally elected Diet members. Hokkaido is seen as such an exceptionally autonomous prefectural branch of the DPJ, with characteristics similar to the LDP (see Ohmura and Machidori 2013). In places like Hokkaido, Aichi, Iwate, Osaka, and Tokyo (where the DPJ had its strongest presence in local legislatures), we expect the local DPJ to diverge from national policy that threatens its particular territorial interests.

Multi-level relations under the DPJ

The DPJ came to power promising many things, but transforming central and local government relations was high on its agenda (*icchōme ichibanchi*). Its so-called 'regional sovereignty reforms' (*chiiki shuken kaikaku*) aimed to decentralize the Japanese state and reduce clientelistic relations between the centre and periphery (Sunahara 2012; Kitamura 2014). These involved a broader promise to shift government spending priorities from 'concrete to people', reducing outlays on wasteful public works and increasing universal welfare programmes, particularly those to children and working mothers. Certain high-profile public works were to be abolished; these included large-scale dams that had been delayed for decades, notably Yamba dam in Gunma prefecture and Kawabegawa dam in Kumamoto prefecture. The party also promised to make highway tolls free, reduce taxes on gasoline, and reduce spending plans for new road infrastructure (DPJ manifesto 2009).

Instead of traditional clientelistic redistribution between the centre and dependent local governments, the DPJ called for establishing greater regional autonomy. Among DPJ measures that were achieved were the institutionalizing of central-local government dispute resolution mechanisms as well as replacing use-specific subsidies with general subsidies that had no strings attached (Kitamura 2014). The DPJ also sought, less successfully, to transform the traditional practice of local interest groups separately and directly petitioning the central ministries through the brokerage of local Diet members. Instead, party secretary-general Ozawa demanded that all budgetary requests and petitions go through the local DPJ prefectural branch and pass through the party secretary general's office. The scheme sought to centralize the traditional LDP system of petitions and clientelist demands under the DPJ leadership (Ito and Miyamoto 2014, pp. 17–18).

All of these initial measures predictably triggered strong opposition from local conservatives and local politicians of specific regions whose territorial interests were threatened by DPJ initiatives. Multi-level conflicts also emerged on issues not directly related to the DPJ's initial manifesto promises. In the later DPJ administrations, local legislatures passed a host of resolutions seeking to stop the government from entering into negotiations for the TPP. Following the nuclear accident in Fukushima in March of 2011, the DPJ administration was not only internally divided over the future use of nuclear power, but clashed with local governments (and local partisans) over its use. There was a sharp row particularly over the restarting of the Oi nuclear power plant in Fukui prefecture in July of 2012, the first to be restarted since all plants were shut down for safety inspections after the Fukushima accident. Finally, the DPJ administration under Prime Minister Noda faced a severe foreign policy crisis over the disputed islands of Senkaku involving the Tokyo governor.

The LDP appeared to quickly unite and rally around the goal of ousting the DPJ from government soon after falling into opposition. In fact, the LDP leadership repeatedly indicated that it viewed local branches as a key resource to

84 *The politics of local opposition*

challenge the DPJ nationally. In October 2009, the party policy chairman at the time (Ishiba Shigeru) advised local prefectural LDP branch policy chairmen to submit written opinions criticizing DPJ policies.[5] Local conservatives complied and kept up a steady barrage of WOs attacking the DPJ for a wide range of its policies as soon as it came to power. The Saga prefectural LDP branch policy chairman's comment captured the perception that this was an effective tactic: 'now that we [the LDP] are in opposition, the submission of written opinions is, instead of petitions, the most effective tool to realize policy'.[6]

As Figure 3.3 in Chapter 3 indicates, the total number of WOs by all prefectural legislatures surged during the DPJ administration. Many prefectures passed the highest number of WOs in its legislature's history in the early months of the DPJ government challenging a host of national policies. These included criticisms of DPJ plans to make highways free, cut gasoline taxes and reduce spending on public works (including highways), expand universal child-allowance, and unify local petitioning through the DPJ. Many of these were redistributive policies directly affecting rural areas and interest groups tied to local conservatives. The LDP local branches, following the national party's request, passed resolutions on matters that did not directly affect its territorial interests in non-redistributive issues as well. These include WOs against the DPJ plans to pass legislation that would grant voting rights in local elections to foreign residents and permit women to keep their maiden names.

For the LDP in opposition, there appeared to be surprisingly little infighting over the future of party direction that appears to plague parties following catastrophic electoral defeats.[7] Soon after the 2009 general election, numerous LDP prefectural branches put forward plans to reform and revive party fortunes, emphasizing the need to restore linkages between the national party leadership, Diet members, and local party organizations. They also demanded HQ reduce dependency on second and third generation candidates, retire old veteran incumbents and replace them with newer blood, expand the party base to non-traditional supporters of the LDP (salarymen and housewives, NGOs and youth), and increase local branch voice in leadership selection.[8]

In the first leadership contest for the LDP held a month after falling into opposition, the party HQ increased the share of votes granted to the 47 prefectural branches for the LDP presidential elections from 141 to 300 votes (against the 200 votes given to parliamentarians) to increase representation of local interests.[9] The local branches largely backed Tanigaki Sadakazu (he had won most regional votes in 44 out of 47 prefectures). Tanigaki spoke of unifying the party, emphasized linkages of '*kizuna*' to regions, and listening to the voice of the LDP grassroots; all of these went down well with the LDP prefectural branches.[10]

In general, local branches of the LDP remained largely loyal to the LDP despite losing access to the national levers of power. There were few defections from the LDP to other parties national or locally. In one notable case of Osaka city and prefecture, however, about 40 local conservatives left the LDP to join the newly established regional party – Osaka Restoration Association (*Osaka ishin no kai*) – founded by Osaka mayor Hashimoto Toru. The defections were

The politics of local opposition   85

triggered by internal conflicts within the local LDP over policy as well as the strong pull of a highly popular local chief executive where levels of party identification for both major parties had fallen (Hijino 2013).

Written opinions under the DPJ

To compare multi-level interactions under the DPJ administration, we take a closer look at written opinions expressing local government positions against national policy.

First, in terms of frequency, as already indicated in Figure 3.2 and Figure 3.3, the absolute number of WOs being passed and submitted by prefectural legislatures as well as being reported by the media reached record levels during the DPJ administration (2009–2012). Compared to other periods of elevated WO activity (1993, 1997, 2001–2005) during the LDP administration, the period of widespread incongruence triggered an even greater number of WOs submitted to the national government. As previously described, LDP HQ encouraged local branches to challenge DPJ policies and local branches complied. Assessed only by the frequency of WO submissions, periods of widespread incongruence under the DPJ have generated more conflictual relations than under periods of congruence, even during LDP administrations with considerable intra-party conflicts, as described in the previous chapter.

Which prefectures have been most prone to passing WOs during the DPJ administration? We have complete data on which prefectures passed WOs for five selected policy areas between September 2009 and December 2012: unifying petitions under the DPJ prefectural branch, entering TPP negotiations, granting foreign residents local voting rights, restarting nuclear power plants, and raising the consumption tax (Table 4.1). If we break down the number of WOs submitted by type of prefecture, we see that most of these WOs were passed in areas where the LDP has been dominant, rather than in areas where it faces stronger competition from the DPJ (and other parties). Divided into urban or rural prefectures, rural prefectures appear far more prone to passing WOs challenging the DPJ than urban prefectures. The tendency of LDP dominant, rural prefectures to take the lead in passing WOs critical of national policy (both in redistributive and non-redistributive policies) is similar under the DPJ administration as under the LDP administration.

Finally, we ask if the DPJ local party groups remained 'loyal' to the national party initiatives by voting against these WOs or if they chose to side with conservatives in backing WOs criticizing the DPJ policies. We predicted that DPJ branches in most regions with a small local presence will be subordinate and lack the autonomy to challenge national policy decisions. But where the DPJ local group is relatively large, we expect they will be more autonomous and prone to challenge national initiatives. Data were collected on how local DPJ groups voted on the WOs in a sample of prefectures on a number of key issues of contention between central and local governments during the DPJ administration (Table 4.2).

Table 4.1 Average number of WOs submitted per prefecture (by strength of LDP in legislature) under DPJ administrations, 2009–2012

	LPD strong	*LDP weak*	*LDP weakest*	*Urban prefectures*	*All*
	32 other prefectures	*Hyogo, Fukuoka, Ishikawa, Shiga, Miyagi, Nagano, Kochi (7)*	*Tokyo, Aichi, Osaka (3)*	*47 prefectures*	
All policies	149	31	21	2	201
Composition percentage	74	15	10	1	100
Average submission per prefecture	4.7	4.5	2.7	0.7	4.3
TPP	2.7	2.4	1.8	0.7	2.5
Foreigner voting	0.9	0.9	0.0	0.0	0.7
Unifying petitions	0.8	0.7	0.4	0.0	0.7
Restarting nuclear plants	0.3	0.4	0.4	0.0	0.3
Consumption tax	0.0	0.0	0.1	0.0	0.0

Source: compiled by author from data provided by National Association of Chairpersons of Prefectural Assemblies.

Note
LDP weakest = lost majority of seats in prefectural legislature over 4 times; weak = 2–3 times; strong = 1–0 times between 1986–2011 (from Tsuji 2015, p. 393). N = 663.

Table 4.2 DPJ local branch support for key national policies as revealed by WOs

	Prefectures where DPJ is strong							Prefectures where DPJ is weak							
	Hokkadio	*Aichi*	*Osaka*	*Iwate*	*Tokyo*	*Mie*	*Totals*	*Aomori*	*Ishikawa*	*Fukushima*	*Gunma*	*Toyama*	*Niigata*	*Miygai*	*Total*
Free highway tolls	O			O				O	O	?	O	?	x	x	2
Unifying petitions	O			O				O	O	?	O	?	O	O	
TPP	x	x		x		O	3	x	x	x	x	x	O	x	6
Foreign voting rights								O	x	x	x	?	O	O	3
Nuclear power	x			x			2			x			x		2
Consumption tax				x			1								
All policies	2	1		3			6	1	2	3	2	1	2	2	13

Source: compiled by author from various homepages of respective prefectural legislatures that provide data of voting behaviour for written opinions by partisan group in legislatures.

Note
O = Supported WOs in line with national DPJ policy; x = Supported WOs against national DPJ policy; Empty cell = no WOs passed; ? = records not available.

88 *The politics of local opposition*

As not all prefectures provide public records on how party groups voted during this period, we have selected a sample from two groups of prefectures which do provide such data during 2009 and 2012. The first group of prefectures is one where the DPJ contingent was weak, including: Aomori, Ishikawa, Fukushima, Gunma, Toyama, Niigata, and Miyagi. The second group of prefectures is one where the DPJ was particularly strong, including: Tokyo, Iwate, Hokkaido, Aichi, Osaka, and Mie. Table 4.2 provides data on how the local DPJ group voted on WOs challenging national policies. The local DPJ group could either vote for or against a WO critical of national DPJ policy, or in some rare cases back a WO which supports national DPJ policy. In some cases, the local DPJ was split in its response (e.g. Ishikawa prefecture where the local DPJ was split into separate local groups – *kaiha* – that took different positions on WOs).

The data show that for the policy of unifying petitions and making highway tolls free, local DPJ contingents in all types of sampled prefectures remained largely 'loyal' to the national party line. They voted against WOs critical of these measures, although failing to stop them in some cases. In rural areas where the DPJ presence was weak – such as Ishikawa, Fukushima, and Gunma – the local DPJ were divided over following national policy over foreign voting rights.

Urban-rural divides were evident for attitudes towards TPP: rural DPJ called for caution or even directly opposing entry into TPP negotiations in Hokkaido and Iwate, but not in urban areas (Osaka and Tokyo) which did not pass any WOs over TPP. WOs calling for caution in restarting nuclear power plants were passed mainly in prefectures with, or bordering prefectures with, nuclear plants – Fukushima, Fukui, Shiga, Kyoto, Hokkaido. Thus local DPJ in directly affected areas were prepared to signal opposition to the policies of their leadership (Kan and Noda were prepared to restart plants). Finally, only Iwate prefecture passed WOs opposing increases in consumption tax, despite the opposition towards raising consumption tax becoming the issue which most divided the national DPJ and the proximate reason for its breakup in 2012.

The data above show that DPJ policy was challenged widely by local legislatures through WOs initiated by and passed by local conservatives. The local DPJ, in turn, did not consistently vote against these motions critical of DPJ plans – at times even joining the local LDP in attacking national policy. Though seen as a 'top-heavy' organization which sought to centralize decision-making, DPJ leadership appears to have been unable to enforce policy unity and discipline over its local branches. Our sample suggests that local DPJ branches diverged from national policy in prefectures where they were relatively strong (Aichi, Hokkaido, Iwate) as well as where they were very weak (Ishikawa, Fukushima, Gunma). And in some prefectures, the local DPJ appeared internally divided over how to vote on a WO (Ishikawa, Gunma) – reflecting internal divisions between more conservative and progressive arms of the party.

Cases of multi-level conflict under the DPJ administration

We turn to more in-depth case studies to trace how local resistance from both local conservatives and their own local contingents affected the DPJ's national policy process. We look at five different instances of multi-level conflict: redistributive policy directly affecting prefectures across Japan (making highway tolls free, unifying petitions, and TPP); policy affecting a limited area (Yamba dam); and non-redistributive policy (granting foreigners voting rights). We briefly provide analysis of how local partisan actions impacted the course of the national policy.

Abolishing highway tolls

In its 2009 manifesto, the DPJ promised to gradually abolish all highway tolls with the aim of reducing transportation and distribution costs as well as stimulating local economies. Highway tolls were mentioned several times as well as included in one of eight central policy promises which were given a timeline (to be gradually implemented from 2010) and expected costs (1.3 trillion yen).[11]

Abolishing highway tolls, along with DPJ promises to cut gasoline taxes, triggered resistance from interest groups connected to the road industry, including local governments dependent on road-related revenues in tax and public works. Following the DPJ's electoral victory in September 2009, local legislatures across Japan passed WOs in opposition to abolishing highways tolls, cutting gasoline taxes, and reducing spending on highway construction. Many of these WOs were similar in wording, suggesting that the activity was coordinated centrally. These WOs claimed, among other things, that making highways free would hurt local public transport businesses, reduce revenues for the construction of necessary highways in the future, and increase traffic and carbon dioxide emissions. The DPJ faced opposition from labour unions related to public transport (e.g. the railway company unions) who lodged concerns that free highways would lead to lower passenger traffic and affect their business.

The plan to abolish highway tolls was implemented initially in June 2010 as a limited 'social experiment' for a limited period and scope. Only a small portion of routes was made free, excluding major routes between urban centres. Following the Great Northeastern earthquake of 11 March 2011, the policy was terminated (officially indefinitely put on hold) in June of the same year to provide funding for reconstruction efforts in the disaster areas.

Although one of its high-profile policy promises, the DPJ cancelled its original plans for making highway tolls free within a year of being in power. There was widespread resistance from local governments led by the LDP, public transport, highway, and road construction companies, unions affiliated with the DPJ, as well as an unexpected exogenous shock in the form of the Tohoku earthquake. The DPJ leadership argued that it was too costly under the circumstances to continue and disbanded the project. Local partisan pressures played only one of many factors leading to the compromises and eventual abandoning of the

90 *The politics of local opposition*

national project. Despite considerable opposition in rural prefectures, including transportation-related unions affiliated to the DPJ, local DPJ were largely loyal to the national party position in this instance.

Unifying petitions under the DPJ

As described earlier, another important bone of contention between local governments and the DPJ administration was an attempt to unify and regulate local petitions. Ozawa Ichiro, secretary general of the party, announced two months after the DPJ came to power that the traditional style of petitioning central ministries for local public works and projects would be replaced by a new system of petitioning controlled and unified under the DPJ organization. The DPJ's nominal goal for this policy was to make local petitions more transparent and fair, centralize budget-process and reduce influence of backbenchers, and end the time-consuming and wasteful effort of 'pilgrimages to Kasumigaseki' by local government executives and interest groups (Sunahara 2012; Ito and Miyamoto 2014).

The new petition method was introduced with the mind to strip the strong links that local LDP Diet members and prefectural politicians had with local interest groups/executives and force them to build new ties with the local DPJ. Moreover, as all petitions were to be routed from the 47 DPJ prefectural branches to the secretary general's office at party headquarters, it was also seen as a way to strengthen the office of Ozawa Ichiro, secretary general at the time and original proponent of this scheme.

The plan soon met with predictably emphatic opposition from local conservatives, with 34 prefectures passing WOs within weeks of the plan's announcement. Media reported LDP headquarters encouraging local LDP groups to submit WOs, while providing a model version of the WO for local legislators to copy. In many of the WOs, the scheme of unifying petitions under the DPJ was criticized as being unconstitutional in that it took away the right of petition guaranteed to citizens and going against the rules of democracy to block channels of access to the public administration.

Ozawa's plans for creating a centralized DPJ network of local petitions was not only challenged, but even flouted by local politicians and eventually abandoned. Soon after announcing the scheme, the Okayama governor (a former construction ministry bureaucrat backed by the LDP) bypassed the local DPJ to directly petition DPJ ministers in the central government about local public works projects. The governor met with DPJ ministers of construction and home affairs as well as other high-level bureaucrats. The local Okayama DPJ branch chairman, who had been bypassed by the governor, claimed he had strongly advised the governor not to petition Tokyo directly and later spoke to media of being in conflict with the local governor.[12] The particular fracas made evident divisions within the DPJ over its petition policy, while highlighting the inability of Ozawa and party leadership to force individual bureaucrats and ministers to comply with their guidelines.

The politics of local opposition 91

As Ozawa's grip over the party organization weakened as a result of his prosecution and change of party leadership during the spring of 2010, the policy of unifying petitions, although not officially terminated, was substantially abandoned. During the traditional petition season (mid-November to December) of finalizing national budgets for 2010 media reported an increasing number of governors as well as industry groups bypassing the local DPJ and going directly to ministries in Tokyo to petition.[13]

The case suggests once again that local resistance to national policy was but one element behind the derailing of DPJ policy. Internal divisions within the DPJ leadership and its inability to enforce policy upon cabinet and top-level bureaucrats appear as important as local intransience. Notably, chief executives from traditional LDP strongholds, such as Okayama and Ishikawa, sought to bypass the local DPJ and link directly to ministers and veteran DPJ politicians nationally. These details highlight the difficulty the DPJ faced in dissolving the clientelistic network and petition practices established by rural conservatives.

Entering TPP negotiations

Both the Kan and Noda DPJ administrations (2010–2012) faced fierce resistance in their initiative to make Japan enter into negotiations to join the TPP. Although both DPJ prime ministers were committed to the process, their efforts were blocked as Japan did not formally join negotiations during their terms. Resistance primarily came from the farming lobby and farmers who feared the trade deal would reduce tariffs and lead to an influx of cheap agricultural products that would devastate local producers. National and local politicians, both those from the LDP and DPJ primarily in rural areas dependent on electoral support from farmers, opposed the process on the ground and in the national policy process (see Mulgan 2013, 2014 and Sasada 2013 for the impact of the farming lobby, rural voters and backbenchers in Diet).

At national level, the DPJ was divided over policy even before Kan Naoto announced intentions to join in October 2010. Diet members and local politicians in urban prefectures and districts with manufacturing industries took a pro-TPP position, as they were dependent on unions which favoured freer trade as members stood to benefit from increased exports (Mulgan 2013, p. 219). DPJ politicians from rural areas and districts, however, largely opposed the TPP, with a sizable group of Diet backbenchers joining groups publically campaigning against it (such as the *TPP wo shinchōni kangaeru kai*). These anti-TPP DPJ parliamentarians used the revived research committees and Policy Research Council groups to sabotage and delay government plans to enter into TPP negotiations (Mulgan 2014).

At local level, the resistance to the TPP was spearheaded by the farmers' lobby group (*zenchū*) who threatened to withhold recommendations and electoral support for politicians who did not openly oppose TPP for local elections.[14] Local politicians, both of the LDP and DPJ, were thus pressed to demonstrate their opposition to the national policy in visible form. Within the year that Kan

92 *The politics of local opposition*

announced intentions to join the TPP negotiations, 39 prefectures passed WOs in opposition to, or calling for caution over, the TPP. A rush of WOs were passed within a month before major local elections, suggesting local DPJ candidates in rural areas were seeking to distance themselves from the unpopular national policy before facing the polls.

According to media reports, DPJ local groups joined the LDP in passing these WOs in 29 of 39 prefectures, demonstrating how a majority of local DPJ had diverged from its leadership over the TPP.[15] Most of these were from rural areas such as Hokkaido, Gunma, and Fukushima, where the DPJ groups joined the LDP in resolutions opposing the TPP.[16] Prior to the 2011 local elections, some DPJ prefectural branches made their anti-TPP position clear, for example Tochigi,[17] or joined anti-TPP rallies held by the farming lobby, for example Miyagi.[18]

Divisions laterally and horizontally were evident in the DPJ response to TPP. In some rural prefectures, such as Aomori, Mie, and Toyama, the local DPJ were split over the vote or were undecided over WOs submitted by conservatives opposing the TPP. These divisions reflect considerable internal divisions among the local DPJ, even in areas where their presence was relatively weak and small. DPJ diet members were also unable to exert discipline over local DPJ. Yamada Masahiro, Lower House member from Nagasaki and chairman of the parliamentary group opposing the TPP within the DPJ, unsuccessfully demanded his prefectural DPJ to pass WOs more critical of TPP. The chairman of this local branch was a former union member, and many of the local DPJ had similar links to the local shipbuilding industry as well as more urban voters in Nagasaki city.[19]

Finally, policy conflicts over the TPP triggered defections locally: in Fukui, three local prefectural DPJ politicians formed a new legislative group (*kaiha*) prior to elections citing the TPP, cuts to public works, and unpopularity of the DPJ locally.[20] The struggle over the TPP was also one of several policy issues (raising consumption tax, restarting nuclear plants, and restarting public works) which were cited as reasons behind defections from the DPJ under the Noda administration to form Ozawa's new party as well as other third parties prior to the 2012 elections (Reed 2013).

In comparing the multi-level response of the LDP and DPJ, both parties faced horizontal and vertical divisions over how to deal with the TPP. Some were under strong pressure from farm lobbyists to commit to opposition while others sought votes of pro-TPP groups and voters in their region. The difference is that under the DPJ administration, the rural LDP was unhindered by party leadership and able to unite in criticizing the TPP locally. At the time, the LDP leadership took a more ambiguous position of opposing participation in the talks, saying it was opposed so long as all tariffs without exception, including agriculture, were to be abolished (Mulgan 2013, p. 217). But once back in power, the LDP had to deal with bridging the gap between the two levels over the TPP. The LDP leadership placed greater pressure on local branches to desist from openly opposing the TPP, though with limited success. In contrast, there

The politics of local opposition   93

was little evidence of the DPJ HQ trying or able to control anti-TPP forces within the party nationally and locally.

Local partisans petitioning and campaigning against the TPP worked together with the farm lobby and Diet members to oppose the DPJ administrations plans for the TPP. Delays to formally entering into negotiations can be explained by these internal party divisions. It should also be explained by how the Kan and Noda administrations re-established a decentralized decision-making process within the party, including the revival of the Policy Research Council, which gave veto power to internal TPP opponents (Mulgan 2014). During this process, the DPJ was unable to control its local branches, even in rural areas where they had a relatively weak presence. As with the LDP, so with the DPJ, local territorial interests trumped partisan loyalty when it came to positions over TPP in rural areas.

Yamba dam

The DPJ administration collided with local governments over region-specific issues as well. They occurred most prominently with the cancellation of public works projects including dams and roads, the restarting of nuclear power plants, and the transferring of US military bases in Okinawa. The latter two will be investigated in greater detail in the next chapter as they heavily involve governors. But here we provide a brief outline of the case of the cancellation and resurrection of one of the most contested public works during the period, the Yamba dam in Gunma prefecture.

In its 2009 general election manifesto, the DPJ had listed the Yamba dam along with Kawabegawa dam in Kumamoto as examples of wasteful public works to be cancelled. Having initially been planned in 1950s, the dam's construction had undergone various changes of plan and delays over its half-century of contestation. Moreover, with total projected costs of nearly half a trillion yen, the Yamba dam project was one of the most costly dam projects in Japan (Nakajima 2012, p. 48). Local DPJ Diet members in Gunma, where the dam was located, had campaigned and gained seats in 2009 on promises to put an end to the project.

Within a month of the DPJ electoral victory, a barrage of criticism erupted from various quarters when construction minister Seiji Maehara announced that the government was cancelling the Yamba dam project. Governors of Gunma and five downstream prefectures which had jointly funded the dam project until then demanded DPJ carry on with the dam. Particularly noteworthy was the fact that the Saitama governor (former DPJ parliamentarian who had been backed by the DPJ in his 2007 election) opposed cancellation of the dam project. The Saitama DPJ prefectural branch was also divided over support for the project.[21] Local residents and chief executives in Gunma opposed the DPJ cancellation of Yamba dam, at the least demanding compensation in its place. The ministry of construction and related branch offices (*kantō chihō seibikyoku*) were one of the main drivers behind the project, with evidence of as many as

94 The politics of local opposition

400 bureaucrats having already 'descended to heaven' to companies related to the pre-planning and pre-construction of the Yamba dam (Nakajima 2012, pp. 168–170).

In the next two years, pro-dam and anti-dam forces (primarily DPJ back-benchers in Gunma) carried out a 'petition war' against the cabinet, policy committees, as well as construction ministry in decentralized fashion. Three governors from Gunma, Saitama, and Tokyo went to the prime minister's office to deliver a letter asking for the revival of the Yamba dam project, while anti-dam elements approached the party's policy chairman and vice-minister of construction to oppose any efforts to revive the dam.[22]

The momentum for reviving the dam accelerated with the arrival of the Noda administration and appointment of a new minister of construction, the fourth one since the DPJ came to power, in September 2011. The new minister, a former construction ministry bureaucrat, eventually announced in December 2011 that the dam would go ahead. Local Diet members from Gunma (led by Nakajima Masanobu) fiercely protested the change of plans, demanding Noda and the government adhere to its manifesto promise to no avail.[23] Nakajima left the party to become an independent to join anti-TPP and anti-consumption tax defectors from the DPJ.

Ultimately, this DPJ initiative was overturned by a change in DPJ leadership (from Kan to Noda) who appeared indifferent or unable to adhere to the party's manifesto. Notably, the party leadership was less responsive to a very vocal group of local DPJ Diet backbenchers who opposed to the project, than to various pressures from local LDP-affiliated chief executives and bureaucrats in support of the dam. Such irresponsiveness suggests the weakness of back-benchers and the lack of integrated channels linking local demands with national policy. Instead, the DPJ's internal divisions and decentralized decision-making allowed for local pressures to upturn policy, leading to further divisions and defections. As with the TPP or unifying petitions, it was not local resistance alone that blocked national policy over Yamba dam, but local pressures working in tandem with national-level disunity over policy.

Foreign resident voting rights

The final case of multi-level conflict under the DPJ involves a non-redistributive issue: i.e. whether to permit foreign residents voting rights in local elections. Unlike previous cases which have direct material implications for local interest groups, this particular policy initiative by the DPJ hinges more on questions of value and ideology.

Local partisans have challenged such policies with no direct redistributive consequences over foreign policy, the role of the Self Defense Forces, collective security, constitutional reform, among other areas. During LDP administrations, more progressive local partisans (socialist, communists, others) have tried to lodge WOs criticizing national policy, for example against the passing of collective security-related laws or special secrets bills. But these resolutions tended

The politics of local opposition 95

to be rejected on the assembly floor as most prefectural legislatures were held by the LDP and its coalition partner. Instead, local conservatives (particularly at the prefectural level) have tended to back resolutions supporting the LDP on foreign policy and value issues in recent years.

During widespread partisan incongruence under the DPJ, LDP local branches actively passed WOs resisting the central government's more ideologically progressive initiatives. These initiatives included the party's plans to grant foreign residents local voting rights as well as permit women to keep their maiden names after marriage. Initially, the DPJ leadership, including Ozawa and Hatoyama, committed to realizing this policy (along with the Komeito which has long supported granting foreigners' voting rights). In contrast, the majority of the LDP and a considerable number of more conservative DPJ members, including its coalition partner People's National Party (*Kokumin shintō*) were strongly opposed to this expansion of suffrage.

LDP HQ requested local branches to submit WOs opposing this legislation. In particular, local LDP branches which had passed WOs in the mid-1990s in favour of such resolutions were asked to reverse their positions by making clear their opposition to foreign voting rights.[24] Thirty-four prefectures complied with many of these rural areas with the LDP holding a single-party majority in legislature. In regions such as Tokyo, Aichi, Osaka Fukuoka, Nara – with large urban centres and high concentrations of foreign residents to be most directly affected by this proposal – such resolutions were not submitted. The small contingent of DPJ prefectural politicians in rural areas tended to vote in line with the national initiative against the LDP (Table 4.2). Although in some prefectures where the DPJ was divided into two party groups (like Ishikawa or Gunma), it appears only the conservative DPJ faction joined the LDP in voting against the policy.

Although not a matter directly affecting local territorial interests, the DPJ administration was opposed by a majority of local LDP forces as well as some of its local branches. The policy to provide foreigners voting rights was largely shelved once Ozawa fell from influence within the party and the leadership faced difficulty securing support of its coalition partner (Kokumin Shinto). Although difficult to measure the exact impact of the local partisans' resistance against the national initiative, the considerable media coverage (Figure 3.2) is likely to have eroded public support for the policy and thereby raised hurdles for the party leadership.

Conclusion

In terms of expectations about greater partisan incongruence leading to more externalized conflict between national and local levels of government, the case of the DPJ administration (2009–2012) appears to have largely confirmed theory. As measured by the frequency of resolutions, the DPJ faced more WOs submitted by local conservatives in prefectural assemblies than LDP administrations faced from the legislatures of similar partisan composition. Local conservatives challenged the national government over both distributive matters

96 *The politics of local opposition*

directly affecting rural areas and more ideological issues such as foreign voting rights. Under the LDP, local conservatives challenged the central government primarily over distributive issues, not ideological matters.

Our expectation that the DPJ would be more subordinate to national policy in regions where its local party organizations were weak and more autonomous where large was largely discounted. In fact, the DPJ local branches were equally 'disloyal' to initiatives proposed by the national leadership regardless of their size and presence. What appeared to determine whether a local DPJ branch diverged from the DPJ administration was the degree to which they perceived themselves to be affected by national policy. Thus DPJ branches in rural regions opposed TPP and in regions hosting or close to nuclear plants opposed restarting nuclear power, with other less affected regions falling in line with national policy. The DPJ simply lacked any coherent and consistent policy unity either laterally or horizontally. Nor did the DPJ leadership try to enforce greater discipline over its diverging internal actors, in contrast to the LDP.

Despite the seeming de-integration and growing distrust between the two levels of the party leading up to the 2009 elections, the local conservatives joined forces to help its national leadership in opposition. The LDP national executive responded to its national collapse by showing contrition and humility to its local base, and more significantly, granting greater voice to local branches over the national party (such as changes in the LDP presidential election rules). These rebuilding efforts from the local branches illustrate how local conservatives still consider the goal of the LDP holding power at national level vital and worth cooperating for. One explanation for this 're-integration' of the LDP in opposition may be that the collapse of the national party in 2009 stripped power resources away from the party leadership and left local branches relatively more powerful. This imbalance of power reduced conflicts and unified the party from bottom-up, at least until it returned to power in 2012.[25]

What impact did local partisans in prefectural legislatures have on the direction of DPJ policy and more broadly on the DPJ administrations at national level? Case studies make evident that local recalcitrance to national policy was only one of many factors affecting the gradual implementation or blocking of national initiatives. In the cases of multi-level conflict under the DPJ, divisions at the national level were prominent and appeared to contribute most proximately to the eventual derailing of the initial policy promises. Exogenous shocks, such as the ousting of Ozawa or fallout from the 2011 earthquake, also played a role in reversing or shaping important DPJ projects. Thus it is unclear how vital the constant criticism levelled at the DPJ from the local conservatives had on DPJ policy. As with the similar intransience of local conservatives under the LDP, one could say national party leadership faced an uphill battle in convincing voters of policies when media reported a majority of local legislatures (however representative they were of popular opinion) opposing national policy.

The case studies also indicated how the actions of governors were prominent in affecting the success or failure of national policy: e.g. the Okayama governor flaunting DPJ requests to direct petitions to local branches or the Gunma and other governors campaigning to revive the Yamba dam. These multi-level conflicts pivoted around actions of local chief executives, informed by their partisan relationship with parties at national and local level. It is to this complex dynamic that we turn in the next chapter.

Notes

1 Numerous articles in the media reported local prefectural branches criticizing party leadership and local Diet members immediately following the ousting of the LDP in national and local party meetings held in September. Some illustrative examples include 'Sōsenkyo de jimin taihai, kenren uramibushi hombu he "Chihō no koe kike"', *Asahi Shimbun*, 2 September 2009; 'Chihō no jimin, gatagata chiji mo kokkaigiin mo zembu minshu he', *Asahi Shimbun*, 5 September 2009; and 'Imai kenren kanjichō, jimintō hombu ni chūmon', *Asahi Shimbun*, 5 September 2009.
2 'Jimin zenkoku kanjichō kaigi chihōsoshiki, tsunoru fuan yatoutenraku', *Yomiuri Shimbun*, 5 September 2009.
3 Conditions of multi-level partisan incongruence in prefectural legislatures existed for major cities during the late 1960s and early 1970s, with progressive parties on the left controlling local legislatures under LDP national administrations. In addition, during the brief 10-month Hosokawa administration in 1993–1994 when the LDP was out of power, legislative incongruence was high. But aside from these periods, there have been very few legislatures where opposition parties controlled local legislatures (even in areas where the LDP has been weakest). As such, the book focuses on the 2009–2012 period where the DPJ faced a majority of LDP-controlled legislatures.
4 The party as an amalgamation of different parties inherited differing local party organizations and cultures. These include: prefectures with a strong inheritance of socialist party organizations and influence of unions either of the JSP or DSP (e.g. Aichi, Hokkaido); regions that are home to conservative DPJ politicians with strong personal electoral machines (e.g. Iwate, Yamanashi); and other prefectures with a very weak and inactive DPJ presence (most rural prefectures) (see e.g. Ito 2008; Tatebayashi 2013; Uekami and Tsutstumi 2011 for discussions of the variation in DPJ local organizations).
5 'Chihō gikai "tsute" motome jimin henka', *Asahi Shimbun*, 25 December 2009.
6 Ibid.
7 The LDP's unity in opposition is in contrast to other notable examples from parliamentary democracies: nearly two decades of internal conflict and ideological divisions of the British Labour Party after its collapse in 1979 which included a damaging split within the party, driven in large part by grassroot activists (1979–1997); and the breakup of the Canadian Progressive Conservative Party after losing 154 out of 156 seats in the federal election of 1993. In Japan, the DPJ underwent a similar party organizational meltdown, which began before its electoral defeat and accelerated after it in 2012. The DPJ was reformed and renamed in 2016.
8 E.g. proposals for party organization reform by LDP prefectural branches were reported widely by media during the year after the LDP fell into opposition. See for example, 'Tanigaki sōsai ni kaikakuan teigen jimin kenren tō saisei iinkai', *Asahi Shimbun*, 12 December 2009 and 'Jimin saisei he kenren ga yōbōsho hombuya shibuchō he tsūretsu hihan', *Asahi Shimbun*, 20 May 2010.
9 See 'Sōsaisen, chihōhyōzou he nittei ni ironmo jimin yakuin renrakukai', *Asahi Shimbun*, 1 September 2009 and 'Jimin sōsaisen chihōjūshi he tōinhyō 300, giinhyō 200 ni', *Yomiuri Shimbun*, 2 September 2009.
10 For example 'Chihōjūshi no shisei wo hyōka jimin sōsaisen, kenren no Tanigakishi shiji', *Asahi Shimbun*, 25 August 2009.

98 *The politics of local opposition*

11 DPJ General Election Manifesto 2009.
12 'Madoguchi ipponka ni minshusōren "Zannen" Chiji ga kuni he chinjō kyōkō daijin-rato menkai', *Yomiuri Shimbun*, 27 November 2009.
13 'Chinjō, yappari kanryō he jichitai, minshushisutemu ni hushinkan', *Yomiuri Shimbun*, 25 December 2010.
14 'Tōitsusen "han TPP" semaru nōgyōdantai shien no "fumie" 100 nin shomei yōseimo', *Yomiuri Shimbun*, 10 March 2011.
15 'Nōkō futamata chihōgikai "han TPP", 39 todōfuken de ikensho', *Asahi Shimbun*, 22 February 2011.
16 Although there is some evidence that local DPJ groups sought in some instances to mollify the wording of WOs that criticized national DPJ leadership too severely. The Hokkaido local DPJ agreed to sign a WO asking the Kan government not to enter into TPP negotiations, but the wording of the WO was edited so that it would not appear to be too strong a criticism of the DPJ government (*Yomiuri Shimbun*, 9 November 2010).
17 'Minshu kenren TPP hantai hōshinkatameru "Tōitsusen taisaku" irokoku', *Yomiuri Shimbun*, 5 February 2011.
18 'Tōhakoe, TPP hantai nōkyōshusai hantaishūkai, kengira dōchō', *Asahi Shimbun*, 24 February 2011.
19 'Nōkō futamata chihōgikai "han TPP", 39 todōfuken de ikensho', ibid.
20 'Minshukei kaiha 3 kengi ga shinkaiha', *Yomiuri Shimbun*, 14 January 2011.
21 'Ba hatsugen "Dam chūshi" chiji hampatsu minshukeikengi ha sampinibuni', *Yomiuri Shimbun*, 18 September 2009.
22 'Yamba seifu ni yōbōgassen suishin, hantai ryōha kokkōshō handan', *Yomiuri Shimbun*, 17 December 2011.
23 'Minshugiin Yamba chūshi yōsei', *Yomiuri Shimbun*, 8 October 2011.
24 Interview with LDP headquarters.
25 The pendulum appeared to swing the other way with the selection of Abe Shinzo over Ishiba Shigeru in the 2012 October leadership selection. In a run-off election, Diet members chose Abe over Ishiba (who had been overwhelmingly popular with LDP prefectural branches). Local LDP branches, in rural areas, responding to these election results complained that the LDP was not necessarily a bottom-up organization if regional votes for a leadership election can be upturned by parliamentarians. See 'Chihō rikkyaku ha maboroshika' jimin kenren uramisuji sōsaisen, Abe shi no "gyakuten" ni fuman zokushutsu', *Asahi Shimbun*, 10 October 2012.

References

Hijino, K.V.L. 2013, 'Liabilities of partisan labels: Independents in Japanese local elections', *Social Science Japan Journal*, vol. 16, no. 1, pp. 63–85.

Ito, A. 2008, *Minshuto: yabo to yago no mekanizumu*, Shincho shinsho.

Ito, M. and Miyamoto, T. (eds) 2014, *Minshutō Seiken no chosen to zasetsu: Sono keikenkara naniwo manabuka*, Nihon Keizai hyoronsha.

Kitamura, W. 2014, ' "Chikishuken" kaikaku', in M. Ito and T. Miyamoto (eds), *Minshutō Seiken no chosen to zasetsu: Sono keikenkara naniwo manabuka*, Nihon Keizai hyoronsha.

Mulgan, A.G. 2013, 'Farmers and agricultural policies', in R. Pekkanen, S.R. Reed, and E. Scheiner (eds), *Japan decides 2012: The Japanese general election*, Palgrave Macmillan.

Mulgan, A.G. 2014, 'Bringing the party back in: How the DPJ diminished prospects for Japanese agricultural trade liberalization under the TPP', *Japanese Journal of Political Science*, vol. 15, no. 1, pp. 1–22.

Nakajima, M. 2012, *Hōkai manifesto: Yamba dam to Minshuto no chōraku*, Heibonsha.

Ohmura, H. and Machidori, S. 2013, 'Minshuto chihō soshiki no rekishiteki kiban: Hokkaido to aichiken no jirei kara', in M. Tatebayashi (ed.), *Seitōsoshiki no seijigaku*, Toyo Keizai shimpo.

Reed, S.R. 2013, 'The survival of "third parties" in Japan's mixed-member electoral system', in K.E. Kushida and P.Y. Lipscy (eds), *Japan under the DPJ: The politics of transition and governance*, Walter H. Shorenstein Asia-Pacific Research Center.

Sasada, H. 2013, 'The impact of rural votes in foreign policies: The FTA policies under the DPJ government in Japan', *Asian Journal of Political Science*, vol. 21, no. 3, pp. 224–248.

Sunahara, Y. 2012, 'Seiken kōtai to reiki yūdō seiji', in T. Mikuriya (ed.), *'Seiji shudō' no kyōkun: Seiken kōtai wa nani wo motarasitaka*, Keiso shobo.

Tatebayashi, M. (ed.) 2013, *Seitōsoshiki no seijigaku*, Toyo Keizai shimpo.

Uekami, T. and Tsutsumi, H. 2011, *Minshutō no Soshiki to Seisaku*, Toyokeizai shinposha.

5 Governors and governments
Multi-level policy conflicts between executives

The governors of Japan's 47 prefectures are vital nodes of representation and power in the local politics of the country. As directly elected executives, they downplay partisan affiliations and portray themselves as impartial representatives of the whole prefecture. Such governors control government budgets and oversee regional economies as large as major countries',[1] and are granted considerable formal powers over initiating and blocking policy.[2]

The wide formal powers ascribed to governors are further amplified by the duration of their terms and the directly elected nature of their office. Japanese governors tend to complete their legally mandated four-year terms, and commonly go on for second and third terms.[3] Unlike national presidents with term constraints,[4] popular governors can be entrenched for three, four terms or longer, developing extensive networks and able to pursue long-term plans. Compared to the volatility of cabinets and short durations of national administrations in recent years, governors clearly enjoy greater stability in their office. Combined with such longevity in office, governors can also point to their democratic legitimacy of being directly elected. Unlike indirectly selected ministers of state, most governors receive more votes in their own elections than Diet members; those from the most populous prefectures, like Tokyo or Osaka, need millions of votes to win office.

From this unique platform of formal power, stability, and popular legitimacy, governors of varying backgrounds have impacted the national political process and discourse. They have been described in popular discourse as being 'more powerful than prime ministers or presidents',[5] 'modern-day *daimyō* lords' (Yawata 2007), and, for the Tokyo governor, the 'second prime minister of Japan' (Sasaki 2011). They are, in other words, a significant force in both the national and local arena of politics. More than local legislatures or local party organizations, these powerful executives arguably play a visible role in defending territorial interests in the national arena. How the governors' relationship to central government has evolved since the 1990s and how their powers impact national policy are the main topics of this chapter.

Types of governors and expected behaviours

A diverse group of high-profile governors has loomed large in post-war history. During the 1960s and 1970s, economists and constitutional scholars became leading progressive governors: Ninagawa Torazo (Kyoto), Minobe Ryokichi (Tokyo), and Kuroda Ryoichi (Osaka). Governors from smaller prefectures later became prime ministers such as Hosokawa Morihiro (Kumamoto) or party leaders such as Takemura Masayoshi (Shiga) who played a central role in party realignment at national level in the early 1990s. Following this period, a surge of non-partisan voters dissatisfied with party politicians and ministry bureaucrats swept celebrities and writers to victory in gubernatorial elections. These include Yokoyama Nokku (Osaka), Aoshima Yukio (Tokyo), Ishihara Shintaro (Tokyo), Tanaka Yasuo (Nagano), and Higashikokubaru Hideo (Miyazaki). In recent years, local chief executives have started their own regional parties, some that have crossed over successfully onto the national stage. These include Hashimoto Toru (Osaka), Kada Yukiko (Shiga), and Kawamura Takashi (Nagoya mayor). Other governors have suffered high-profile scandals, such as the three governors of Fukushima, Wakayama, and Miyazaki prefectures who were arrested for construction-related bid-rigging crimes in 2006, as well as two successive Tokyo governors who stepped down on misuse of political funds in 2013 and 2016. Although the proportion of former bureaucrats among governors remains high (Figure 5.1) throughout the post-war period, there has been a fair share of former national and local politicians as well as non-politicians who have become governors.

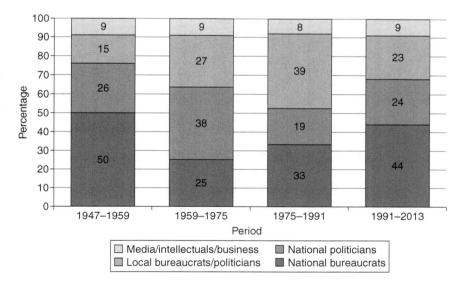

Figure 5.1 Career backgrounds of governors.
Source: compiled from Tsuji (2015, pp. 53–54).

102 *Governors and governments*

Regardless of their background, governors individually and collectively have over the years played a key role in major confrontations with the national government. The progressive government era (1965–1975) centred on governors and mayors in major urban areas backed by non-LDP parties and opposition forces. Local executives, not legislatures, led the charge against the national conservatives' agenda of runaway economic growth and called for greater welfare and environmental regulations for residents. Since the 1990s, governors worked together through national umbrella organizations in defending local government interests; in particular, against central government attempts to reduce subsidies and grants through fiscal decentralization.

Individual governors have also collided with the central government over national policies which directly affect their prefectures, with what appears to be increasing frequency and intensity from the mid-1990s. Among notable examples, this period has seen severe clashes between Okinawa governors and the capital over US base policy; recurring and public conflicts over the funding of national projects; and successful resistance against major public works, including the construction of national dams and blocking the restarting of nuclear power plants.

The relationship between governors and the national parties has also been changing. An increasing number of gubernatorial candidates are refusing nominations and the support of national parties and their headquarters, choosing to stand as independents or with the backing only of local branches of the national parties (see Figure 2.5 in Chapter 2). Related to these developments, high-profile governors/mayors have established their own local parties in legislature and sought to expand these forces upwards into the national arena and influence national policy.

Our theoretical and historical discussion in earlier chapters claimed that national and local governments have been decoupling because of decentralization since the 1990s, which combined the expansion of local autonomy with reduced fiscal support/clientelism from the centre. Such decoupling is expected to lead to less cooperation and more critical/conflictual attitudes among national and local governments in general. Local executives, leading these local governments, are thus expected to be more willing to challenge the national government over national policy direction. This is expected to be particularly the case for the increasing number of governors who are less dependent on the ruling party at national level for re-election or policy implementation at local level.

We try to provide evidence for these hypotheses by focusing on three areas. First we look at the changing overall dynamic between individual governors and the central government, specifically using data of governor meetings with the PM over time. Second we look at the evolving role and behaviour of the National Governors' Association (NGA), a key actor representing the collective interests of the regions, as well as the use of more institutionalized frameworks for inter-governmental interaction. Third, we investigate cases of major conflicts led by individual governors against the national government to better assess the

Governors and governments 103

origins, processes, and outcomes of these multi-level conflicts. By weaving together these different sets of evidence, both capturing changes over time for all governors and between governors with different characteristics, the chapter will show how interactions between governors and central government have become less stable and less cooperative.

PM meetings with governors

How have the relations between national and local executives changed over time? Governors interact with the central government through different channels and in different capacities. They may meet with higher-level national bureaucrats, ministers, and local Diet members to petition for local projects or influence national policy. In some cases, the governor will take their case directly to the prime minister. Among these interactions, nation-wide data of how often a governor meets with national ministers, Diet members, or bureaucrats are not readily available. Each of the 47 prefectures keeps past records of governors' official visits, but not their informal meetings, and past records are available only through information disclosure requests. In comparison, the daily movement and meetings of the Japanese prime minister are comprehensively recorded, archived, and made public by the major newspapers. As a data source, the so-called 'daily movement of prime ministers' has been effectively mined by other researchers to capture the changing leadership style of PMs (e.g. Machidori 2012). The author similarly collected and analysed this data to capture the changing overall relationship between PMs and governors.

Using the *Asahi* newspaper database and searching all articles recording the PM's daily schedule between 1985 and 2015, the author found 1,645 unique meetings involving a PM and a governor (1,307), a vice-governor (64), a gubernatorial candidate (216), or multiple governors (58).[6] From these 1,645 meetings, the author counted the frequency of meetings (by dividing the duration of the administration by the number of PM-governor meetings during that administration) (see Figure 5.2 below). It is evident that the frequency of meetings has generally fallen throughout this period, but with particularly low frequency of meetings with governors under the Koizumi, Fukuda, and Aso administrations as well as under the three DPJ PMs (2009–2012). Although the frequency of governor and PM meetings recovered somewhat under Abe's second term in office (2012–), they remain lower than in the 1980s and 1990s.

This general decline in frequency of PM meetings with governors can be interpreted as an expression of the growing distance between national and local governments, with direct interactions between the executives of the two levels diminishing. Moreover, the very infrequent meetings between the DPJ PMs and governors comes as little surprise. The previous chapter explained how the DPJ sought to end traditional petitioning (including those from the governor) and force local demands to be channelled through formal procedures with their local branches. The sharp drop of governor meetings since 2009 is likely a result of this DPJ policy.

104 *Governors and governments*

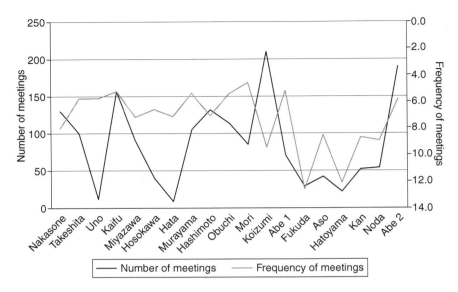

Figure 5.2 Changing frequency of meetings between PM and governors.
Source: compiled by author from *Shushō dōsei* data from *Asahi Shimbun*, 1985–2015.
Note
N = 1,645 meetings.

The author also categorized the 1,645 meetings into whether they took place at the PM's official locations (PM's official residence *kantei* and, in his capacity as leader of the LDP, at the LDP party headquarters or the Diet offices) or elsewhere (on campaign tour, some site inspection, at a conference outside of the capital, or at some informal location such as a hotel in Tokyo) (see Figure 5.3). Since 1985, it is clear that fewer governors are coming to the capital to visit the PM in his official residence, at Diet, or in LDP headquarters. Rather it is the PM who has been increasingly going out to the provinces and meeting governors during these tours.

The newspaper records of the PM's daily schedule sometimes detail the purpose or nature of the meeting between the PM and the governor (or governors). The author categorized the governor meetings into three types and recorded the proportion of these meetings for each of the PMs, tracing changes over time (see Figure 5.4 below). The first type are meetings between the PM and governor that relate to elections; these include meetings in which the PM in his capacity as the leader of the LDP (or DPJ) would: formally hand over party nominations to candidates (*suisenjō no tewatashi*); campaign on their account in their prefectures (*senkyo ōen*); meet a governor who had come to thank the PM for support after an election (*senkyo aisatsu*); and meet governors on the road when doing a campaign tour for national-level elections. The second are those in which the PM meets a governor during official business or ceremonies. These

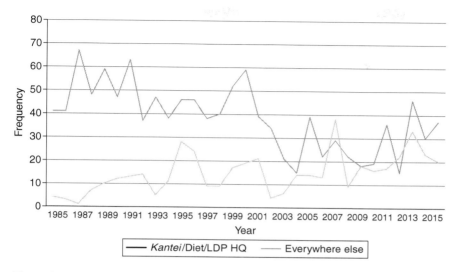

Figure 5.3 Frequency of meetings between PM and governors by location.
Source: compiled by author from *Shushō dōsei* data from *Asahi Shimbun*, 1985–2015.
Note
N = 1,645 meetings.

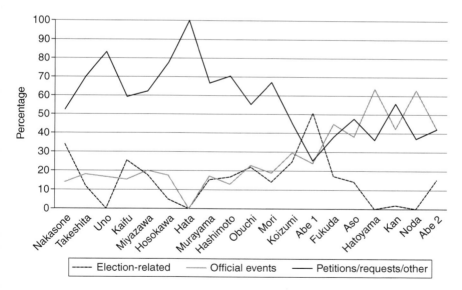

Figure 5.4 Proportion of meetings between PM and governors by category.
Source: compiled by author from *Shushō dōsei* data from *Asahi Shimbun*, 1985–2015.
Note
N = 1,645 meetings.

include: attending National Governors' Association meetings; attending various ceremonies and conferences; visiting prefectures for inspection tours or after natural disasters; or receiving guests of honour that are escorted by the governor to the PM's residence. Finally, the third type of meetings include any meetings in which: there is an explicit reference to some policy petition or demand (22 meetings); the only explanation for the meeting is that it was a lunch/ dinner meeting (42 meetings); or there is no explanation given for the meeting (838 meetings). The majority of these meetings, in which the newspapers do not record the explicit nature or purpose of the governor visiting the PM, are intriguing. The author assumes that many of these are meetings in which the governors petition for local projects or negotiate about national policies which affect their prefectures, bringing their case directly to the PM.

Figure 5.4 above demonstrates some clear trends for the three types of PM/ governor meetings since the mid-1980s. First, successive PMs are meeting governors for official occasions more, as a proportion of all their governor meetings. At the same time, PM meetings with governors concerning petitions or other matters not on official business are declining over time. From Nakasone to about Mori (1985–2000) meetings with governors on unofficial business (and those held at the *kantei* or LDP headquarters) were at high levels. Since Koizumi, these types of meetings have declined (while more and more meetings are held increasingly outside of the PM's official locations). This trend could be interpreted as a growing distance and formalization of ties between PM and governors, with fewer instances of the governor coming to the *kantei* to negotiate or petition national policy at the top level. Finally, the proportion of electoral-related meetings varies across administrations, but clearly the three DPJ administrations met hardly at all with governors to campaign for them or provide nominations, etc. This is not surprising considering the difficulty the DPJ had in nominating DPJ gubernatorial candidates, even during their term in power (Hijino 2014).

The final set of data analyses the proportion of PM meetings with specific types of governors, namely: those from the PM's own home prefecture (e.g. Nakasone's home prefecture is Gunma, so any meeting between PM Nakasone and the governor of Gunma); those from Okinawa prefecture; and those governors who did not receive nominations from the LDP headquarters for their elections (i.e. non-LDP governors) (see Figure 5.5).

The trends here corroborate the themes of growing distance between national and local governments as well as growing tensions with specific prefectures. PMs are meeting less and less with home-prefecture governors, with the proportion of such visits falling under 10 per cent since 2000. Meetings with Okinawa governors have increased since the Hashimoto administration had to deal with a crisis over US base issues under Governor Ota (meeting Ota or the vice-minister 23 times, or 20 per cent of all governor meetings). The increasing frequency of meetings with Okinawa governors reflects the growing tensions between Naha and Tokyo over base issues since that time. Finally, the proportion of PM meetings with non-LDP governors has clearly surged from under

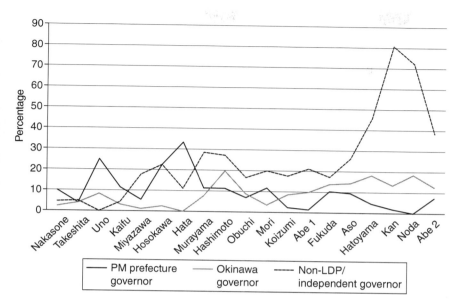

Figure 5.5 Proportion of meetings between PM and governors by category II.
Source: compiled by author from *Shushō dōsei* data from *Asahi Shimbun*, 1985–2015.
Note
N = 1,645 meetings.

20 per cent in the 1980s and 1990s to around 30 per cent for Aso and Abe to over 50 per cent since 2009. This increase reflects the greater prevalence of such non-LDP governors in general (see Figure 2.5 in Chapter 2).

The changing frequency and types of PM and governor meetings from 1985 to 2015 illustrate a number of trends in the evolving relationship between central and local governments as expressed in the interaction of executives from both levels. Primarily, meetings have become fewer in frequency and more formal in nature (ceremonies, tours of inspection, emergency meetings over natural disasters). At the same time, fewer of these meetings relate to either local petitioning/influencing national policy.

Aside from the clear increase in meetings with Okinawa governors since tensions heightened over US military bases in the mid-1990s and relations unravelled over relocating the Futenma air base from 2009, the PM meeting data cannot – by itself – capture increased tensions or conflicts between governors and PMs. What it does reveal, however, is the growing distance between governors either less willing (or no longer invited, as in the DPJ) to bring their case to Tokyo. Concerned about media relations and publicity, increasingly 'presidentialized' PMs (Krauss and Nyblade 2005; Machidori 2012) appear to be taking to the road to make more frequent stops in prefectures resulting in incidental meetings with governors outside of Tokyo. PMs are also less attached to their home prefectures, meeting with governors from their prefectures far less. There also appears to be an overall weakening of providing electoral support for governors in later administrations, as more governors distance themselves from the national parties. Executives of the two levels are delinking and direct channels of communication between the PM and individual governors thinning out.

Although a very crude indicator of the changing relations between governors and PMs, the author searched for articles in the major dailies (*Asahi Shimbun* and *Yomiuri Shimbun*) that included the terms 'criticize', 'governor', and 'prime minister's official residence (*kantei*)' (see Figure 5.6 below). The results included articles that were not related to relations between governors and the PM, but the majority of them were articles in which governors criticized or questioned national policy. In both newspapers, the frequency of articles with those search terms increased at a similar rate: sharp increases in 1995, 2001–2004, 2007, and after 2009. Each of these peaks reflects different issues of contention between the two levels of government, but the overall trend is clear: governors are generally more critical of the central government executive, with much of these increases occurring after 2000. Together with the PM meeting data, the frequency of such articles further corroborates the interpretation that relations between executives at both levels have become more tense and confrontational.

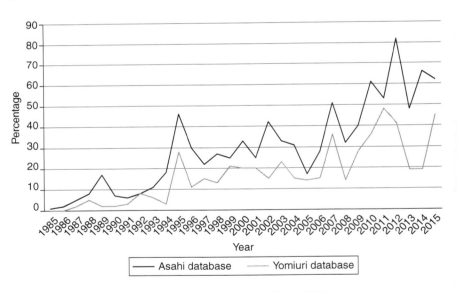

Figure 5.6 Media reporting on governors criticizing cabinet/PM and vice versa.

Source: compiled by author from *Yomiuri Shimbun* database (*yomidasu*) and *Asahi Shimbun* database (Kikuzo II).

The National Governors' Association and collective bargaining

Since the post-war period, local governments have been organized into national umbrella associations which act collectively to bargain and pressure the central government. All 47 governors are members of the National Governors' Association (*zenkoku chijikai*), while the chief executives of cities as well as towns and villages have their own national associations (*zenkoku shichōkai* and *zenkoku chōsonchōkai*, respectively). In addition, the prefectural, city, and village-level legislatures have their own legislative chairman's associations (*zenkoku todōfukengikai gichōkai*, *shichōgikai gichōkai*, and *chōsongikai gichōkai* respectively). These associations are linked together as the Six Associations of Local Government (*chihō rokudantai*) which serves as a kind of interest group for local governments, jointly petitioning and proposing policies to the central government on commonly shared issues (Kanai 2008, p. 92).

The collective bargaining process by these groups has changed considerably since the mid-1990s. The changes in the internal organization of the NGA, their relations with successive administrations, as well as the powers and roles of other collective bargaining channels are investigated in this section. These observations are provided to further bolster the argument that the relations between executives and governments at national and local levels are becoming more antagonistic and that these tensions are being channelled into more institutionalized fora.

According to Asano Shiro, Miyagi governor and one of the NGA's active members since the mid-1990s, the NGA biannual meetings were traditionally ceremonial events orchestrated by the Ministry of Internal Affairs and Communications (MIC). Governors presented prepared statements and petitions for the national government, while substantial issues were not discussed or decided.[7] This role, however, has changed considerably since the mid-1990s with the emergence of more proactive and vocal governors pushing for further decentralization[8] as well as in reaction to top-down policies which threatened local interests.

The NGA was particularly active, together with other local government associations, in negotiations over fiscal decentralization reforms under the Koizumi administration (2000–2006). In these negotiations, local governments sought to abolish conditional grants and gain greater discretion over spending, while the central government aimed to slash subsidies and general grants while minimizing the transfers of taxing powers. Local distrust towards the capital mounted as the Koizumi administration cut back both subsidies and grants sharply, creating a sudden and unexpected shortage in local finances (see discussion in Chapter 2).

Under this tense context, the NGA meeting hosted by Gifu prefecture in 2003 was unofficially but popularly called 'the NGA which fights' (*tatakau chijikai*) presumably for local interests against the centre. During this Gifu meeting, prepared statements were replaced by free debates and the rules for selecting the NGA chairman were changed from discussion to majority vote.[9] The NGA meetings have increased in frequency since this year from biannual to bimonthly under the Gifu governor, Kajiwara Taku, who became the first NGA chairman to be selected under the new election procedure.[10] The central government also passed a cabinet decision in 2003 and 2004 to host an annual government-hosted NGA meeting (*seifu shusai no zenkoku chijikaigi*) (Kanai 2008, p. 91), institutionalizing collective bargaining with governors.

The NGA also became increasingly active in publically pressuring the central government over various national policy decisions. Notable actions of the NGA at the time include preparing a list of national ear-marked subsidies to be abolished and transferred as general grants as well as pushing for the establishment of a formal forum of inter-governmental discussion. Figure 5.7 shows how the NGA has increasingly held meetings as well as passed resolutions and made public appeals (many of them labelled 'emergency' appeals or demands) against national policy since 2000. The association for governors also stepped away from maintaining strict partisan neutrality by beginning in the 2005 general election for the first time to assess party platforms and manifesto promises relating to decentralization and local government.[11] The NGA has continued with this practice of evaluating party manifestos. In fact, prior to the 2009 general elections, Osaka governor Hashimoto Toru suggested the association publically back either the

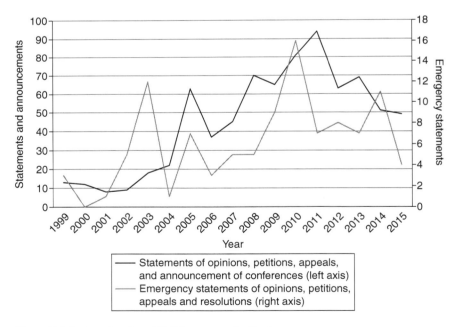

Figure 5.7 Actions listed on NGA homepage by fiscal year.
Source: '*Katsudōkenkyū shiryō yōbōsho/teiansho (kakunen)*', National Governors' Association.
Note
www.nga.gr.jp/data/document/index.html.

Governors and governments 111

LDP or DPJ in order to pressure the two parties to be more responsive to local government demands. This proposal was rejected by other governors, although the NGA asked and did hold open debates with party leaders on their position on decentralization.[12] These increasingly public and politicized actions over national policy of the NGA, in contrast to its former role as a mere ceremonial forum for petitioning, can be interpreted as a result of increasing distance and tensions between governors and their traditional partners, the ruling conservatives.[13]

Frustrated by having their proposals over fiscal decentralization ignored by the ministries, the 'fighting governors' association' under Kajiwara demanded a venue to voice their demands over central government policy. Under instructions of the PM, local and central government representatives[14] were given a chance to meet and discuss the contents of fiscal decentralization. The first such 'forum of discussions between central government and regions' (*kuni to chihō no kyōgino ba*) was held in September 2004 and took place 14 times until 2006. Various observers and participants claimed this forum for central-local discussions over national policy ultimately failed to reflect local government preferences. The forum, having no legal basis and thus unable to bind policy decisions, became merely a place for local governments to express their preferences, rather than a place where decisions took place. Fiscal decentralization policy was determined ultimately in the more powerful Council of Fiscal and Economic Policy without accommodating to local government proposals and demands (Kanai 2008, pp. 98–100).

Following this initial failure, the NGA sought to institutionalize the 'forum of discussions between central government and regions' by demanding the government pass a law giving legal basis to these formerly ad hoc meetings. The aim was to create a forum where local governments could discuss national policy-making on equal footing with the central government on matters which directly impinged on local governance, and influence national policy (Kitamura 2011). The DPJ administration promised and passed a law to institutionalize these meetings in 2011 and, since then up to 2015, there have been about 2–8 annual meetings a year.

Evaluations of how effectively local governments have been able to collectively bargain for their interests in this forum remain divided. Significantly, the 1,850 or so local governments are not a monolithic entity and interests between wealthier urban local governments and smaller, poorer rural local governments diverge (as do the interests between the associations representing legislatures and executives). These internal divisions weaken the bargaining power of the local government representatives by limiting what kind of demands and pressures they can place on the central government.

Although the overall effectiveness of these institutionalized forums for securing local government interests is unclear, these developments in collective bargaining should be interpreted as a result of reactions to growing tensions between national and local governments since the 1990s. From below, governors have collectively reacted to less fiscal support from the centre by politicizing its national association and demanding more channels for participation in

112 *Governors and governments*

national policy. From above, administrations have tried to contain this tension by setting up institutionalized forums of 'discussion on equal footing', based on the outward principle of decentralization reform, without necessarily committing themselves to local demands.

Cases of conflict: origins, process, and outcomes

Types of conflicts and overview of cases

The historical data so far capture how the relationship between governors and central governments has shifted to a weakening of informal links, growing tensions over national policy, and more institutionalized interactions. These developments occurred contemporaneously with trends of decentralization, weakening clientelism, top-down policy-making from above, and the emergence of non-partisan governors from below. The changing relations between levels of government, like all broad historical change, is driven by intertwined, multiple variables having multiple, inter-related outcomes. Yet such a description of messy covariation lacks analytical rigour in terms of causality. Moreover, not all governors became uncooperative towards the central government overnight. Some governors opposed national policy while others didn't, even if all local governments were more or less affected similarly by administrative decentralization in 2000 or reduced fiscal support since that time.

What, then, makes some governors, under this new institutional context more likely to resist national policy publicly? In this section we try to sharpen the causal argument to this question. First, after describing what sort of actions by governors can be construed as challenges to the central government, we provide a table of major challenges by governors since 2000 over a range of national policies. The governors who challenged national policy in this list are then analysed in terms of two variables – their party affiliation and fiscal wealth – and compared to the national average for all governors. This comparison is done to see if governors engaged in multi-level conflict tend to be of a particular partisan affiliation or wealthier/poorer than the national average. The rest of the chapter explores cases of multi-level conflict involving governors to show what resources and channels were used to resist national policy and to what degree they succeeded in this local resistance.

What types of actions constitute conflict or resistance from local chief executives against the central government over national policy? The following list captures, from a survey of past cases, the potential routes used by governors to challenge the centre.

1 Petition and influence the central government (ministers and bureaucrats) through local Diet members, local bureaucrats, or through direct meetings with central government representatives as individual governors.
2 Petition and influence the central government through the NGA (or other regional governors' associations) collectively.

Governors and governments 113

3 Make personal and public statements (in press conferences, in media interviews, on personal blogs/social media) challenging or opposing national policy.

4 Use executive powers as governor (propose budgets, seek by-law changes, retract permits, use the National and Local Government Dispute Resolution Council, sue the central government) which seek to block or influence national policy.

The list is, intuitively speaking, on an escalating scale of seriousness in terms of raising the stakes of conflict. We have already captured how informal meetings between governors and PMs (channel 1) have weakened as well as how collective bargaining routes (channel 2) have become more intense and institutionalized since the mid-1990s. We turn to how individual governors have opposed national policy by going beyond channels of petitioning to publically challenge and oppose the central government (channels 3 and 4).

We select multi-level conflicts over national policy which triggered resistance from some governors but not from others to ensure variation in outcome (e.g. unlike the collective responses from all governors such as on fiscal decentralization). The cases selected are particularly high profile and well publicized, reflecting the intensity and high stakes of the conflict for both national and local politicians. The time period is between 2000 and 2016 under the new institutional context following the start of decentralization reforms. The policy conflicts can be divided into conflicts over public works (dams or nuclear power plants), disputes over funding of shared facilities, and security issues. The 15 cases in Table 5.1 are categorized by the policy area, what major actions were taken against national policy, the governor who took these actions, their prefecture, years of conflict, the governors' partisan background, and the fiscal strength of their prefecture.

The data point to two observations. First, the fiscal strength of a prefecture seemed unimportant in determining whether its governor was likely to challenge national policy. Prefectures highly dependent on central government transfers such as Tokushima, Okinawa, and Niigata appeared prepared to challenge the centre as frequently as wealthier prefectures such as Tokyo, Osaka, Kyoto, or Shiga. Second, governors that were not backed by LDP headquarters tended to engage in conflicts against the central government. During 1999–2015, 48 per cent of all governors (98 out of 188) were not backed by the national LDP (they were either backed only by the local LDP, backed by other parties locally or nationally, or had no partisan affiliation). In the conflicts sampled here, 80 per cent (12 out of 15 cases) involved were non-national-LDP governors.

The finding that such governors less dependent on the national ruling party more frequently challenge national policy is not in itself surprising. The surge of these types of governors since 2000 thus explains how multi-level conflict has generally increased during this period. What is curious is that such combative governors have emerged both in richer and poorer regions. Our expectation that lack of fiscal strength, because it decreased local autonomy, would make governors less prone to challenging the centre was not supported in these cases.

Table 5.1 Challenges made by governors against national policy

Case number	Policy area	Main actions taken by governor against national policy	Governor	Prefecture	Period	Partisan affiliation of governor	Financial strength of prefecture
1	Dam projects (prefectural)	Cancel dam projects/Dismiss public works section manager	Tanaka	Nagano	2002–2006	independent	lower
2	Yoshino moveable weir	Seek project termination	Ota	Tokushima	2002–2003	non-LDP	lower
3	Ootogawa dam	Seek project termination	Kada	Shiga	2006–	other	higher
4	Kawabegawa dam	Seek project termination	Kabashima	Kumamoto	2008–	local LDP	lower
5	Pluthermal nuclear project	Withdraw agreement to plan	Sato	Fukushima	2002–2006	LDP	lower
6	Restarting nuclear power plants	Oppose restart of plants	Izumida	Niigata	2011–	LDP	lower
7	Restarting nuclear power plants	Oppose restart of plants in other prefectures/Demand safety agreements with utility company	Izumida	Shiga	2011–2012	other	higher
8	Restarting nuclear power plants	Oppose restart of plants in other prefectures/Demand safety agreements with utility company	Mikazuki	Shiga	2015–	non-LDP	higher
9	Restarting nuclear power plants	Oppose restart of plants in other prefectures/Demand safety agreements with utility company	Yamada	Kyoto	2011–2012	local LDP	higher

10	Stopping nuclear power plant in operation	Submit request to utility company to stop nuclear power plant	Mitazono	Kagoshima	2016–	non-LDP	lower
11	Special Local Corporate Tax	Announce opposition and official protest	Ishihara	Tokyo	2008–2012	local LDP	higher
12	Hokuriku Shinkansen construction costs	Refuse to pay obligatory local contributions/Use National and Local Government Dispute Resolution Council	Izumda	Niigata	2009–2012	LDP	lower
13	Olympic facility costs	Refuse to pay obligatory local contributions	Masuzoe	Tokyo	2015–2016	local LDP	higher
14	Obligatory local contributions	Refuse to pay obligatory local contributions/Protest through NGA	Hashimoto	Osaka	2009–2012	other (originally local LDP)	higher
15	Futemma base transfer to Henoko	Withdraw permit for construction/Use National and Local Government Dispute Resolution Council	Onaga	Okinawa	2012–2016	Non-LDP	lower
	Total by cases					LDP (3), local LDP (5), independent or non-LDP (8)	Higher than national average (7) vs lower (8)

Source: compiled by author. Partisan affiliation of governor is taken from Tsuji (2015, pp. 73–74) as well as *Asahi* reporting on individual elections; fiscal strength of local governments calculated by the Financial Capability Index (*zaiseiryokushisū*) being higher or lower than national average for the starting year of conflict. Data from Somusho E-stat database: www.e-stat.go.jp/SG1/estat/eStatTopPortal.do.

116 Governors and governments

There are two potential explanations for this unexpected outcome. First, governors in poorer regions no longer expect to receive fiscal support from the centre (having seen it cut sharply since 2000) by remaining loyal to Tokyo. Thus they see little to lose by challenging the central government. And second, many of these non-LDP governors who later on challenged Tokyo had specifically campaigned in opposition to these national projects. Opposition to these projects has become sufficiently strong and widespread in the prefectures to over-ride concern of reduced fiscal support from the centre. Having once turned off the fiscal tap to its most traditionally loyal regions, the centre can no longer ensure obeisance when trying to implement unpopular national policy programmes in these regions.

Central-local relations over controversial national policies have changed abruptly and dramatically in some prefectures through gubernatorial elections as well. As we will see below, e.g. in Nagano, Tokushima, Shiga, Kagoshima, and Okinawa, the birth of a non-LDP governor resulted in a sudden reversal of past prefectural positions accepting national programmes or projects. In these cases, non-partisan governors – with little dependence on the national ruling party for re-election – have chosen to take on a combative relationship to the national government. In some rare cases, such as in Fukushima or Niigata, governors initially backed by the HQ of the national ruling party have later hardened against national programmes. We look more carefully at some of these cases of conflict, focusing on how governors fight back and whether they succeed.

Public works: dams and nuclear policy

Local opposition movements against national public works projects such as dams, airports, and nuclear plants have always been a recurring fixture in post-war politics. Notable protests include the Shimouke dam protests (1959–1964),[15] local struggles against construction of the Narita airport (Sanrizuka struggles, 1960–), as well as numerous local opposition fights to nuclear plant sites across Japan since the 1970s (Aldrich 2016). In these earlier conflicts, the struggles occurred mainly between the ministries (central government) and opposition movements at local level. Conservative governors, who were involved in petitioning the centre to bring these major national projects to their prefecture, tended to back these national infrastructure project in these conflicts.

Entering into the late 1990s and early 2000s, however, governors emerged across Japan who campaigned and won elections in opposition to national public projects, criticizing them as both economically unsound (waste of tax money) and environmentally damaging. Such governors emerged in a number of regions, but most dramatically in Nagano, Tokushima, Shiga, and Kumamoto where governors sought to halt long-standing national plans to construct dams.

In Nagano, author Tanaka Yasuo who had formerly organized opposition to the construction plans of Kobe airport in the mid-1990s, became governor in 2000. He had campaigned against public works projects as wasteful and economically inefficient, pointing to prefectural debts resulting from the

Governors and governments   117

construction boom for the Nagano winter Olympic games. After making a 'declaration of quitting dams', Tanaka halted the construction of all major dam projects in Nagano. Although most of the cancelled dams were prefectural projects, subsidized by the central government, Tanaka came into direct conflict with the local LDP and construction ministry officials in support of the dams. The governor cut the budget for dam construction and fired a ministry of construction bureaucrats seconded to the prefectural government.[16] Tanaka faced strong opposition in the local legislature, dominated by conservatives, who passed multiple votes of no-confidence, but he was able to stop prefectural dams and delay national dams in Nagano during his term.

In the traditionally conservative stronghold of Tokushima, an LDP-backed governor was arrested and later charged for bid-rigging of public works in 2002. In the ensuing gubernatorial elections, Ota Tadashi, a former Social Democratic Party of Japan (SDPJ) prefectural assembly member, received backing from parties on the left, campaigned against wasteful public works, and defeated the LDP-backed candidate. Ota declared an end to a long-standing national movable weir project on the Yoshino river which had been opposed in local referendums by a wide majority. Despite majority opposition, the weir plans had not been officially terminated by the ministry of construction who held final discretion over the continuation of the project.[17] Like Tanaka in Nagano, Ota faced severe resistance from the local conservative-dominated assembly which sought to revive the project and passed votes of no-confidence against the governor, resulting in his early ousting in 2003. During his term, Tanaka sought meetings with the minister of construction, but was refused.[18] The project remained delayed, however, and was finally cancelled under the DPJ government in 2010.

In Shiga, Kada Yukiko, a former academic and environmental activist backed by neither LDP nor DPJ in her 2006 gubernatorial race, came to power criticizing public works on the slogan of '*mottainai*' (don't be wasteful). Once in office, she sought to halt construction of nationally funded dams and a *shinkansen* station in the prefecture, but faced the foot-dragging of the local legislature controlled by conservatives. After leading a regional party (*Taiwa de tsunagu shiga no kai*) to victory and pushing the conservatives into a minority in the legislature in 2007, Kada was able to terminate the *shinkansen* station construction plans (Hijino 2014). The national dam projects (Daidogawa and Niu dams), however, being far larger in scale and budget size, proved more difficult to stop. In 2008, Kada joined with governors of Kyoto, Osaka, and Mie (prefectures down-river of the dam project) to submit a joint statement to the ministry of construction opposing the Daidogawa dam project. The DPJ government announced the project 'frozen' in status in 2009, but since the LDP government returned to power, there is evidence of the central government trying to 'thaw' the dam project back to life.

In Kumamoto, Kabashima Ikuo, a political scientist, became governor in 2008 with the support of the local LDP. Once in power, he announced opposition to a long-standing national dam project (Kawabegawa dam). The project

118 *Governors and governments*

which had been delayed for decades as a result of strong local opposition was re-assessed, with the governor concluding that such a dam was unnecessary. The DPJ government which had campaigned in 2009 promising to terminate the dam halted the project officially in 2010. Opposition by the governor (as well as local mayors) to Kawabegawa dam was in contrast to another similar-sized and controversial dam project in Gunma, the Yamba dam. Here, the pro-dam local governor, together with local conservatives, was able to revive the national project despite DPJ promises to terminate it along with Kawabegawa (see Chapter 4).

In sum, governors in rural areas have emerged on the back of a mood of hostility to wasteful public works projects, defeating LDP-backed candidates. Once in power, these governors have declared opposition to major national projects which have been delayed for years by municipal-level opposition movements. Though lacking legal authority to terminate these national projects, the emergence of governors opposing these long-standing national projects has led to delays and eventual termination.[19]

Following the explosion and meltdown of the Fukushima Daiichi nuclear plant in March of 2011, governors across Japan voiced doubts about restarting existing and building new nuclear power plants.[20] The DPJ Noda administration (2011–2012) and succeeding LDP Abe administration (2012–), however, sought to restart some of the 54 plants across Japan which had been stopped since the earthquake on 11 March 2011. In the process, a handful of governors from prefectures hosting the plants (as well governors from prefectures such as Kyoto, Shiga, and Osaka close to prefectures with numerous plants) openly challenged national energy policy of restarting nuclear plants. Notable among these cases were the host prefectures of Niigata and Kagoshima. Though governors have no legal powers to stop the operations of an existing nuclear power plant, they can refuse to sign a so-called 'safety agreement' with the utility companies operating the plants made before operating the nuclear reactor.[21]

In Niigata, Governor Izumida, who had been backed by the LDP in his re-election in 2008, repeatedly criticized the utility and regulators over its handling of the nuclear accident. Izumida opposed restarting of the nuclear power plants in the prefecture by refusing to sign the safety agreement as well as to accept safety inspections and construction of additional safety features on the Niigata plants.[22]

In Kagoshima, Satoshi Mitazono campaigned in 2016 to stop a nuclear plant currently in operation in the prefecture, becoming the first governor to win by campaigning against nuclear power in a host prefecture. Mitazono's predecessor had given the green light to restarting the nuclear power plant and stated intentions to allow the plant to run for the next 30 years. Once in power, Mitazono stated that he would ask the utility company to halt the local nuclear power plant, although the governor has no legal powers to enforce this request.[23]

As with the construction of national dams, governors do not have full authority to stop the operations of nuclear power plants that are regulated by the energy agency. Yet vocal opposition against nuclear power from high-profile

Governors and governments 119

governors – both in host and neighbouring prefectures – boosted the legitimacy of popular opposition and made it difficult for utility companies to restart plants. These cases show how governors have influence beyond their formal powers, stemming from their democratic legitimacy and media impact. Even when lacking ultimate legal authority, governors, as concentrated nodes of political representation, can shape national policy.

Conflicts over shared funding

Money, being the source of most social conflicts, has unsurprisingly been a recurring flash point for inter-governmental relations in Japan. Local governments have collectively and individually clashed with the central government over funding levels for locally administered public services mandated by national law, discretion to issue local debts, and obligatory local contributions for national public works projects. Some of these long-standing struggles re-emerged and were resolved during the post-decentralization period.

In the 1970s, progressive governors from large cities clashed with the ruling party over the right to raise taxes on corporations (*chōka kazei hōshiki*), a right which they eventually won and was extended to all local governments throughout Japan. During that time, the progressive Tokyo governor Minobe Ryokichi also famously tried to challenge the central government through courts to allow local governments to raise debts without central government permission. The struggle, the so-called 'debt issuance litigation' (*kisai soshō*) incident, was 'a war of independence to realize genuine self-rule' for local governments (Sasaki 2011, p. 129). Minobe's challenge was defeated after resistance from the central ministries and ruling party squeezed Tokyo government finances. It also met with unexpected sabotage from the New Liberal Club faction in the Tokyo metropolitan legislature which blocked Minobe's litigation against the central government. The right of local governments to raise debts without central government permit was finally granted in 2006, although the central government retained rights to intervene through a system of prior negotiations[24] (Sasaki 2011, pp. 130–131).

Another long-standing struggle over money between national and local governments has been controversy over local contributions to the construction and maintenance of national infrastructure projects such as dams, roads, bridges, and harbours. Based on local finance law,[25] local governments are obligated to contribute between one-third to 45 per cent of the construction and maintenance of projects directly managed by the central government (*chokkatsujigyō chihō futankin*). This obligatory local contribution has been a source of inter-governmental tension since early in the post-war period, with the NGA making a collective petition in 1959 and 1962 to reduce and abolish these practices.[26] Despite continued protests by the NGA, the co-payment rates remained largely unchanged until the 1980s, when rates were moderately reduced.

The local contribution issue re-emerged onto the national scene in 2009, when the high-profile Osaka governor Hashimoto Toru made headlines by

120 *Governors and governments*

refusing to pay part of the local contribution bill for the year for Osaka, citing lack of transparency in the calculations. In typical populist fashion, Hashimoto appealed to the press by comparing the way central ministries send these obligatory payments bills to local governments for national projects as being similar to the unfoundedly expensive bills given customers at a 'rip-off bar' (*bottakuri* bar). His acerbic metaphor made the rounds, with criticism erupting from numerous other local governments about the practice.[27]

Renewed hostility to this local contribution system stemmed from the reduced flow of money overall to regions since around 2000. Central government subsidies for locally managed construction projects had been slashed, while the budget for national projects (and hence local contributions) remained largely unchanged (Yamazaki 2009, p. 83). Local governments were now receiving fewer subsidies, but footing the same costs for national projects and feeling unfairly squeezed. They thus took collective action, following the lead of Osaka governor Hashimoto.

Through the year, the NGA, together with a government committee on decentralization, pushed for change. The NGA demanded formal discussions over the local contribution system with the relevant ministries, made an emergency appeal to abolish the system, and demanded the national parties to include reform of this system in their general election manifestos (Yamazaki 2009, pp. 89–90). The DPJ administration came to power in 2009 and abolished the local contribution system of maintenance fees for national projects, but the practice of local contribution for construction of national projects remains.[28]

There have also been other similar struggles over shared funding of national/local projects. In Niigata, governor Izumida initially refused to pay for a part of the obligated one-third co-payment for the construction costs of a new *shinkansen* bullet train through his prefecture in 2009. Local bureaucrats told media that the governor may have been pushed to these actions in the face of reduced overall subsidies and grants from the central government, while facing unchanged co-payment costs for national projects.[29] An additional factor enabling this combative behaviour was the existence of a bullet train line already connecting Niigata to Tokyo.

Izumida had also earlier challenged the government to arbitration by the National and Local Government Dispute Resolution Council (*kunichihō keisōshori iinkai*) over the central government's approval of the bullet train construction plans. The council rejected the arbitration request, stating that the central government had not directly intervened in Niigata prefecture, but merely approved a railway company's plans. This was the second time that a local government took a dispute to this arbitration council, which had been set up as part of the decentralization reforms to ensure inter-governmental disputes be resolved on equal footing. The first occurred when the Yokohama city government challenged the MIC minister for refusing to allow the city to tax horse-race facilities. Yokohama city lost. The third occurred under the tensions between Okinawa governor and the central government after 2015 (see opposite).

Governors and governments 121

In Tokyo, Governor Masuzoe baulked at contributing payments to the construction of the new national stadium for the 2020 Tokyo Olympics. Masuzoe questioned the ballooning costs of the project, arguing that no formal agreement had been made by his predecessor over shared costs. Through the spring and summer of 2015, the governor criticized the Ministry of Education, the Japan Olympic committee, and even the prime minister over the ever-growing construction costs for the project, refusing to meet the ministry officials who were prepared to 'explain' the costs.[30] The ministry of education responded by threatening to pass special legislation to ensure that local governments, including Tokyo, would be compelled to contribute to the construction of national stadiums.[31] In turn, Masuzoe appealed to the public through the media, attacking the central government over an issue which most voters were sympathetic about. The popular uproar eventually resulted in the education minister resigning and the PM calling for a new, less expensive stadium plan in December 2015. Masuzoe, however, was forced to resign half a year later when a scandal of improper use of political funds emerged. In the same month, a cabinet decision was taken compelling Tokyo to pay a quarter of the total costs of the construction of the stadium.[32]

Though tensions over who pays for what in inter-governmental relations are not unique to Japan (see Chapter 6), the highly fiscally centralized structure and dependency of a majority of local governments on central transfers and subsidies has kept such challenges under check in the post-war period. Not surprisingly, it had been wealthier local governments – Tokyo, Osaka, and other urban centres – that sought greater fiscal autonomy. In the post-2000 period, such wealthier local governments have again taken the lead in demanding more freedom to raise and spend monies. But notably, poorer prefectures have also fought back to pay less for national projects. Similar to opposition against long-standing national dam projects and nuclear plants, the new combative and assertive local posture towards shared funding of projects reflects an overall weakening of clientelistic links between the two levels.

Security: base relocation in Okinawa

The final case of local resistance to national policy is perhaps the most substantial and vital for it concerns national security, specifically multi-level conflicts related to US military bases in Japan.

Although US base issues exist in other prefectures, the intense and complex multi-level conflict between Okinawa and the central government make it the most significant. Unlike the mainland, Okinawa has a distinct cultural and historical trajectory, experience of US land invasion at the end of the Pacific War, and 27 years of US occupation. Since gaining independence, Okinawa, with only 0.6 per cent of the landmass of Japan, hosts three-quarters of all US military installations in the country. The island prefecture is also one of the poorest in terms of per capita income and depends heavily on revenues related to bases and central government transfers.

122 *Governors and governments*

The intensity of the conflicts over base issues compared to other multi-level challenges adds to this uniqueness. As such, the case needs to be treated with caution in terms of comparing it with the dynamics of other multi-level conflicts. With this in mind, we demonstrate some of the ways in which partisanship and fiscal dependence has affected relations between Okinawa and the central government. Finally, we see how two Okinawa governors (Ota and Onaga) who were most prominently in conflict with Tokyo sought to resist and influence central government policies.

The partisan affiliation of Okinawa governors has swung in pendulum fashion between 1972 and 2015. Progressive governors backed by opposition and regional parties (Yara and Taira 1972–1978; Ota 1990–1998; and Onaga 2014–) have alternated with LDP-backed conservative governors (Nishime, 1978–1990; Inamine and Nakaima 1998–2014). The swinging partisan dynamic was also reflected in the legislature where progressives and a regional party (Shakai Taishuto) sought expulsion of US bases against conservatives who accepted US military bases. In the post-Cold War period, this progressive-conservative cleavage blurred, with both sides increasingly linking demands for economic support with accepting some level of US base burden (Sakurazawa 2015, p. 237). In this context, refusal to comply with Tokyo's requests on bases resulted in threats to retract or offers to provide economic stimulus packages to Okinawa.

In 1996, Governor Ota refused to sign off on land leases for US military bases and was sued by the national government in courts. During the stand-off, individual negotiations with Ota and PM Hashimoto resulted in an offer of a large stimulus package which pushed Ota to finally comply with national government requests (Sakurazawa 2015, pp. 250–252). Similarly, in 2012, Governor Nakaima who had previously refused to provide a permit to begin construction of a relocation base in Henoko Bay for the Futenma airbase acceded to government demands after being offered, what he called, the 'largest stimulus package in history' (Sakurazawa 2015, pp. 313–314).

In the ongoing stand-off between Governor Onaga (2014–) and the Abe administration, both partisan affiliation and financial resources also play key roles. Onaga was formerly a veteran LDP prefectural legislator, mayor for Naha, and campaign manager for the former governor Nakaima. He stood against Nakaima and was backed by parties on the left (including communists) but also a handful of local LDP legislators opposing relocation of Futenma to a new base in Henoko bay (see Chapter 3). The so-called 'all Okinawa' non-LDP coalition swept Onaga to victory in 2014, ousted LDP MPs in Okinawa constituencies for both houses of Diet (2014 and 2016), and expanded the non-LDP majority of the prefectural assembly (2016).

From this strong position of united partisan opposition to Tokyo, Onaga has confronted the ruling party and capital by retracting the permit given by the previous governor to construct the base in Henoko bay (October 2015). The Abe administration responded initially by repeatedly refusing to meet with Onaga for negotiations as well as reducing budgetary spending for the prefecture (Onaga 2015, pp. 27–30). The central government (the construction

Governors and governments 123

ministry and defence agency) has also sued the governor's retraction of a construction permit, while Onaga responded in kind by suing the Defence Agency. The governor has also brought the matter to the Dispute Resolution Council on three occasions, but the council has refused to arbitrate, citing an inability to judge on the matter. During this period, the construction on Henoko has been further delayed, with local citizen groups clashing with police and security officers at the construction site. The Fukuoka local court called for the central government and Okinawa to settle out of court, and temporarily stop construction work at Henoko (March 2015). The Abe administration momentarily accepted this settlement offer, but has re-litigated against Okinawa prefecture (immediately after the Upper House elections in July 2015) and the matter remains pending.

Beside the executive powers of retracting permits for construction, Governor Onaga writes that he, together with the Nago mayor where Henoko bay is located, have counted up to ten areas under their jurisdiction (requiring local government permits) which can be used to delay and stop construction work at Henoko (Onaga 2015, pp. 96–97). If so disposed, Onaga believes he can further delay and block national plans to relocate the base. In the meantime, Governor Onaga has opened up further fronts by engaging in local government 'paradiplomacy'. The governor has visited the US to speak at the United Nations Human Rights Council to raise awareness about Okinawa base issues as well as met with US congressmen to discuss US base policy.[33]

Although the Okinawa case has only been investigated perfunctorily, the data lead to three main observations. First, and unsurprisingly, the greatest multi-level tensions occurred when non-LDP governors assumed office. Furthermore, in recent years, local LDP in legislatures have been less loyal to the national leadership (see Chapter 3), resulting in the birth of a rogue LDP governor in 2014 opposed to national policy. Second, the central government has used Okinawa's fiscal dependence as a tool to ensure compliance on base policy. Though it has been effective in past cases, it appears that buying compliance has become less effective recently, with Okinawa voters booting out a governor (Nakaima) after he had secured one of the largest fiscal packages from the capital in the prefecture's history. Finally, the Okinawa governor certainly does not have direct vetoing power of US base policy (security is an exclusively national policy area), yet it has used various local by-laws such as those regulating public works to effectively delay national policy of the highest importance for as long as 20 years.

As Onaga has claimed, if the Okinawa governor and local governments chose to actively resist by blocking various construction projects, an endless series of litigation will take place and confound the central government. Full-on conflict involving Okinawa local executives and legislatures against the central government has emerged under the Onaga governorship. The dynamic demonstrates the inherent formal and informal powers which Japanese local government, if pushed to the limit, can use to quite effectively and surprisingly derail national policy.

Conclusion

The chapter demonstrated, through a wide range of evidence and case studies, how relations between governors and the central government have changed since the mid-1990s. Individually, governors have less personal contact with the prime minister, as fewer and fewer of them are backed by the national ruling party. Collectively, governors have become more active in protecting local interests by politicizing and institutionalizing the governor associations in the face of top-down decisions by LDP administrations. The case studies involving key flash points of public works (dams and nuclear plants), shared funding, and US base issues demonstrated how partisan affiliation of the governors was more predictive of multi-level conflicts than the fiscal autonomy (wealth) of the prefectural government.

Finally, governors are successfully challenging the centre, but not through new powers or institutions granted to them through administrative decentralization. Among the new tools used by governors was the Dispute Resolution Council, established as part of the decentralization reforms in 2000. The council has only been used by local governments three times and on two of these occasions the council has refused or failed to arbitrate multi-level conflict. Instead, fiscal decentralization (and reduced clientelistic practices) has made governors from both richer and poorer regions more willing to challenge the centre because they face less risk of being disloyal to Tokyo. In this context, governors are using executive powers and their informal power of popular legitimacy, resources available in the past, to challenge the centre. Whether driven by genuine opposition or strategic positioning, these governors are choosing to represent territory, rather than the partisan links to either ruling or opposition parties. Increasingly, campaigning against Tokyo has become a successful vote-winning strategy in post-decentralization Japan, feeding multi-level conflict and disequilibrium.

Notes

1 As of 2012, Tokyo's economy (by gross regional product) was larger than the GDP of Indonesia, Holland, Turkey, Switzerland, and Sweden. Aichi's economy is larger than Austria. Even the smallest prefectures like Tottori are comparable to the economies of Estonia or Iceland in pure size. See data from the *Shakai jitsuzō data zuroku* website. Available from www2.ttcn.ne.jp/honkawa/4550.html [accessed 20 October 2016].

2 Unlike US presidents, for example, the Japanese governor has the right to submit legislation (by-laws) and has exclusive right over the drafting and submission of the local government budget. The Japanese governor, unlike most presidential systems, also has the power to dissolve the elected legislature, if the legislature passes a motion of no-confidence against them.

3 Yawata (2007) calculates that the re-election rate for incumbent governors is over 90 per cent and the average number of their terms is just above three between 1947 and 2007.

4 Presidents in US, France, Germany, Austria, Brazil, and Finland have two-consecutive terms as limits.

Governors and governments 125

5 'Tokyo tochijino kengen wa "Daitoryō nami" yosan 13 chōen, Sweden ni hitteki', *Asahi Shimbun*, 5 February 2014.

6 Using the *Asahi* Kikuzo II database, the author searched for *shushō dōsei* articles which capture the daily schedule of the PM. If the PM met with the same governor on two consecutive days (e.g. during a visit to some conference/symposium stretching over two or more days) this was counted as a single meeting of the same governor.

7 Asano Shiro, 'Shissō 12 nen kara dai 5 kai zenkokuchijikai', *Kahoku shimpo*, 11 February 2006.

8 These so-called 'reformist governors' (*kaikakuha chiji*) – Kajiwara Taku (Gifu), Hiashimoto Daijiro (Kochi), Asano Shiro (Miyagi), Kitagawa Masayoshi (Mie), Masuda Hiroya (Iwate), and Katayama Yoshihiro (Tottori) – emerged in the late-1990s. They formed various unofficial study groups, such as *Chiiki kara kawaru nihon suishin kaigi* and *Chihō bunken kenkyūkai* with pro-decentralization scholars and took the initiative to pressure the central government for more powers and resources (Kawatake 2012).

9 Asano Shiro, 'Shissō 12 nen kara dai 5 kai zenkokuchijikai', *Kahoku shimpo*, 11 February 2006.

10 'Masuda shi, makikaeshi kenmei kōkaitōronnado shikake zenkokkuchijikaichōsen/ Iwate', *Asahi Shimbun*, 13 February 2005.

11 The NGA assessed the party manifestos for the 2005 elections of the LDP, DPJ, and Komeito, and publicized and submitted the assessment to the parties prior to the election in an effort to pressure national parties to commit to providing local government powers and resources. www.nga.gr.jp/data/document/2005/1396012233294. html [accessed 20 October 2016].

12 'Seitōshiji hyōmei, miokuri Hashimoto Osaka chiji, chijikaini dōchō', *Asahi Shimbun*, 30 July 2009.

13 The combative approach of the 'fighting governors' to Tokyo was not shared by all 47 governors. After Kajiwara's chairmanship of the NGA in 2006, many of the more active, reformist governors claimed that the NGA had reverted to its more ceremonial role, following the script created by the MIC (see Sato 2009, pp. 149–152 and Kawatake 2012, p. 175).

14 The local government side was represented by the representatives of the six local government associations and the central government side was represented by the chief cabinet minister as well as relevant ministers (Harada 2010).

15 The local opposition movement to the Shimouke dam (Kumamoto) had barricaded themselves on the dam wall in a 'wasp nest'-like fortress (*hachinosujo*), but were eventually evicted through land expropriation laws. See http://yabusaka.moo.jp/hachinosu.htm [accessed 20 October 2016].

16 'Chiji tokubetsuhisho ga rihan, ken dobokubuchō ha kōtetsu. Tanaka Yasuo, kubikiri urabanashi', *Asahi Shimbun*, 23 March 2001.

17 Governors must be 'consulted' over dam and other construction projects conducted by central government agencies which oversee rivers designated as national ones. The national law for rivers states that the central government agency must ask for the agreement of the governor on any public work plans (such as dams), but it is unclear if the results of such consultation are legally binding (River law *kasenhō* articles 10.4 and 16.5).

18 'Jimin sōryoku, Iizumi Kamon shi hatsutōsen denaoshi Tokushima chijisen', *Asahi Shimbun*, 19 May 2003.

19 It is important to note that there was growing opposition to wasteful public works since 2000 in the national party leadership and public mood. Administrations after Koizumi were disposed to ending these projects as part of their drive to slim down the state and, under DPJ, to shift investments from 'concrete to people'. In this sense, the governors' resistance to national projects did not face direct opposition from the party executive, merely from local MPs and assembly members as well as ministries benefitting from these public works.

126 *Governors and governments*

20 Until the Fukushima accident, governors in prefectures hosting the plants tended to promote nuclear power even against local and national protest movements against nuclear energy use. An early and rare example of conflict between a governor and the nuclear regulators (METI) and utility companies occurred earlier in Fukushima under governor Sato Eisaku (1988–2006). Sato had earlier accepted the government's pluthermal nuclear fuel programme in 1998, but withdrew this agreement in 2000 after utility companies were found to be hiding accidents and fabricating data. Sato continued to refuse national plans for pluthermal power, until his arrest on charges of political corruption in 2006 (Sato 2009, pp. 49–116).

21 This 'safety agreement' (*anzen kyōtei*) is one that takes place between the utility company, host prefecture, and the host municipality. Described as a 'gentlemen's agreement', it does not have any legal foundation or binding powers, and theoretically a nuclear power operator can over-ride local government opposition to restarting a plant.

22 Ikeda Nobuo, 'Izumida Niigata kenchiji wa naze gempatsuno anzen shinsa ni hantai surunoka', *Newsweek Japan*, 6 August 2013.

23 Okada Hiroyuki, 'Kagoshima ken ni datsugempatsuchijiga tanjō shitanowa shōgekida', *Toyokeizai*, 14 July 2016.

24 Entering the 2000s, the Tokyo governor Ishihara sought to implement new local taxes on banks (2000–2002) as well as to openly fight against the partial nationalization of the local corporate tax (*chihō hōjin tokubetsuzei* 2008). The new tax scheme was designed to redistribute local corporate tax revenues from wealthier to poorer local governments with the Tokyo government losing a large share of its local revenue (see Sasaki 2011, pp. 137–140).

25 Article 17 sections 2, see Yamazaki (2009).

26 P.T. Zenkokuchijikai, 2009, 'Chokkatsu jigyōni kansuru sankōshiryō' (p. 4). Available at www.nga.gr.jp/ikkrwebBrowse/material/files/group/3/5shiryou3090316.pdf [accessed 20 October 2016].

27 'Bunkenito chijira taggu kunino chkkatsu jigyō, hihōfutan minaoshihe', *Asahi Shimbun*, 27 March 2009.

28 Prefectures most dependent on national public works projects are reluctant to abolish this system. They fear that abolishing the local government contribution system may result in the central government quitting national projects altogether. Around the time of this policy debate, the construction ministry published (in timely and threatening fashion) the predictions that if local governments stop contributing, the overall size of the budgets for nationally managed projects may fall by more than one-third (Yamazaki 2009, p. 92).

29 'Chihōbunken kunino tsuke, zaisei chokugeki/Niigata ken', *Asahi Shimbun*, 11 August 2009.

30 'Tochiji, Monkashō no setsumei kyohi Shinkokuritsu kyōgijō no hiyōfuran mondai', *Asahi Shimbun*, 30 May 2015, and 'Shinkokuritsu, shiminno koega ugokasu "Sekininno shozai hakkirito" "shijiritsu agetai noka"', *Asahi Shimbun*, 18 July 2015.

31 'Shinkokuritsu kyōgijō no tofutan, Monkashō Konkyo to naru hōseibi', *Asahi Shimbun*, 9 June 2015.

32 'Shinkokuritsu hiyōfutanwo kakugikettei', *Mainichi Shimbun*, 28 June 2016.

33 'Henoko "Henkō dekiru". Beigiin, phillipines no rei age chijini genkyū', *Ryukyu Shimpo*, 18 May 2016.

References

Aldrich, D.P. 2016, *Site fights: Divisive facilities and civil society in Japan and the West*, Cornell University Press.

Harada, M. 2010, 'Chihōkōkyōdantai no kokusei sanka wo meguru giron', *National Diet Library Reference*, vol. 60, no. 9, pp. 117–127.

Hijino, K.V.L. 2014, 'Intra-party conflicts over gubernatorial campaigns in Japan Delegation or franchise?', *Party Politics*, vol. 20, no. 1, pp. 78–88.

Kanai, T. 2008, '"Kuni to chihō no kyōginoba" no seiritsu to satetsu', in A. Morita, T. Kanai, and K. Taguchi (eds), *Bunkenkaikaku no dōtai (Seiji kūkan no henyō to seisaku kakushin)*, Tokyo daigaku shuppankai.

Kawatake, D. 2012, *Kaikaku ha chiji no jidai*, Minaminokaze sha.

Kitamura, W. 2011, '"Kuni to chihō no kyōgino ba ni kansuru hōritsu" no seiritsu ni yosete', *Toshi to Governance*, no. 16, pp. 3–8.

Krauss, E.S. and Nyblade, B. 2005, '"Presidentialization" in Japan? The prime minister, media and elections in Japan', *British Journal of Political Science*, vol. 35, no. 2, pp. 357–368.

Machidori, S. 2012, *Shushō no seidobunseki*, Chikura shobo.

Onaga, T. 2015, *Tatakau min'i*, Kadokawa shoten.

Sakurazawa, M. 2015, *Okinawa gendaishi*, Chuko shinsho.

Sasaki, N. 2011, *Tochiji: Kenryoku to tosei*, Chuo kouron shinsho.

Sato, E. 2009, *Chiji massatsu: tsukurareta Fukushima oshoku jiken*, Heibonsha.

Tsuji, A. 2015, *Sengo nihon chihō seijishiron: Nigen daihyōsei no rittaiteki bunseki*, Bokutakusha.

Yamazaki, O. 2009, 'Chokkatsujigyō kōfukin seido no minaoshi', *National Diet Library Reference*, vol. 59, no. 10, pp. 79–97.

Yawata, K. 2007, *Nihonzenkoku Gendaino tonosama retsuden: Rekidai chiji 300 nin*, Kobunsha shinsho.

6 Multi-level conflicts in Canada, Germany, and the UK

Theoretical expectations that greater local autonomy and weaker party-political linkages between levels of government would trigger more conflictual relations have largely been confirmed thus far in our investigations of Japan. Do these patterns of multi-level conflict apply to countries elsewhere? Are cooperative multi-level relations more commonly found where national and local governments are inter-dependent, both administratively and through partisan channels? Contrariwise, do lack of partisan congruence, vertically integrated parties, or high levels of local autonomy necessarily lead to greater multi-level conflict?

This chapter[1] seeks to broaden and deepen these arguments about the importance of local autonomy and partisan linkages in multi-level conflict. We do this by looking at central-local government dynamics in other developed and established democracies beyond Japan. We select comparative case countries that manifest very strong features on the two dimensions of importance: the degree of local autonomy (how much discretion and independent resources local governments possess) and the degree of partisan inter-linkages (vertical integration of individual parties and the congruence of party control of national and local governments).

Canada, Germany, and the UK were selected for comparison with Japan to test whether similar dynamics are at work in generating conflictual or cooperative inter-governmental relations (IGR).

The first case, Canada, is chosen for being an outlier on both dimensions of local autonomy and multi-level party integration. Canada's provincial governments are highly autonomous in that they have large areas of exclusive jurisdiction, while the Canadian federal and provincial party systems and parties are highly separated and lack integrative links.

The second case, Germany, is chosen as an antithesis to the Canadian case on these two dimensions. The federal German government and its regions are highly inter-linked in the national legislation process as well as local administration, while its party systems have tended to be highly symmetrical and vertically integrated. Post-unification Germany since 1990 has seen these integrative and cooperative relations under pressure as a result of diverging territorial interests.

The third case is the United Kingdom. During the 1980s, the UK became one of the most centralized unitary states among advanced democracies, providing local authorities with very little autonomy. Its two major parties reflected

Multi-level conflicts in Canada, Germany, UK 129

this unitary structure of the state, with the national party executive imposing tight control over regional and local constituency organizations. Post-devolution UK since 1997 resulted in greater local autonomy for the new regional governments of Scotland, Wales, Northern Ireland, and London, with national parties also decentralizing moderately to adapt to emerging territorial competition.

Selecting and comparing these cases which show strong variation on key dimensions strengthens the validity of our model. From our expectations, Canada should tend to highly conflictual multi-level relations, Germany should tend to less conflictual relations, and the UK should tend to show partisan incongruent multi-level conflict under centralization and more territorial multi-level conflict following devolution. Moreover, for all these countries, the degree of local autonomy and partisan linkages, rather than other factors, should be causing the tendency to conflict or cooperation. Our cases of conflict for each of the countries will seek to confirm this causal link and its mechanisms.

In each of the country sections that follow, a discussion of the institutional and socio-economic context of central-local dynamics will be provided before prominent cases of multi-level conflict are analysed. In conclusion, we briefly compare these three countries with Japan to draw some inferences on how differences in how institutional and party organization structures feed into multi-level conflict.

Contexts and cases of multi-level conflict

Canada

Canada has been characterized by numerous observers as leaning towards the 'more competitive, if not conflictual, end of the spectrum' of federalism compared to that of Germany and Switzerland (Atkinson *et al.* 2012, p. 8). Some have even claimed that 'conflicts among federal and provincial governments constitute one of the prime dynamics of Canadian governance' (Wolinetz and Carty 2006, p. 67). Intense centre-local conflicts have emerged periodically throughout Canadian history over constitutional change, economic control particularly over natural resources, as well as fiscal equalization (e.g. Mallory 1981; Watts 1989; Lecours and Béland 2009).

This tendency towards multi-level conflict has been explained by both institutional structures comparable to other countries as well as socio-economic conditions unique to Canada. These include: the territorial diversity of Canadian provinces with various cross-cutting cultural, economic, and social cleavages; the 'separated' nature of Canadian federalism with few concurrent jurisdictions; majoritarian parliamentarianism which concentrates power in federal and provincial executives; and a lack of a party system at both levels which integrates the two levels. We briefly introduce these arguments here, before considering the conditions and process of multi-level conflict over fiscal equalization.

Canada is composed of territories with diverse interests and a constantly changing and expanding population. Various territorial cleavages exist: between

French speakers in Quebec and English speakers in the rest of the country; between natural resource-rich provinces in the West and more industrial and service-oriented provinces in the East; between more traditional and established political cultures in the older provinces (Atlantic, Ontario, Quebec, etc.) as opposed to the pioneer and frontier provinces in the West; between indigenous, early, and later immigrant populations. Overall, the electorate has grown rapidly and unevenly, with the Atlantic regions depopulating and those in the West rapidly expanding. Combined with the influx of different immigrants, this constant and rapid demographic change has transformed party systems and organizations (Carty 2015, pp. 4–9).

These socio-economic conditions have generated cross-cutting cleavages mobilized by national and local parties. Thus tensions have emerged between regions, but also vertically between federal governments which offer compromises (or less rarely, form majority coalitions of the provinces) to keep the country together, and in the process dissatisfy some provincial governments.

> Canada is divided by multiple cleavages which feed into political life in different ways. These include class, religion, ethnicity, language and region. None overshadow the others; instead, ethnicity, religion, class, centre-periphery and rural-urban divisions all are salient ... Inevitably, dissatisfaction with the limited packages offered by the two major parties has left room for the entry and survival of federal or provincial parties taking different points of view. It has provided an incentive for provincial actors to stake out positions in opposition to the federal government in Ottawa.
> (Wolinetz and Carty 2006, p. 68)

Overlaid on to this highly diverse country are institutional structures which further encourage territorial competition and multi-level conflict between national and local governments. First, Canada is considered one of the most decentralized federations in the OECD[2] in terms of the range of policy responsibilities and extent of financial autonomy possessed by the provinces. Canadian provinces have exclusive jurisdiction over crucial spending areas such as education, health, and social welfare (Wolinetz and Carty 2006, p. 67). Equally important is the very small range of so-called concurrent jurisdictions in which federal and provincial governments share authority and decision-making over a particular policy area. Compared to Australia, Germany, and the United States, the Canadian constitution has a very limited list of concurrent jurisdictions (Atkinson *et al.* 2012, p. 5). This lack of shared powers (which means both levels of government possess large areas of exclusive jurisdiction over policy domains) has been described as 'jurisdictional federalism'. The wide policy and fiscal autonomy of local governments in Canada have arguably expanded 'the incentives for the political elite to exploit regional conflicts' and led to 'political advantages for provincial leaders to fight Ottawa' (Chandler and Chandler 1987, pp. 93–94).

Another salient feature of Canada is that it combines federalism with a majoritarian electoral system in a parliamentary form of government for both national

Multi-level conflicts in Canada, Germany, UK 131

and subnational levels. The use of single-member districts in a parliamentary system generates strong majority governments in which power is concentrated in the executive. Together with tight party discipline, policy-making has been concentrated in the executive leadership at both levels (the prime minister and his cabinet in Ottawa/the provincial premiers and their cabinets in the 11 provinces). Moreover, the weakness of the Canadian second chamber as a legislative channel for expressing and inputting territorial interests in federal policy (unlike Germany, see below), leaves the local political elite with few legislative channels to influence national policy. Negotiations and conflicts between levels of government have therefore centred on a proliferation of federal-provincial conferences, committees, and liaison agencies and the like dominated by executives, side-stepping the influence of legislatures (Watts 1989).

Though there appears to be debate over the impact of executive federalism on the degree of conflict in Canadian inter-governmental relations, many authors have claimed that this mode of executive interaction has fuelled multi-level conflicts and competition. In comparison to the United States and Switzerland, 'in general, executive federalism in the parliamentary federations has been marked by a considerably higher degree of inter-governmental conflict and confrontation' (Watts 1989, p. 15). Unlike in the US, where power is dispersed across separately elected executives and legislatures (as well as powerful state and federal judiciaries) at both levels, Canadian parliamentarism focuses power on the political executive. This concentration of powers at the provincial level is compounded by the fact that there are only 10 provinces in Canada as opposed to 50 states in the US. As a result of majoritarian politics at both levels and the paucity of provincial governments, 'conflict is focused on a small universe of monolithic actors' (Mallory 1981, p. 231).

Finally, Canadian parties and party systems at federal and provincial level lack strong integrative links, failing to provide an effective partisan channel to bridge policy differences vertically and horizontally. Wolinetz and Carty (2006) explain how the Canadian party system at national and local level is characterized by low congruence: the number of parties, type of parties competing in them, and the ruling parties at both levels are often divergent. Moreover, 'even where parties of the same name and origins exist at the two levels, there is often no significant organizational connection between them' (Wolinetz and Carty 2006, p. 60). The causes for this disconnect between federal and provincial party competition are various: they include the structure of Canadian federalism, the multiple cleavages cross-cutting the nation and how they are mobilized by parties at both levels, episodic party membership, and an electorate with generally weak party identification (ibid., pp. 66–73). The lack of strong integration within parties and high incongruence of party systems across levels mean there are few partisan channels to constrain conflicts. As others have observed, 'political parties have therefore had a limited capacity for effecting the resolution of inter-governmental conflicts through intraparty relations' (Watts 1989, p. 11).

How do multi-level conflicts manifest themselves in Canada? We turn to a case study from Lecours and Béland (2009) of an extended conflict over fiscal

132 *Multi-level conflicts in Canada, Germany, UK*

equalization policy during the mid-2000s. Although struggles over constitutional reform and the status of Quebec may be the most prominent, and perhaps vital, issue of conflict between federal and provincial governments (as well as between provinces) in Canada, we chose to look at fiscal equalization instead for two reasons. First, ethno-territorial conflicts are relatively muted in Japan (though there are signs of them emerging in Okinawa) and so the dynamics of separatism is difficult to compare. Second, fiscal centralization and distribution remain a central source of multi-level conflict in all states, federal and unitary, with or without separatist movements.

As in most states, the question of fiscal redistribution between regions has been a key source of multi-level tension and conflict in Canada.[3] The fiscal equalization programme in Canada, created in 1957, is funded and administered by the federal government to provide payments to provinces poorer than the national average. During the early 2000s, growing pressures to alter the equalization programme emerged from the provinces led by Quebec which complained of 'fiscal imbalance' in Canada's federalism. The imbalance referred to a situation where the federal government was enjoying fiscal surpluses (raising more money than needed to fulfil constitutional responsibilities) while provinces faced shortfalls in funding their own programmes.

In 2004, the federal government under the Liberal Party administration of Paul Martin (2003–2006) proposed reforms to the fiscal equalization programme in order to shore up his faltering minority government. Strong complaints emerged from a majority of provinces who feared uncertain and/or lower equalization payments as a result. Facing provincial discontent, the federal government set up a panel composed of regional representatives to review the programme and suggest changes. By the time the panel delivered recommendations for the equalization scheme in 2006, the Martin government had been ousted. The succeeding Conservative administration of PM Stephen Harper (2006–2015) implemented the panel's recommendations. Harper's decision triggered sharp criticism from both richer and poorer provincial governments who felt unfairly treated. The unhappy provinces saw changes to the fiscal equalization scheme as unfairly benefitting Quebec and Ontario which were vital electoral regions for the federal Conservative party.

Provincial premiers led the charge in politically attacking the prime minister over the changes to the equalization scheme. The Newfoundland Premier Danny Williams, leader of the provincial Progressive Conservative Party, took out a newspaper advertisement to denounce the Conservative Prime Minister Harper. He urged voters not to support his federal counterpart party with an online campaign entitled 'Anything but Conservatives' in the 2008 federal elections. The Saskatchewan premier threatened to launch a constitutional lawsuit against the federal government over equalization payments. Other provinces, such as Nova Scotia, were also prepared to take on the federal government, accusing it of 'betrayal', and threatened electoral problems for federal Conservative party.

Two salient points about multi-level conflict are deduced from this case.

Multi-level conflicts in Canada, Germany, UK   133

First, the proximate cause of these conflicts was the federal government's strategic attempts to secure territorial support by favouring some provinces at the expense of others. In both the Martin and Harper administrations, the federal executive used its discretion over fiscal equalization policy to favour provinces that were seen as vital in forthcoming elections, while undercutting provinces that were seen as electorally expendable. Conflict during this period was 'heavily guided by an appreciation of which province is going to be most displeased and what that displeasure could mean for the federal party in power' (Lecours and Béland 2009). Deals and negotiations were primarily made bilaterally between executives at both levels, rather than through collective bargaining. The provincial leaders in turn responded to the politicization of the equalization programme by 'pressuring the federal government to amend the program to their advantage' (Lecours and Béland 2009). Using courts, campaigns against the federal ruling party, and threats of non-cooperation in other policy areas, the provincial premiers pushed backed individually, not collectively, against undesired changes.

Second, as provincial and federal party systems and organizations are so autonomous from each other, conflict was not based on partisan lines. In the case, a conservative prime minister was ready to over-ride opposition from a vocal conservative premier, who in turn openly and aggressively opposed his federal counterpart. Partisan incongruence or congruence become irrelevant in ensuring inter-governmental cooperation under Canada's disconnected multi-level party system. Instead, provincial executives, regardless of partisan affiliation, either claimed credit for benefits gained in negotiations or overtly blamed the federal government for unfair treatment.

> Provincial governments in Canada know they are very likely to get support from their constituents in a public dispute with the federal government. In this context, provinces have an incentive to be aggressive when they deal with the federal government on issues they can frame as affecting their interests and/or identities.
>
> (Lecours and Béland 2009)

Germany

Germany is often treated as a counterpoint to Canada despite both states sharing the two fundamental institutional features of federalism and parliamentary democracy (Chandler and Chandler 1987; Watts 1989). Relations between the federal government in the capital of Berlin and the 16 Länder across Germany have been characterized as 'cooperative' in contrast to Canada's competitive federalism. Various arguments have been put forward for this divergence, including Germany's relatively homogeneous socio-economic conditions, widely shared jurisdictions over policy, highly symmetrical party organizations, and vertically integrated party organizations across levels of government – all features absent in Canada's case. We cover the key institutional explanations for

134 *Multi-level conflicts in Canada, Germany, UK*

lack of overt conflict first. We then turn to a discussion of the breakdown of socio-economic homogeneity and the territorial cleavages emerging from the unification of West and East Germany in 1989 which are threatening to disrupt this multi-level stability.

The large portion of shared policy responsibilities, along with the existence of a powerful second chamber that gives regional governments a veto over federal policies, are two structural features often cited as sources of German federalism's cooperative mode. Since the post-war period, the federal government has taken over responsibility for legislation in an increasing number of policy areas[4] while regional governments became responsible for implementing these federal programmes (Detterbeck and Renzsch 2003, p. 263). Combined with the growing number of concurrent responsibilities, divided 'functionally' between the two levels, the existence of the Bundesrat – Germany's second chamber – has ensured that Länder governments can shape federal legislation in their interests. The powerful second chamber is composed of delegates sent by the Länder governments and thus directly linked to outcomes of regional elections. The Bundesrat possesses veto power over federal law that affects regional governments.[5]

With more than 60 per cent of all federal legislation subject to an absolute veto by the Bundesrat, ruling parties are incentivized to adopt a consensual style of politics.

> As neither the federal nor the regional government can pursue their policies without the consent of the other political level in many policy areas, intergovernmental conflicts are either solved by political negotiations or lead to the political blockade of policy decision making.
>
> (Detterbeck and Renzsch 2003, p. 263)

The existence and design of this second chamber has in turn significantly affected the behaviour of national parties to local elections. As local governments, through direct representation in the Bundesrat, are capable of derailing federal legislation, this has led to federal parties paying keen interest to regional elections. The Bundesrat 'not only sensitized national governments to state interests, but has also integrated closely the national and Land parties in the resolution of the issues' (Watts 1989, p. 11).

Such structural incentives have pushed the German parties to be organized as vertically integrated parties which seek representation at all levels. Formal and informal linkages in organization, personnel, finances, and political programmes across levels of government integrate the federal and regional arms of the party. German parties also seek to constrain conflicts between different levels by integrating regional leaders into the national party leadership and by providing a career ladder from regional to federal level (Detterbeck and Renzsch 2003, p. 265). The highly integrated German party organizations mean 'disputes between different levels of the political system or between different regions have often been resolved within the parties ... and thereby increased the workability of cooperative federalism in Germany' (Detterbeck and Renzsch 2003, p. 265).

Multi-level conflicts in Canada, Germany, UK   135

While intra-party conflicts were defused through integrated party organizations, the potential for inter-party conflicts was reduced by the necessity for compromise at federal level. Incongruent majorities in the Bundestag and Bundesrat have been a common feature in Germany (particularly in the 1970s and since 1990 to currently). Such incongruence stemmed in part from the well-documented German voter tendency to punish the ruling party at federal level by backing opposition or minor parties at regional elections, using regional elections as midterm referenda – so-called 'second-order elections' – on federal government performance (Hough and Jeffery 2006). Opposition parties would thus often gain control of Länder governments and send deputies to form a majority in the Bundesrat, resulting in 'divided' governments with different majorities in both chambers. Using its strong vertical links, a federal opposition party could theoretically demand its integrated regional branches to 'blockade' federal policy through the Bundesrat.

Yet such party-political instrumentalization of the Bundesrat has been 'rare and often exaggerated and is in any case inherently limited by a tradition of broadly consensual party politics' (Jeffery 1998, p. 2). The lack of overt conflict has been explained by the constant threat of a veto which generates pre-emptive compromise from the federal governments. As Auel writes, 'if faced with an opposition majority in the Bundesrat, the federal government tries to find (often heavily watered down) compromises acceptable for the opposition long before bills go to the Bundesrat' (Auel 2014, p. 434).

The features of functional federalism, joint decision-making of federal and regional governments, highly integrated parties, and symmetrical party systems have contributed to 'cooperative' relations in much of the post-war period in Germany. Yet numerous observers have suggested 'an erosion of federal-Länder linkages' (Detterbeck and Renzsch 2003; Hough and Jeffery 2006; Auel 2014) in the post-unification period since 1990. We turn briefly to identify how these changes are interpreted as raising the potential for more overtly conflictual relations across levels of government.

Although institutional structures affecting inter-governmental relations remained largely unchanged, German unification has significantly altered the socio-economic context of party competition. As a result, the party system has become more diverse and territorially differentiated, with the two dominant parties on the left and right losing ground to new parties at federal level. In particular, Greens in the west and the successor party to East German communism in the east have eaten into the weakening support of the major parties (Hough and Jeffery 2006, p. 129). At the regional level, there have been fewer Länder mirroring the federal-level coalitions, resulting in more diverse regional coalitions governments that cut across the federal government and opposition (Detterbeck and Renzsch 2003, p. 263). Party organizations have also begun to adjust to diversifying territorial competition, providing greater autonomy to local branches in terms of policy and choice of coalition partners.

This growing territorialization of German politics stems from socio-economic trends of the post-unification period: the financial burden of unification, growing divide between rich and poor Länder (an issue in existence before unification, but accelerating with the entry of the five much less developed former East German Länder); growing social heterogeneity, not just but mainly in the cultural difference across East and West Germany (Detterbeck and Renzsch 2003, p. 264). Economic divergence between the two areas of the country have led to conflicting policy interests as well as controversy over large fiscal transfers from richer to poorer states. In this context, 'solidarity between the Länder has become increasingly strained, raising doubts about whether cooperative federalism remains appropriate as a method and ethos of government' (Jeffery 1998, p. 14).

The divergence in economic and financial incentives across these territorial divides has triggered more diverse competition, emergence of smaller protest parties focusing on region-specific issues, and tensions on federal-regional relations. As regional governments and party organizations have become more focused on territorial interests, coordination across Länder – vital for pressuring the federal government in Bundesrat – has become more difficult. These territorial tensions have also made intra-party coordination more difficult, and in consequence 'the ability of the parties to integrate interests and defuse conflicts throughout the system has weakened' (Auel 2014, p. 437).

The post-unification period has thus seen more wrangling between regions with richer Länder seeking reform of federal structures. In 1998, three Länder in the wealthy south sought greater autonomy and fiscal authority by filing a claim with the constitutional federal court over equalization (although this claim failed) (Auel 2014, p. 438). So far, it appears that reform of the federal structure – particularly ongoing fiscal transfers from richer to poorer Länder – remains blocked. The poorer Länder have managed to use their numerical advantage in the Bundesrat to veto for fundamental change despite growing demands from richer Länder for greater autonomy and a more competitive form of federalism (Auel 2014, p. 441).

Socio-economic change has thus placed greater tensions on the cooperative nature of German federalism. Rising conflicts over federal policy between richer and poorer Länder appear to be placing tensions on traditional channels of internal adjustment within parties or through coordination and compromise between parties before legislation. Despite these pressures, the Bundesrat has continued to provide a strong institutional veto for the majority of regional governments to ensure arrangements remain in their interests. As regional interests are directly integrated into federal decisions, emerging territorial tensions in post-unification Germany appear less vertical (not between federal and regional governments) and more horizontal (between different regions) in nature. Under this institutional structure, minority Länder seek routes outside the normal legislative procedures – such as resorting to court challenges against fiscal equalization schemes – to combat federal decisions legislated by the majority Länder in the Bundesrat.

United Kingdom – ideological clashes under Thatcher

In contrast to the constitutionally protected status of regional governments in federal states, local governments in unitary states have a far weaker legal basis to protect local interests against central government intervention. Among unitary states, the UK has often been referred to as one of the most centralized in the world. Local government in the UK has been 'out of step' with its increasingly decentralizing European neighbours (Crouch and Marquand 1989; Travers and Esposito 2003). The two main UK parties have reflected this centralized and unitary state structure in their party organizations to a large extent. They are dominated by the national party executive with control over local constituency and regional party organizations. The combination of a highly centralized unitary state and highly centralized parties has shaped the nature of multi-level conflicts in the UK.

This section explains the sources of both state and party organization centralization, and how the central government crushed local government opposition during the Conservative administration years (1979–1997). These multi-level conflicts during Thatcher's 'eleven-year war on local government'[6] were as much ideological and partisan rather than territorial in nature.

In the succeeding section we investigate briefly how the ongoing devolution process begun at the turn of the century changed these inter-governmental dynamics. The creation of regional assemblies in Scotland, Wales, Northern Ireland, and London during the Blair administration (1997–2007) re-animated and politicized existing territorial cleavages within the UK. This in turn has generated multi-level conflicts within the organizations of major parties and tensions between London and the regions over policy.

In a unitary state that embodies majoritarian government, lack of a written codified constitution, and a tradition of 'parliamentary sovereignty', local governments in UK theoretically can exist and act only at the pleasure of parliamentary legislation. Local governments have traditionally only been allowed to do what statutes (national law) permits, under the principle of *ultra vires*. Although the Local Government Act of 2000 aimed to expand their powers, local governments still do not have the power of general competence to act over local issues or, more vitally, raise and spend money freely (Wilson 2005, p. 156). Indeed, the centralization of UK local governments is most clearly manifested in their very low levels of self-raised revenues, constrained discretion over setting local tax rates, and strict scrutiny and caps over how money is spent locally (Travers and Esposito 2003; Wilson 2005, pp. 160–161). Although UK local authorities had traditionally been more self-sufficient financially, since the 1970s local self-raised revenues have continued to decline and are now among the lowest in OECD states.[7] Even the devolved regional governments were, at least initially, tightly controlled fiscally and dependent heavily on fiscal transfers from the central government.[8]

UK local governments[9] are also vulnerable to drastic top-down changes in their structure and financing as they have no constitutional protections from

138 *Multi-level conflicts in Canada, Germany, UK*

central government intervention. The number of local authorities in the UK have decreased steadily in the quest for economies of scale since the mid-1970s, falling from 1,855 in 1974 to 521 in 1990 (Wilson 2005, p. 161) and 418 as of 2016.[10] Numerous re-organizations, introduction of new administrative regions, as well as abolition of local authorities have occurred during this time. The local government tax system has also been vulnerable to rapid and frequent overhauls from the centre, as was revealed under the Conservative government in the 1980s and 1990s (see below). This included the introduction of a poll tax and the non-domestic rate (or business rates) (1989), as well as replacement of the unpopular poll tax with a council tax (1993) (Travers and Esposito 2003, pp. 54–56).

> The lack of constitutional underpinning of the finance system in England puts local government directly under the whim and control of the central government in power. This has contributed to the relentless reform of the finance system and the structure of local government institutions since the 1950s, and also saw local government's main form of taxation change three times in the space of three years in the 1990s, something which is very unusual by international standards.
>
> (Travers and Esposito 2003, p. 57)

Reflecting these unitary traditions, the two main British parties have traditionally maintained highly centralized organizations granting little autonomy to constituency organizations over policy, candidate, and leadership selection. Greatly simplified, trade unions, providing both membership and funding, and the national party executive have dominated the Labour Party organization, while the national party leadership and to a less formal extent, private donors, have dominated the Conservative Party organization. Local constituency organizations as well as regional party organizations in the devolved regions do not have formal and ultimate control over candidate selection, policy setting, and the raising and use of financial resources (Clark 2012; Detterbeck 2012). Essentially, the party organizations of both Labour and Conservative are vertically and hierarchically integrated with party leadership controlling local organizations and backbenchers. Such internal party discipline and party label unity is seen as integral elements of the British Westminster model of two-party politics.

Under this dual centralization, multi-level clashes have been infrequent and contained, but have occasionally erupted over partisan lines. In its quest for smaller government, the Conservative government under Prime Minister Margaret Thatcher (1979–1990) clashed with local governments frequently and bitterly. During her first term, the Conservative government slashed funding for councils, imposed compulsory competitive tendering (CCT) for local authorities which weakened local public sector unions, and imposed a new system of grant penalties on councils that had exceeded expenditure limits (Butler *et al.* 1994, pp. 25–27). In 1984, the Conservative government proposed a bill enabling it to cap local rates (local taxes) and put ceilings on budgets to restrict local

Multi-level conflicts in Canada, Germany, UK   139

government spending. As promised in its manifesto for the general elections of 1983, the attack on local government was not just one against 'extravagant' authorities, but against Labour-controlled ones. The Conservative manifesto[11] claimed 'a number of grossly extravagant Labour authorities whose exorbitant rate demands have caused great distress both to businesses and domestic rate-payers'. It promised 'to legislate to curb excessive and irresponsible rate increases by high-spending councils' and limit rate increases for all local authorities.

Following passage of the bill, the government announced 18 local authorities to be rate-capped for the 1985 budget. Of these, 16 had councils controlled by Labour majorities including Greater London, several London boroughs, and Sheffield city. The Labour councillors fought back; many saw themselves as 'warriors' of the left against Thatcher's neo-liberal attack on local democracy and the public sector. These rebellious councils coordinated amongst each other to refuse to set any tax rate for the coming budget year, rather than accept the lowered legal limit. The key Labour strongholds of Liverpool, Manchester, and Birmingham also joined in the so-called rate-capping rebellion to form a coalition against the central government. The two local authorities which acceded to the rate-capping were Brent (with no majority in the council) and Portsmouth (with a Conservative majority).

The central government retaliated by conducting extraordinary audits of the councils that had refused to set a rate. This eventually resulted in a number of Liverpool and Lambeth councillors to be charged surcharges individually for losses in delay of passing the local budget and evicted from office. Eventually, all of the rebelling Labour-controlled councils backed down and passed legal rates. The local Labour councillors folded in part due to strong pressure from the administration, including the threat of personal indemnity. Equally important was the fracture within Labour, with the national leadership under the moderate Neil Kinnock hostile towards the Labour council's militant, non-compliance tactics.[12] The Labour national executive suspended the Liverpool district Labour branch, conducted an investigation, and eventually expelled leftist faction (Militant Tendency) leaders and members from the local organization.[13] To prevent a recurrence of this type of local rebellion, the Conservative government passed several laws including legislation which set a deadline on setting rates as well as giving auditors greater powers over local council decisions.

The Thatcher government next unilaterally abolished metropolitan governments in London and northern England also controlled by hostile Labour councillors. The Conservatives had promised to end this tier of local government in its manifesto in 1983 arguing that: 'The Metropolitan Councils and the Greater London Council (GLC) have been shown to be a wasteful and unnecessary tier of government.' The Labour council leader and socialist Ken Livingstone of the GLC had also repeatedly antagonized the Conservative government through high-spending welfare policies as well as meetings with IRA leaders, among other actions. Thatcher's plans to abolish the GLC triggered strong opposition from Labour leadership, but also from within the Conservative Party as well as

140   *Multi-level conflicts in Canada, Germany, UK*

public protests by public sector unions and residents. The government nonetheless forced through a bill abolishing the GLC and other regional metropolitan counties with a bare majority in 1986.

The final battle against local government involved the introduction of the community charge, or what is more commonly referred to as the poll tax, in 1989–1990. The community charge replaced a local property tax (domestic rates) calculated on the notional rental value of a home, with a flat-rate per-capita tax to be set by local authorities. The highly regressive tax measure was extremely unpopular and turned the public sentiment strongly against the central government, rather than the local authorities. Implementation of the community charge resulted in mass non-cooperation and organized refusals to pay the tax. Councils and police authorities were unable to enforce or arrest those who refused to pay, and major riots erupted through the UK, including the largest one converging on Trafalgar Square in London in March 1990. The huge public opposition against the poll tax and central government contributed to Thatcher's resignation the following year. 'No government since has failed to be cautious in dealing with local taxation. Thatcher's legacy to local governments was increased centralisation and the willingness of her successors to cap, limit and control local democracy in England.'[14]

United Kingdom – territorial conflicts after devolution

The multi-level conflicts under Conservative centralism were essentially fought along partisan and ideological lines: Labour-controlled, socialist local councils fighting neo-liberal policies of the Conservative government. In contrast, devolution and the creation of regional assemblies by Tony Blair's Labour government generated territorially driven multi-level tensions and conflicts in the UK.

The Labour government came to power with a manifesto in 1997 promising a number of changes to local government: to devolve further powers to Scotland and Wales; allowing innovations in local democracy such as directly elected mayors (albeit retaining controls over local councils in terms of spending and enforcing performance targets introduced by the Conservatives); and to re-establish a directly elected government in greater London.[15]

Following successful referendums on devolution for both Scotland and Wales, both regions were devolved powers to their newly created regional assemblies. Scotland gained primary legislative powers in a wide range of policy areas and some limited power to vary income tax. Wales was granted more limited secondary-legislative powers, with their budgets to be funded entirely from the central government (Bradbury 2006, p. 215). Northern Ireland gained an elected regional parliament with limited legislative powers under the 1998 Good Friday Agreement. Finally, the Greater London Authority was established in 2000 with a directly elected mayor and assembly and strategic responsibility to oversee transport, policing, fire and emergency, as well as economic development over Greater London Area. All four of these newly formed local authorities adopted more proportional electoral systems[16] than the majoritarian one in

Multi-level conflicts in Canada, Germany, UK   141

use in the House of Commons, and diverges in electoral cycles from national elections.

Despite conventional views of British party politics as being highly nationalized in a two-party contest over an economic dimension, there has 'long been a territorial dimension to British politics' (Bradbury 2006, p. 215). Party support has varied for Labour and Conservatives across the different territories: with Labour stronger in London, the industrial areas and cities in northern England, Scotland, and Wales while Conservatives predominated in rural England and the south-east (Radice 1992; Morgan 2006; Radice and Diamond 2010). Non-state-wide regional parties such as the Scottish National Party, Welsh Plaid Cymru, and Irish Democratic Union Party and Sinn Fein have won seats to the national legislature.

Following devolution, these regional parties have gained ground, securing majorities in the regional legislature with the SNP becoming the largest party in the Scottish assembly since 2007. The regional parties have also captured the major parties' constituency seats in the regions, with the SNP notably capturing most of the Scottish parliamentary districts in the 2015 general election.

These mounting regional party threats have affected the behaviour and strategy of the national party locally and triggered tensions within the same parties. Various studies point to how both the major parties adapted their party organizations to the challenge of more regionalized competition following devolution (Bradbury 2006; Laffin *et al.* 2007). London, Wales, and Scotland have been vital bases for Labour's parliamentary majorities. As such Labour, much more so than the Conservatives, has had to adjust its party strategies to the devolved regions.

In the early years of devolution, party executives followed centrist impulses to impose control over candidate and policy positions in their regional branches, triggering multi-level intra-party conflict. In Wales, Scotland, and London the Labour Party leadership at first took a heavy-handed approach in selection of local candidates for the first regional elections in 1999. In Scotland party executives in London vetted out left-nationalists such as Dennis Canavan from the candidacy list for the Scottish parliamentary elections and some candidates closer to New Labour Blairite positions. Despite losing his Labour nomination, Canavan stood as an independent and won with overwhelming support. In Wales, the party backed their own preferred candidate (Michael Alun) over the locally popular Rhodri Morgan for Labour leader of the Welsh assembly. Alun's leadership was later overturned by the assembly in a vote of no-confidence and replaced by Morgan. Morgan declared that Welsh Labour will put 'clear red water' between it and the market-embracing policies of New Labour, protecting traditional welfare policies and avoiding privatization programmes undertaken nationally (Laffin *et al.* 2007). A similar clash occurred over the selection of a mayoral candidate for the first Greater London Authority elections in 2000. The New Labour leadership campaigned against the candidacy of left-winger Ken Livingstone (the former GLC Labour Party leader). Livingstone was expelled from the party for running as an independent, but he went on to win the

142 *Multi-level conflicts in Canada, Germany, UK*

London mayoralty comfortably against the official Labour candidate (Van Biezen and Hopkin 2006, pp. 26–29).

These multi-level intra-party conflicts over the selection of regional party leaders triggered local backlashes involving grassroots members that the party executives were unable to contain. The conflicts over candidates stemmed from resentment against 'control freakery'[17] from the centre as well as preferences for the policy positions of the locally backed candidate against those of the preferred candidate from central office. Following these initial clashes, the Labour national executive softened its strategy. More autonomy was granted to its Scottish and Welsh organizations on policy formulation and positions for the regional legislatures. These distinctive policy positions were permitted 'so long as they threaten no major political embarrassment ... to the national party' (Laffin *et al.* 2007, p. 100). The national executive, however, retained ultimate powers of intervention through control over party rules of candidate selection, leadership elections, staffing, and finances. The party has thus come around to strategically and pragmatically decentralizing the party organization in order to combat nationalist-regionalist parties energized by devolution (Laffin and Shaw 2007, p. 69).

Devolution has not just heightened intra-party tensions, but also inter-governmental tensions between the government in Westminster and the regional executives. Partisan congruence marked the initial years of devolution between 1999 and 2007. Both Scottish and Welsh assemblies were controlled by Labour majorities while the UK government was held by the Labour Party. Although tensions existed within parties as described above, this congruence limited tensions and pushed inter-governmental relations to a more cooperative nature. 'When party congruence prevailed, co-operation rather than confrontation was the norm. Central and sub-state governments shared a determination to make devolution work, and avoidance of disputes in IGR was a clear objective' (McEwen *et al.* 2012, p. 328). Moreover, such cooperation was achieved through informal party channels, while formal mechanisms of IGR were rarely used – including the Joint Ministerial Committee (JMC), a key executive body set up to resolve IGR disputes following devolution (ibid., p. 325).

Following the 2007 regional elections, however, multi-level congruence was lost.[18] In particular, the Scottish regional government was held by the SNP, a party committed to regaining the independence of Scotland and ready to challenge existing arrangements with London. The incongruence did lead to a moderate increase in the use of more formal institutionalized channels (including the JMC) as well as greater assertiveness of the Scottish executive to challenge national policy and fiscal equalization compared to the party congruent period (McEwen *et al.* 2012, pp. 326, 330).

Yet the extent of inter-governmental conflict appears to have been dampened by other factors. These include the continued dependence of regional governments to Westminster for both policy and fiscal resources, the lack of a constitutional basis for regional governments to effectively challenge the centre, and the existence of a neutral and strongly inter-linked civil service at both levels (McEwen *et al.* 2012, pp. 332–337). Pragmatic actions prevailed over conflictual relations even when the UK and Scottish/Welsh governments came under control of different partisan forces post 2007. Rather than leading to more conflict, 'the mode of IGR became moderately more institutionalised, with more use of formal multilateral fora, although bilateralism has remained the dominant mode' (Bolleyer *et al.* 2014, pp. 545–546).

Following devolution, regional governments have thus pursued a pragmatic approach to dealing with London, seeking compromises and striking bilateral bargains as possible with their still limited authority.

Conclusion

The multi-level conflicts in the three cases of Canada, Germany, and the UK largely confirm our theoretical expectations, albeit with some important caveats, while highlighting some elements unique to Japan.

The Canadian case demonstrated how the lack of shared federal-provincial administrative functions and party channels connecting the two levels lead to local elites mobilizing territorial interests against state policy. Both when providing compromise packages and strategically favouring some provinces over others in national policy, the federal government would generate some level of dissatisfaction among territories. Few administrative or partisan linkages exist to prevent such dissatisfaction from becoming externalized. In the event, deals were cut bilaterally. Some provinces would win and others lose, depending on the federal government's strategy and the importance of the region to the balance of the federal ruling party's electoral majority.

The German case demonstrated the inverse situation: strong party linkages and the joint decision-making process between federal and regional governments facilitated cooperation. The key institution of the Bundesrat which fuses national and local governments systems ensures federal policy reflected the interests of (the majority of) regional governments. This means that federal legislation unacceptable to the regions does not get passed. In other words, German bicameralism prevents situations in which the central government initiates policy which over-ride local preferences and later trigger resistance from below, as was prominent in the Canadian, UK, and Japanese experience. Coordination between regions and vertically among the national and local arms of parties further ensures that any policy differences are negotiated within parties, rather than erupt as externalized conflict. Although expanding territorial differences post-unification have increased pressure on the federal dynamic, the Bundesrat appears to block any major conflicts between federal and regional levels. Recent dissatisfaction over fiscal policy among minority Länder has fed horizontal tensions between regions, rather than becoming vertical conflicts.

Finally, the UK case has demonstrated how multi-level conflicts could emerge even when parties are integrated (centralized hierarchically in this case) and local autonomy is extremely low. In this case, party incongruence triggered very bitter, ideological clashes between central and local governments, although the centre prevailed in abolishing and fundamentally altering local authorities

144 *Multi-level conflicts in Canada, Germany, UK*

repeatedly. Under such a system, local authorities resist infrequently and when they do they are over-ridden. Expansion of local autonomy following devolution generated some of our expectations about multi-level conflict: intra-party conflicts between the Labour national executive and its regional organizations increased and relations between London and the devolved regions became somewhat tenser, particular under conditions of partisan incongruence.

Two significant caveats to our argument appear from the comparative investigation.

First, partisan incongruence does not necessarily lead to clashes between levels of government. In Germany, incongruence was a common occurrence, resulting in opposition parties at federal level controlling the majority of Länder and thus the upper house. This incongruence however did not lead to 'blockading' the federal government at every turn through the Bundesrat: instead the federal government pre-empted the regional veto and provided policies acceptable to the Länder. In the UK, incongruence under Thatcher led to an all-out ideological war between national and local governments, but incongruence between the SNP-controlled Scottish regional government and London was a much more pragmatic one based on compromise. For local authorities in unitary states, even those with devolved powers, the central government controls key fiscal and legislative powers. These can be used, as under Thatcher, to over-ride even the fiercest of local resistance. Following devolution, both London and regional governments have sought to avoid any overt and politically costly conflicts.

The second caveat is that, even if local governments lack autonomy and are unlikely to prevail, they may choose to resist central government policies if local actors feel they have little to lose. The behaviour of the more militant Labour councils under Thatcher illuminates this point. Although initially crushed, the rate-capping rebellion and opposition by the GLC and other councils against top-down emasculation of local authorities was not completely futile. Ultimately the fiasco of the poll tax (reforming local authority taxes) contributed to the eventual resignation of Thatcher and, when the Conservative government was replaced by Labour, the central government re-instated the London authority and devolved powers to regions.

The three cases have also raised a number of issues in multi-level dynamics which the Japanese experience did not do so prominently. The first is the issue of how the concentration of power in the political executive at both levels affects inter-governmental dynamics. The IGR between single-party governments emerging from majoritarian electoral rules at both levels (in Canada and most of the UK) appears to differ from the interaction of coalition governments under proportional electoral rules at both levels (in Germany). Furthermore the differences between multi-level relations between parliamentary executives and presidential executives are unclear. Japan's unique configuration of both national parliamentarism and local presidentialism (with a very strong executive) needs to be compared and put in such a context. When contrasted with the London mayor – another directly elected executive dealing with a parliamentary executive nationally – Japanese governors tend to have greater powers and authority to

Multi-level conflicts in Canada, Germany, UK 145

challenge the centre. Both UK mayors and Japanese governors have thrown a spanner into the vertical integration of national parties (Hijino 2014); how this affects IGR is a topic awaiting further systematic comparative investigation.

Finally, the role of a national second chamber in incorporating regional interests into national policy needs better theorizing. Where a strong second chamber exists that channels local preferences, as in Germany, it appears multi-level conflicts are reduced. In the UK and Canada, the upper houses were largely irrelevant in the multi-level equation. In Japan, the upper house is designed to give weight to regional interests by guaranteeing each of the prefectures an electoral district.[19] This means the House of Councillors plays an alternate voice to channel regional interests. But unlike the Bundesrat where regional legislatures send delegates to veto and check national policy, the HoC politicians are directly elected national figures without necessarily being linked to or beholden to prefectural interests. How HoC reflects Japan's diverse regional interests – and how different HoC members from rural to urban prefectures coordinate over territorial interests – awaits investigation.

Despite these unanswered questions and the fact that the chapter only looks at a limited selection of countries, Japan's experience of increasing multi-level conflict is echoed in the dynamics of the three countries. Naturally, such a brief comparative study cannot confirm the validity of our model for the whole universe of federal and unitary states. Nor does this book make such a broad claim. There may be exceptions and cases that do not fit, as a result of unique institutions or socio-economic conditions which cause multi-level relations to be more or less conflictual than our model would predict. Nonetheless, a comparison of the three cases above with Japan provides evidence that local autonomy and partisan inter-linkages are vital elements shaping how cooperative or conflictual relations are in both federal and unitary states.

Notes

1 Research for this chapter was conducted in part by funding from JSPS grant number 26885038 – 'Ideational analysis of decentralization in developed democracies' (2013–2015) and JSPS grant number 15H03311 – '*Giin kotairitsu ni kansuru hikaku kenkyu*' (2015–2018).
2 Using benchmarks indicators of sub-state powers over key areas as well as a more simpler indicator based on percentage of total government revenues before intergovernmental transfers (Atkinson *et al.* 2012, pp. 10–11).
3 The account and analysis of the conflicts below over the Canadian equalization scheme are taken from Lecours and Béland (2009).
4 This expansion was driven by the need to maintain nationalized standards of policy delivery as the welfare state expanded in the post-war period. Article 72 of the Basic Law was used to justify 'federal legislation wherever it is deemed necessary to maintain "equivalent living conditions" throughout the federation' (Jeffrey 1998, p. 2).
5 In order to maximize the Länder's influence on federal policy-making through the Bundesrat, Länder have sought to act collectively, creating horizontal linkages of regional ministers and the like for coordination as well as through partisan linkages (Jeffery 1998, pp. 7–8).
6 'Local government: Margaret Thatcher's 11-year war', *Guardian*, 9 April 2013.

146 *Multi-level conflicts in Canada, Germany, UK*

7 As of 2011 the proportion of tax set in the UK at a subnational local or regional level was 1.7 per cent of GDP. This compared with 15.9 per cent in Sweden; 15.3 per cent in Canada; 10.9 per cent in Germany; and 5.8 per cent in France. See Communities and Local Government Committee, 2014, 'Devolution in England: The case for local government'. Available at www.publications.parliament.uk/pa/cm201415/cmselect/cmcomloc/503/50305.htm#n33 [accessed 20 October 2016].

8   The London Chamber of Commerce and Industry (LCCI) described London compared with other capital cities as an 'extreme outlier'. It noted that Madrid looked to the state for 37% of its funding, New York 30.9%, Berlin 25.5% and Tokyo 7.7%. London, in contrast, required central government funding totaling 73.9%.

(Communities and Local Government Committee, 'Devolution in England: The case for local government' 2014)

9 The British local government system is a complex patchwork combining unitary authorities (with only one level of local government), upper-tier counties, lower-tier metropolitan and non-metropolitan boroughs and districts, as well as the three devolved regions and the Greater London Authority.

10 House of Commons Library, 2016, 'Local government in England: Structures'. Available at http://researchbriefings.parliament.uk/ResearchBriefing/Summary/SN07104#fullreport [accessed 20 October 2016].

11 Conservative General Election Manifesto 1983. Available at www.margaretthatcher.org/document/110859 [accessed 20 October 2016].

12 'Kinnock opposes illegal action on rate-capping', *Financial Times*, 2 February 1985.

13 'The English city that wanted to "break away" from the UK', *BBC Magazine*, 8 November 2014. Available at www.bbc.com/news/magazine-29953611 [accessed 20 October 2016].

14 'Local government: Margaret Thatcher's 11-year war', *Guardian*, 9 April 2013.

15 Labour General Election Party Manifesto 1997. Available at www.webarchive.org.uk/wayback/archive/20100608091221/www.politicsresources.net/area/uk/man/lab97.htm [accessed 20 October 2016].

16 STV for Northern Ireland and AMS for the other regions.

17 Term used by the Labour Scottish National Party chief executive to describe Blair's attempts to impose Blairite candidates for leadership in the regional Labour organizations. See 'Blair's man scrapes home in Wales', *Guardian*, 21 February 1999. Available at www.theguardian.com/politics/1999/feb/21/wales.devolution [accessed 20 October 2016].

18 The SNP captured minority (2007) and then majority (2011) government control of the Scottish assembly seats, with Plaid Cymru joining a coalition with Welsh Labour in the Welsh assembly (2007, 2011), while the national level was under the Labour administration of Gordon Brown (2007–2010) and later the Conservative administration of David Cameron (2010–2016).

19 The institutional practice persisted until the 2016 Upper House elections, when redistricting merged Tottori and Shimane prefectures as well as Kochi and Shimane prefectures into two SMDs.

References

Atkinson, M.M., Marchildon, G.P., Béland, D., Phillips, P.W., Rasmussen, K.A., and McNutt, K. 2012, *Governance and public policy in Canada: A view from the provinces*, University of Toronto Press.

Auel, K. 2014, 'Intergovernmental relations in German federalism: Cooperative federalism, party politics and territorial conflicts', *Comparative European Politics*, vol. 12, no. 4, pp. 422–443.

Multi-level conflicts in Canada, Germany, UK 147

Bolleyer, N., Swenden W., and McEwen, N. 2014, 'Constitutional dynamics and partisan conflict: A comparative assessment of multi-level systems in Europe', *Comparative European Politics*, vol. 12, pp. 531–555.

Bradbury, J. 2006, 'British political parties and devolution: Adapting to multi-level politics in Scotland and Wales', in D. Hough and C. Jeffery (eds), *Devolution and electoral politics*, Manchester University Press, pp. 214–247.

Butler, D., Adonis, A., and Travers, T. 1994, *Failure in British government: The politics of the poll tax*, Oxford University Press.

Carty, R.K. 2015, *Big tent politics: The Liberal Party's long mastery of Canada's public life*, UBC Press.

Chandler, W.M. and Chandler, M.A. 1987, 'Federalism and political parties', *European Journal of Political Economy*, vol. 3, no. 1, pp. 87–109.

Clark, A. 2012, *Political parties in the UK*, Palgrave Macmillan.

Crouch, C. and Marquand, D. 1989, *The new centralism: Britain out of step in Europe?* (Vol. 60), B. Blackwell.

Detterbeck, K. 2012, *Multi-level party politics in Western Europe*, Palgrave Macmillan.

Detterbeck, K. and Renzsch, W. 2003, 'Multi-level electoral competition: The German case', *European Urban and Regional Studies*, vol. 10, no. 3, pp. 257–269.

Hijino, K.V.L. 2014, 'Intra-party conflicts over gubernatorial campaigns in Japan Delegation or franchise?', *Party Politics*, vol. 20, no. 1, pp. 78–88.

Hough, D. and Jeffery, C. 2006, *Devolution and electoral politics*, Manchester University Press.

Jeffery, C. 1998, *Multi-layer democracy in Germany: Insights for Scottish devolution*, The Constitution Unit publications. Available from: www.ucl.ac.uk/spp/publications/unit-publications/26.pdf. [accessed 20 October 2016].

Laffin, M. and Shaw, E. 2007. 'British devolution and the Labour Party: How a national party adapts to devolution', *The British Journal of Politics and International Relations*, vol. 9, no. (1), pp. 55–72.

Laffin, M., Shaw, E., and Taylor, G. 2007, 'The new sub-national politics of the British Labour Party', *Party Politics*, vol. 13, no. 1, pp. 88–108.

Lecours, A. and Béland, D. 2009, 'Federalism and fiscal policy: The politics of equalization in Canada', *Publius: The Journal of Federalism*, vol. 40, no. 4.

Mallory, J.R. 1981, 'Conflict management in the Canadian federal system', *Law and Contemporary Problems*, vol. 44, no. 3, pp. 231–246.

McEwen, N., Swenden, W., and Bolleyer, N. 2012, 'Intergovernmental relations in the UK: Continuity in a time of change?' *The British Journal of Politics & International Relations*, vol. 14, no. 2, pp. 323–343.

Morgan, K. 2006, 'Devolution and development: Territorial justice and the North-South divide', *Publius: The Journal of Federalism*, vol. 36, no. 1, pp. 189–206.

Radice, G. 1992, *Southern discomfort* (No. 555), Fabian Society.

Radice, G. and Diamond, P. 2010, *Southern discomfort again*, Policy Network.

Travers, T. and Esposito, L. 2003, *The decline and fall of local democracy: A history of local government finance*, Policy Exchange.

Van Biezen, I. and Hopkin, J. 2006, 'Party organization in multi-level contexts', in D. Hough and C. Jeffery (eds), *Devolution and electoral politics*, Manchester University Press, pp. 14–36.

Watts, R.L. 1989, *Executive federalism: A comparative analysis* (Vol. 26), IIGR, Queen's University.

Wilson, D. 2005, 'The United Kingdom: An increasingly differentiated polity', in S.A.H. Denters and L.E. Rose (eds), *Comparing local governance: Trends and developments*, Palgrave Macmillan, pp. 155–173.

Wolinetz, S.B. and Carty, R.K. 2006, 'Disconnected competition in Canada', in D. Hough and C. Jeffery (eds), *Devolution and electoral politics*, Manchester University Press, pp. 54–75.

Conclusion

How can local politics matter?

We conclude by revisiting our initial question and summing up the book's findings and its implications. Our first conclusion is that local politics matters, not always, but more often than not. Under various conditions and through different channels, local political actors have found ways to reflect their preferences in vital national decisions. At times this influence works through internal channels before national decisions are taken, at others times they work in the form of overt challenges to national policy after decisions are taken. Second, local political processes and the territorial aspect of national political competition has become increasingly vital as the ability of state-wide parties to broker territorial divides weakens. Claims about the 'nationalization' of Japanese politics need to be modified by a better understanding of local political dynamics. Third, we point out how the influence of local politics on national policy weakens the decisiveness of Japanese democracy in general. Despite institutional reforms aimed at making a more majoritarian system that concentrates powers in the central government executive and party leadership, Japan's local government system serves as a damper on centralized decision-making.

Following these three concluding observations, we end by highlighting some relevant developments in central and local government relations in Japan, as of writing in 2016. Some speculations are made briefly on how the current disequilibrium should be dealt with.

Assessing local politics in national policy

Our first finding is the conditions which lead to more cooperative or more conflictual relations between central and local governments. We observed Japanese inter-governmental relations since the 1990s after institutional changes and socio-economic developments eroded central-local inter-dependence. During this period, more frequent and intense local resistance to national policy emerged and manifested itself in three ways. The growing conflicts manifested themselves primarily within the vertical relations within a ruling party organization which continued to dominate local legislatures. These multi-level conflicts

150   Conclusion

were primarily territorial in nature, with local party branches (usually of rural areas) seeking to defend region-specific interests, rather than being conflicts of party ideology or programmatic policy. Such tensions and conflicts also emerged frequently between national and local legislatures and executives. During periods of partisan incongruence, opposition parties in local legislatures mounted nation-wide challenges, including over ideological/programmatic policies against the centre with legislative resources. Finally, an increasing number of directly elected local executives less beholden to the national ruling party also threatened to block national initiatives through executive powers. Moreover, our comparative investigation into three other countries (Canada, Germany, and the UK) further demonstrated how these dimensions of local autonomy and multi-level partisan linkages/party congruence strongly determine how conflictual multi-level relations become, as we found in the case of Japan.

In all three manifestations of multi-level conflict – within party organizations, between legislatures, and between executives – the driving forces were the same: the divergence of national and local preferences, combined with reduced incentives to maintain cooperative relations in the long term. Yet when these multi-level conflicts surface, predictions about whether local actors will win or lose the struggle (i.e. whether local politics can effectively shape important national policy) were far harder to generate.

Our case studies in Japan and the comparative countries demonstrate that multiple forces and conditions impinge on outcomes of such conflict. The degree of unity within each level of government is one variable shaping outcome. The national executive may be united behind the proposed policy or divided by reluctant coalition partners/ministers/backbenchers; the local government may also be united or divided, facing a sympathetic or hostile legislature in its position towards national policy. Equally important in such multi-level conflicts is the extent to which the proposed national policy and administration is popularly supported (and how close the policy positions held by local political representatives are to voter preferences). The ability of local governments to be able to resist national policy may also depend on how effectively they can link vertically with sympathetic forces nationally and laterally with other local governments. This capacity to link and collectively bargain may be determined by existing institutions and arenas for IGR as well as partisan affiliations of other local governments. And so on and so forth, the kaleidoscopic combination of relevant conditions limit general predictions about whether a specific local opposition to national policy will succeed or fail.

Our cases of local political actors resisting undesirable national policy in Japan and elsewhere provided a mixed picture of local success. At times, central governments have overtly crushed and ignored local opposition to implement policies. Widespread local protests over the Koizumi administration's privatization of postal services or fiscal decentralization did not halt these policies; although visible resistance by locally elected actors arguably resulted in the weakening of legitimacy for these administrations in the long term. More frequently, both central and local actors have reached compromise positions, with local challenges resulting in compensation from central governments on unpopular national policy. Conflicts over the sharing of costs for national projects and resistance to the TPP have generated compromise solutions. In other cases, the central government has been forced to shelve or delay unpopular but vital national policy in the face of local opposition. Strong resistance from local executives led to over two decades of delay on US base relocation plans in Okinawa, continued closure of nuclear power plants (such as those in Niigata), and the termination or revival of major public works projects (such as Kawabegawa and Yamba dams).

A similar variation in the ability of local governments and actors to influence national policy emerged in our investigation of other countries with different institutional and socio-economic conditions to Japan. Even in highly centralized unitary states such as the UK, local resistance could eventually undermine strong executives (local government rebellions under the Thatcher administration) or lead to compromise positions (such as with regional parliaments in Scotland). Where local governments have very strong constitutional and formal channels to shape national policy as in Germany, local preferences are pre-embedded in national policy. Under these conditions, multi-level conflicts have been rare. In a highly decentralized and fractured system like Canada, multi-level conflicts were more common and outcomes variable. Provinces may be successful or not in securing preferred policy and resources depending on the electoral strategy of the federal government at the time (such as conflicts over fiscal equalization under the Harper administration).

What can be inferred is that local politics can matter in a variety of institutional contexts. Both in Japan and elsewhere, through formal legal powers and partisan channels, local politics possesses surprising resilience to push back against top-down decision-making.

The 'nationalization' of politics?

Local politics thus matters. It matters, after all, because preferences over national policy differ considerably across different territories. If voter preferences were distributed homogeneously – i.e. all provinces or districts across a nation have the same proportion of supporters for different parties and/or policies – local politics would be irrelevant. But this is not the case. In the countries we observed, a persisting territorial divide exists between wealthier and poorer regions (often times overlapping with urban and rural divides) where economic, demographic, and perhaps even cultural differences result in voter preferences to diverge on public works, market regulations, trade policy, welfare policy, etc. Other, more granular territorial differences also exist: e.g. regions hosting undesirable facilities (such as nuclear power plants) and those neighbouring and/or benefitting from such facilities; areas with high concentrations of foreigners and those without; large cities and smaller cities; industrial areas vs service-industry regions. Geography is diverse across Japan as it is in most countries, and most policies (from public works, trade, energy, tourism, immigration) have a heterogeneous impact on these different regions. When specific policies benefit more

152 *Conclusion*

people in some territories/regions/districts than others, it is only natural to expect policy preferences (of the majority or median voter in a particular territory) to diverge across territories.

These divergent territorial interests are than represented and institutionalized, at local level, through local elections, governments, and party organizations. That these local interests are not just represented at national level by legislators from electoral districts representing specific territories, but also locally is a very important distinction. Throughout the book, the existence (regardless of their actual formal powers) of directly elected legislatures and executives as well as local branch organizations of national state-wide parties gave greater voice and channels for local preferences. In Japan's case, the existence of powerful and high-profile chief executives (governors and mayors of large cities and prefectures) played a particularly vital role. They have often acted as nodes which concentrate and direct local interests towards central governments. Local legislatures, less powerful, have also made public their discontent with national policy such as through the passing of local resolutions. Local party organizations, when integrated to the ruling party executive, possessed strong influence over the direction of national policy. Though top-down decision-making style and vertical de-integration of party organizations have weakened these channels, local party branches still served as a base of revolt for territorial interests against such top-down decisions (and party rebuilding during times of opposition).

These observations about the continuing importance of local political actors and territorial interests lead us to question the claims of a 'nationalization' of Japanese parties and electoral politics. The nationalization thesis of electoral politics, encapsulated and most prominently espoused by Caramani (2004), claims three dimensions of change: (1) a homogenization of turnout and support for political parties across all territories in a state; (2) national political factors/forces becoming more important than local factors/forces for determining voting behaviour; (3) uniform response to political forces, as seen by uniform swings between subsequent elections across all territorial units (Caramani 2004, p. 36).

In a highly 'nationalized' system of party competition, territorial interests are dissolved under national issues and the distribution of preferences among voters for policies/parties becomes homogeneous across all territorial units. Local politics thus becomes unimportant or largely non-existent. Such claims have naturally been challenged by the recent expansion of theoretical and empirical work in multi-level relations, party organizations, and local elections (see Detterbeck 2012, pp. 8–12 for an overview).

In the context of Japan, recent observers (e.g. Rosenbluth and Thies 2010; Scheiner 2012; McElwain 2013) have also suggested that Japanese elections and party systems are becoming more 'nationalized'. Primarily through electoral reform in 1994 that created a more majoritarian electoral system, Japanese politics was being transformed into a system of roughly two parties equally competitive throughout the country. Voters were paying less attention to local/district level issues or the quality of individual candidates, and more on party

Conclusion 153

programmes. Weakened incumbency advantage, increased floating voters, and the reduction of malapportionment between rural and urban votes, had flattened the electoral playing field. Parties were thus incentivized to target 'nationalized' voters with more homogeneous preferences across regions with common universalistic programmes (e.g. welfare, foreign policy) rather than clientelistic, territorially targeted policies. Moreover, as both parties converged on median voters and policy programmes became hard to differentiate, national party executives focused on attracting voters by emphasizing competency of the party leadership and party image.

These claims about the nationalizing trends of politics in Japan need to be modified in light of this book's findings.

The first point is that although the nationalization thesis claims increasing homogeneity of support and turnout across territorial units in Japan,[1] this is hardly the case for local-level elections. As the book has evidenced clearly, the DPJ has dismally failed to secure legislative majorities in most prefectural legislatures, particularly in rural areas, as well as for major city legislatures. A majority of local executive offices (governors and mayors) are held by candidates backed by either national or local LDP branches or independents, with the DPJ often unable to nominate and support their own nominates. The opposition has a 'hollowed out' and very erratic local party organization in contrast to the stable, institutionalized, and often dominant LDP organizations across 47 prefectures. The nationalization thesis looks strictly at national electoral outcomes and voter behaviour, but this is a very narrow conception of party competition. When one looks deeper – that is at local election results and local party organizations – it is clear the 'nationalization' of Japanese politics is only skin-deep.

Some may argue that it is only national electoral results and voter behaviour which matter, and that local elections are an irrelevance. But the book has demonstrated how local political actors affect not only the direction of national policy, but also national electoral outcomes. Parachuted national candidates and those campaigning against local policy preferences may face local branches who refuse to provide electoral support. In the worst cases, they may face independents backed by local branches to whom, in some cases, they lose (e.g. consider parachuted candidates against local postal rebels backed by local party organizations in the 2005 general elections). Since the local party system and party organization strengths in Japan are not homogeneous across territories (or even symmetrical with the national level), territorial differences play a role in national electoral competition.

Finally, the notion that voters are increasingly homogeneous and concerned primarily or only about national issues is unconvincing in light of the many territorially divergent challenges against national policy discussed in the book. Although our empirical focus was on local political elite – not voter – behaviour or preferences, we provided countless evidence of local representatives from select regions diverging from the national executive's preferences. Either these local politicians are not representative of the majority of voters in their regions (which is possible for local legislatures, less so for directly elected local

154 *Conclusion*

executives). Or more likely, the preferences for national policy in one region as reflected by its local representatives differ from the national executive position (which may or may not proximate the national median voter position). Our book demonstrates how these territorial differences, unable to be resolved internally within party channels or through redistributive compensation as in the past, triggered significant multi-level conflict.

Although Japan's party system has not re-organized across territorial cleavages, as some more regions in traditionally 'nationalized' party systems like the UK[2] appear to be doing, it sits uncomfortably astride numerous territorial divisions, including a persisting rural-urban (overlapping wealthy-poor and populating-depopulating) cleavage. The emergence of new parties such as Osaka Restoration Association (*Osaka ishin no kai*) later Japan Restoration Party (*Nippon ishin no kai*), Tax Reduction Japan (*Genzei nippon*), and Your Party (*Minna no tō*) representing primarily urban voters and preferences, as well as those focused on rural interests such as PNP (*Kokumin shintō*), People's Life Party (*Seikatsu no tō*), and New Party Daichi (*Shintō daichi*) testifies to the possibility of territorially based parties even in a primarily majoritarian system.

With national parties facing great internal tensions and lacking the ability to effectively broker deals over rural and urban as well as other territorial differences (through traditional redistribution or solidary benefits appealing to ideology), the possibility of the party system splintering into territorial-based parties is not negligible. Consider the strange evolution of the model Westminster state. Despite being idealized as a unitary and nationalized two-party system, the UK has recently experienced a resurgence of territorialization in its party politics. The UK appears to be split into regions dominated by regional parties (Scotland) and state-wide parties with persisting geographic bases (as Labour has been in Northern England and the Tories in the South for long). One can imagine Japan, with an even less majoritarian system and tradition of centralization, further territorializing in party competition.

Decisive or resolute democracy?

Our final observation of how local politics matters is its impact on democratic governance: local politics matters for the 'decisiveness' of Japan's political system.

From around 2008 to 2012 or so, under the 'twisted Diet' (*nejire kokkai*) conditions of different partisan majorities controlling upper and lower houses and consequent gridlock in policy-making, a debate emerged about the problem of 'indecisive politics' (*kimerarenai seiji*). Newspaper editorials, books, and popular discussion griped about the ills of institutional gridlock caused by the vetoing power of the Upper House. High-profile local executives such as Osaka mayor/governor Hashimoto Toru whose reforms were blocked by recalcitrant local assemblies further fuelled debate about gridlock in decision-making. Even foreign observers joined the debate, with a US state department official publishing a book entitled *The Japan That Can't Decide* (Maher 2011).

Such discussion on Japan's indecisive political system focused primarily on the design of Japan's national legislature in terms of the strength of its Upper House to veto policy and the slow and inefficient legislation process in the Diet itself (Nonaka 2013). Unlike past and similar discussions of the weakness of Japanese leadership in the late 1980s which triggered electoral reforms in the mid-1990s, factionalism and intra-party indiscipline was seen as less of an issue in terms of formulating and implementing policy. The role of local governments and local party organizations has also largely not been part of the recent debate concerning limits to Japan's majoritarianism, although notable exceptions include Machidori (2015, pp. 180–183).

Our book, however, has illustrated how local politics played an important role in slowing, delaying, and shaping significant national policy initiatives at various stages of its life cycle. Albeit not as powerful a veto player as the Upper House, the behaviour of local party branches, local legislatures, and most importantly local executives has certainly made national executives less decisive than they wished. Delays in the TPP, restarting nuclear power, and relocating the Futenma base are but the most visible and important effects of local veto power.

Following the LDP's control over the two houses in 2013, however, the Abe administration used its absolute majorities in Diet committees and plenary sessions to force through a number of controversial bills (such as the state secrecy law in 2013 and the collective security-related bills in 2015). This active legislation has in turn been criticized from some quarters as a 'politics that is too decisive' (*kimesugiru seiji*).[3] Once again, these assessments of decisiveness have failed to take into account the brake which local politics has served on a supposedly over-decisive prime minister and his office. Although Abe may have restored control over both houses of Diet since 2013, he has faced difficulty in a number of areas seen as vital policy goals (such as agricultural trade liberalization, Okinawa base policy, and nuclear energy) from local politics. Japan's political system is not as majoritarian as past observers have suggested or certain political actors wish it to be. Local politics is an often overlooked element of these checks on a centralized policy-making process.

Whether a proliferation of veto players, including autonomous local political actors, which make governments less decisive is a desirable thing or not is another matter altogether. The desirability to concentrate powers and decision-making (in majoritarian systems) or to deconcentrate powers and decision-making to allow for a wide range of actors to participate in policy-making (in consensus systems) is a long-standing and core debate in institutionalist democratic theory (e.g. Powell 2000; Lijphart 2012). In terms of local politics, providing greater local autonomy deconcentrates power and thus pushes democracies to a more consensus, less decisive system (Lijphart 2012, pp. 174–188). Normatively, a long-standing tradition has claimed that guaranteeing such strong autonomy to local governments prevents central government tyranny and protects local communities' freedom. Riker was most critical of this 'ideological fallacy … that federal forms are adopted as a device to guarantee freedom' and has shown how federalism has not prevented tyranny or abuse of freedoms

156   *Conclusion*

(Riker 1987, p. 14). In the US, federalism allowed for the continuation of racist policies in Southern states, preventing progressive policies and protection of human rights to be implemented by the federal government nationally (Riker 1964). Divided powers can thus prevent 'good policies' as much as enable 'bad ones'.

As with Fukuyama's elegant formulation below, choosing between institutions that offer 'decisiveness' or 'resoluteness' (reached when the numerous veto players in a consensus system have come to an agreement after a long process of negotiation) really depends:

> Institutions are only enabling devices; those that facilitate or encourage strong and decisive political decision-making are only as good as the policies being pursued. ... Constitutional rules that amplify executive power by reducing veto gates can produce policies that come to be regarded as illegitimate; without a broader underlying social consensus, reforms are likely to be undermined over time.
>
> (Fukuyama 2006)

It seems that Japanese observers, voters, and politicians have not fully grasped the implications of the above logic. Instead, proposals for institutional reform conflate mechanical effects of institutional design with desired policy outcomes: both critics and supporters should well remember that decisiveness does not ensure preferred policy outcomes or that divided powers prevent only undesirable policy outcomes.

Moreover, observers and participants in Japan need a clearer understanding of the capacity of local governments to stop both desirable and undesirable national policies. Discussions and reforms of decisiveness without taking account of the vital local/territorial elements of politics will be incomplete. Finally, Japanese actors need to better engage with the mixed nature of Japan's current political system with strong majoritarian and consensus elements. In terms of local government, this indeterminacy must be negotiated carefully: ruling parties must build 'a broader underlying social consensus' through material compensation or appeals to principle, if they wish to decisively implement desired national agendas.

Future of local politics in Japan

All of which leads us to how the current Abe administration (2012–) has been managing this tricky disequilibrium with local governments.

Abe's first two years in office focused on national-level macroeconomic, fiscal, and security matters, and by and large paid relatively little attention to regional issues. Instead, Abe's initial regional policy was a narrow focus on reviving traditional public works spending. In the 2012 campaign, the LDP called for spending up to 200 trillion yen over the next ten years to strengthen Japan's resilience towards natural disasters. The LDP expanded public works for the 2013 and

Conclusion   157

2014 budgets, reversing a general downward trend. These increases in public works, although still far below peak levels in 1998, have been criticized as a return to the old LDP of wasteful and ineffective pump-priming measures. Moreover, the sudden surge of public works spending has resulted in a shortage of construction labourers and rise in construction material costs, with record levels of unused budgets and uncompleted construction orders.

Thus the LDP was in search of a new approach to regional issues. The publication of a high-profile article – the so-called 'Masuda report'[4] – in May of 2014 on rural depopulation provided a cue. In the article, Masuda and his research team recalculated future demographic predictions based on the assumption that the population inflow from rural to major urban areas would continue. Under this scenario, half of Japan's municipalities would see the portion of their 20–39 year old women (child-bearing population) fall below half of current levels by 2040. These 896 municipalities were deemed to become potentially 'extinct',[5] while 523 of them with a population of under 10,000 were deemed to have a very high likelihood of becoming extinct. The predictions estimate that 80 per cent of municipalities in Hokkaido, Aomori, Iwate, Akita, Yamagata, and Shimane – including larger cities such as Akita, Aomori, and Hakodate – were at risk of becoming extinct due to a shortage of child-bearing women (Masuda 2014, p. 30).

The article also linked the mechanism of this depopulation to over-concentration in the metropolitan regions. Tokyo, with the lowest fertility rate of all prefectures (1.13 compared to the national average of 1.41), was sucking in younger generations like a demographic 'black hole' who on arrival were not bearing children, resulting in a demographic 'polar society'.[6] Compared to other developed economies, Japan was exceedingly concentrated in Tokyo: 30 per cent of its population was living in the capital region, compared to between 5 and 15 per cent for Paris, London, New York, Rome, and Berlin (Masuda 2014). This trend has continued, with Japan's population declining for the fifth straight year while Tokyo's population has increased and 39 of Japan's prefectures declined in 2014.

By publicizing a list of municipalities at risk of extinction, and applying the dramatic term 'extinction' (*shōmetsu*) in contrast to past terms of 'marginalizing' (*genkai*) or 'depopulating' (*kaso*) for rural municipalities, the report triggered a flurry of news reports, editorials, and television documentaries. Soon after publication, local assemblies deliberated the matter in their assembly sessions, while governors responded to the article by declaring a state of emergency concerning depopulation.

To reverse regional depopulation, the Masuda report recommended the creation of compact and core cities in regions to act as 'dams' to stop the outflow of young people from rural to urban areas. These ideas have been linked to proposals from the Ministry of Internal Affairs and Communications and the Ministry of Land, Infrastructure and Transport to select and focus administrative resources on select cities (with proposals including the creation of 60 or so core designated cities) as well as promote municipal coalitions. The Masuda report,

158   *Conclusion*

however, was explicit in arguing that counter-depopulation policies should not rely on decentralization, which could potentially weaken regions and accelerate the population shift to Tokyo (Masuda 2014, p. 38). In September 2014, a Cabinet council on depopulation and local economy[7] was established with former LDP chairman Shigeru Ishiba as special minister in charge.

Prior to the dissolution of the Lower House, the ruling party passed a bill for regional development (*machi hito shigoto sōsei hō*). Proposals included dispatching central ministry bureaucrats to local governments, the creation of special deregulatory zones, and providing new block grants to fund proposals from local communities. In general, however, these were criticized as a rehash of past policies and leading to uncoordinated distribution of subsidies. Editorials and analytical pieces doubted whether the measures could generate enough employment in rural communities to stem the continued population exodus to the cities.

The language and content of Abe's flagship regional policy of *chihō sōsei* (revitalizing regions) reveals much about the administrations' strategy to local government. In the pamphlet[8] provided by the Cabinet explaining the long-term regional revitalization project, the government hopes to reduce the influx of people from rural areas to metropolitan areas in order to stop Japan's overall depopulation. This goal will be achieved by creating jobs in regions and encouraging people to stay, or move, to these depopulating areas. On the principles of 'autonomy, future-mindedness, localness, regional-ness, and emphasis on results', the pamphlet claims, 'local governments will draft and take charge of its revitalization strategy'. The central government will provide support in terms of information, finance, and personnel. All local governments will be expected to draft a regional revitalization plan which 'takes into account local conditions to ensure effective policies' for reviving their economies. These local government plans will be assessed by a new metric of key performance indicators (KPI). Deregulatory regions will be promoted and created according to local demand. A new system of local subsidies would be put in place, with funding to local governments adjusted according to the performance achievements of their revitalization plans.

During the 2014 general elections and 2015 local elections, the 'local revitalization' project was sold to the public in PM speeches, in manifestos, and various public forums. A number of key words and concepts were repeated in the discourse including: 'regions as protagonists' (*chihō ga shuyaku*) and emphasizing the 'effort' (*doryoku*), 'passion' (*jyōnetsu*), and 'creativity' (*sōi kufū*) of localities.[9] The central government would 'back up' (*shien*) and 'aid' (*ōen*) the 'ambitious challenges' (*iyokuteki na challenge*) taken on by local governments who should strive to make 'unique regions' (*kosei yutaka na chihō*).[10] In a government-sponsored TV series[11] providing examples of *chihō sōsei*, local residents were urged to 'engage in community-building not depend on city hall' and 'make pro-active efforts at community-building' claiming that 'independence leads to rebirth'. The minister in charge of local revitalization, Ishiba Shigeru, commented in the media that disparities which emerge as a result of

Conclusion 159

competition among local governments were 'to be expected' (*tōzen*). He added that if the state treated local governments which made an 'effort' in the same way as those which didn't, the 'whole state would go bust' (*kuni zentai ga tsubureru*).[12]

Thus the discourse surrounding local policy under Abe centred on themes of autonomy, self-effort, competition, and accountability of local governments. At the same time discussion of decentralizing powers and resources under the Abe administration have retreated and fallen off the active agenda (Hijino 2016). Unlike decentralization reform, the *chihō sōsei* project is selective in providing discretion (through deregulation) and resources (through new selective subsidies) to certain local governments that make efforts to change. Such a dynamic mirrors to some extent the lateral competition among local governments petitioning the central government for subsidies and developmental projects in the high-growth period (Muramatsu 1988). But there are important differences. Unlike competition in the past in which local governments petitioned to attract developmental projects from a menu offered by central ministries, the responsibility of drafting and implementing regional revival plans is now hoisted onto local governments. At the same time, local government competition in the growth era sought additional benefits from a growing pie; in other words, it was a race to the top. The current competition is one of avoiding a slide to the bottom, menaced by central government threats of reducing subsidies through strict performance assessments. It is a race of local governments seeking to 'maintain its current status in size and resources' and not fall behind (Yamashita and Kanai 2015, pp. 177–182).

It is unclear whether such a project of emphasizing inter-regional competition with selective central government support would lift the many Japanese local communities out of their severe demographic and socio-economic crisis. Even if encouraged 'to work together towards realizing regional revitalization',[13] some regions will inevitably lose. For many residents and regional politicians who have seen conditions worsen under decentralization since the 2000s, there is perhaps more fear than hope in the face of such exhortations to become more independent.

Most crucially, it is not at all evident that local communities and politicians are actively seeking greater autonomy and discretion. No one has asked if local communities really want or have the capacity to be responsible for their own economic revival. Abe's regional revitalization plans reflect the underlying problem of disconnected national and local actors described through this book: local preferences have not been seriously considered and embedded in the policy programmes emanating from the centre.

As of writing, it is unclear how this centre-local linkage will be restored as the ruling party executive and local party organizations remain de-integrated, opposition parties lack a foothold locally and are crumbling nationally, and local governments are increasingly controlled by non-partisan actors distant to the centre. For national agendas to work, both central and local governments need to restore channels to ensure cooperative, not conflictual, relations over major

160 *Conclusion*

policies. The Abe administration has restarted traditional construction-related pork and provided ideological exhortations of local diversity and community-building to secure territorial consensus and support. The results, so far, seem limited. One hopes for more creative and convincing attempts, from the ruling party and opposition parties, to bridge the gap between centre and periphery in the future.

Notes

1 Weakening incumbency advantage of LDP candidates in rural areas has been provided as one set of evidence for the 'nationalizing' of Japanese elections between 2000 and 2009 (McElwain 2013). In the 2012 and 2014 elections, however, it appears the LDP regained its advantage in the most rural SMDs and 'won big' over the DPJ in them.

2 Labour and Conservative support has always shown geographic concentrations, with Labour strong in the Northern England, Scotland, Wales, and industrial areas and Conservatives dominant in the South and South-east (Radice 1992; Radice and Diamond 2010). Recently the weakening and collapse of Labour in Wales and Scotland respectively to regionalist parties highlights the new territorialization of politics in the model two-party Westminster system.

3 ' "Kimeru seiji" shikaku wa naika', *Nihon Keizai Simbun*, 20 July 2014.

4 The article, published in in *Chuō kōron* magazine, was authored by Hiroya Masuda, former Minister of Home Affairs and Communications, and researchers at the Japan Policy Council. It was entitled 'Stop the rapid depopulation society: Realizing the people's desired fertility rate and creation of core regional cities' and later published in book form (Masuda 2014).

5 The term *shōmetsu jichitai* was used originally, directly translating to 'municipalities that become extinct'.

6 Tokyo, in turn, is also facing a demographic crisis of its own, as its population ages rapidly. Currently new nurse homes are being built around Tokyo which are drawing in nursing care-workers from rural areas (in effect depopulating rural areas for which there exist few other job opportunities for young women). Eventually, however, this pool of younger female workers from rural areas will also be depleted, leaving Tokyo with a host of old people unable to receive old-age care (Masuda 2014).

7 Council on Overcoming Population Decline and Vitalizing Local Economy in Japan.

8 'Machi hito shigoto sōsei "chōki vision/sōgō senryaku" ', Cabinet Office, 13 February 2015. Available at www.kantei.go.jp/jp/topics/2015/panf20150213.pdf [accessed 20 October 2016].

9 Prime Minister Abe's policy speech to the opening of the 189th Diet, 12 February 2015.

10 Prime Minister Abe's policy speech to the opening of the 187th Diet, 29 September 2014.

11 *Chihō no susume: Chihō no genki saizensen* (ten-part mini-TV series about regional vitalization). Available at www.gov-online.go.jp/cam/chihou_sousei/event/BS/ [accessed 20 October 2016].

12 'Ishiba chihō sōsei sō: Kakusa "Atarimae da", chihō jichitai wa kyōsō wo', Bloomberg News, 26 January 2015. Available at www.bloomberg.co.jp/news/123-NIKJY96JT-SEB01.html [accessed 20 October 2016].

13 Prime Minister Abe's policy speech to the opening of the 190th Diet, 22 January 2016.

Conclusion 161

References

Caramani, D. 2004, *The nationalization of politics: The formation of national electorates and party systems in Western Europe*, Cambridge University Press.

Detterbeck, K. 2012, *Multi-level party politics in Western Europe* (Vol. 2), Basingstoke: Palgrave Macmillan.

Fukuyama, F. 2006, 'Do defective institutions explain the gap between the United States and Latin America?', *The American Interest*, vol. 2, no. 2. Available at www.the-american-interest.com/2006/11/01/do-defective-institutions-explain-the-gap-between-the-united-states-and-latin-america/ [accessed 20 October 2016].

Hijino, K.V.L. 2016, 'Selling the idea of local power: Decentralization reforms since the 1990s', in G. Steel (ed.), *Power in contemporary Japan*, Palgrave Macmillan, pp. 219–237.

Lijphart, A. 2012, *Patterns of democracy: Government forms and performance in thirty-six countries*, Yale University Press.

Machidori, S. 2015, *Daigisei minshushugi*, Chuko shinsho.

Maher, K. 2011, *Ketsudan dekinai nihon*, Bunshu shinsho.

Masuda, H. 2014, *Chihō shōmetsu: Tokyo ikkyoku shūchū ga maneku jinkou kyūgen*, Chuo Koron shinsho.

McElwain, K. 2013, 'The nationalization of Japanese elections', in K.E. Kushida and P.Y. Lipscy (eds), *Japan under the DPJ: The politics of transition and governance*, Walter H. Shorenstein Asia-Pacific Research Center.

Muramatsu, M. 1988, *Chihōjichi*, Tokyo daigaku shuppankai.

Nonaka, N. 2013, *Saraba Galapagos seiji: Kimerareru nihon ni tsukurinaosu*, Nihon Keizai Shimbun shuppansha.

Powell, G.B. 2000, *Elections as instruments of democracy: Majoritarian and proportional visions*, Yale University Press.

Radice, G. 1992, *Southern discomfort* (No. 555), Fabian Society.

Radice, G. and Diamond, P. 2010, *Southern discomfort again*, Policy Network.

Riker, W.H. 1964, *Federalism: Origin, operation, significance*, Little, Brown.

Riker, W.H. 1987, *The development of American federalism* (No. 342.24 (73)), Kluwer Academic Publishers.

Rosenbluth, F.M. and Thies, M.F. 2010, *Japan transformed: Political change and economic restructuring*, Princeton University Press.

Scheiner, E. 2012, 'The electoral system and Japan's partial transformation: Party system consolidation without policy realignment', *Journal of East Asian Studies*, vol. 12, no. 3, pp. 351.

Yamashita, Y. and Kanai, T. 2015, *Chihou sōsei no shōtai: Naze chiiki seisaku wa shippai surunoka*, Chikuma shinsho.

Index

Page numbers in *italics* denote tables, those in **bold** denote figures.

Abe Shinzo 72–3, 79n31, 98n25, 103, **104**, **105**, 107; administration 42, 57, 64–5, 67, 74–5, 78n21, 118, 122–3, 155–6, 159–60; flagship regional policy 158; policy speech 160n9, 160n10, 160n13

agricultural 73; cooperatives 75, 79n30; products 91; regions 78n23; trade liberalization 46, 67, 72–3, 155

agricultural reform 79n35; cooperatives 73, 79n30, 79n35

agriculture 47, 72, 92

anti-TPP 92–3; DPJ parliamentarians 91, 94

Asano, M. 45, 71

Atkinson, M.M. 129–30, 145n2

Auel, K. 135–6

autonomy 1, 18, 20, 31n4, 32n6, 82, 138, 142, 158–9; central government 19; delegating 32n7; expanded 7, 40; fiscal 8, 121, 124, 130; granted 138, 142; greater or increased 22, 30, 135–6; guaranteeing 155; lacking 19–20, 24, 85, 144; levels of 11; limited or low 3, 43; local 4, 21; local government 18, 25, 37–8; national 53; policy 7, 25; regional 21, 83; *see also* local autonomy

backbenchers 44–5, 60, 138, 150; Diet 91; DPJ 94; reduced influence 90

bicameral system 24; bicameralism 11, 143

Blair, T. 140, 146n17; administration 137

Blairite candidates for leadership 146n17; New Labour Blairite positions 141

Bolleyer, N. 15, 24, 143

Bradbury, J. 140–1

Bundesrat 19–20, 134–6, 143–5, 145n5

Calder, K.E. 6, 50

campaign 69, 75, 77, 106; 2012 156; against national-level policies 57; finance reforms 45; key electoral themes 76; local-level planning 49; locally 32n6; manager 122; material 73; mobilization 25; national contents *60*; online 132; personal machines 10, 44; promises 57, 62; reform 65; support 47; against Tokyo 76; tour 104

campaigning 49, 79n35, 80, 91, 97; against LDP candidates 72; against local policy preferences 153; against nuclear power 118; against Tokyo 124; against TPP 93; local 10; local politicians 32n4; policy 32n5, 57, 61

Canada 8–9, 26, 128, 131, 145, 150; IGR 144; federal and provincial governments 20; local government system 28; multi-level relations 129–30, 132–3, 143, 151; tax 146n7

Canadian 143; constitution 130; equalization scheme 145n3; federalism 129, 131; party systems and parties 128, 131; Progressive Conservative Party breakup 97n7; provincial–federal relations *27*

candidate selection 32n5, 32n6, 59–60, 82, 138, 141–2; procedures 10, 80

candidates 44, 51; Blairite 146n17; characteristics 46; conflicts over 142; DPJ 92; first-time **48**; gubernatorial 48–9, 57, 60, 69, 73, 75, 102–3, 106; independent 53n8, 72; LDP 160n1; LDP-backed 50, 117–18; national 1, 44, 48, 59–60, 62, 153; nominations 45, 76, 104; non-LDP 75; non-partisan

Index 163

30; parachuted 153; progressive 49–50; quality 77, 152; rebel 71–2; second and third generation 84; strategies 52

candidates, official 60; Labour 142; LDP 57–8, 62, 71–3, 75

Caramani, D. 152

Carty, R.K. 32n7, 129–31

central government 3, 5, 7–9, 14–19, 21, 26, 27, 28, 29, 38, 43, 46, 49–50, 53, 75, 77, 90, 95–6, 100, 103, 109–13, 116, 119, 121–4, 125n8, 125n14, 126n28, 139–40, 143, 150–2, 158; agencies 125n17; control 144; control of standards and levels 39; executive 108, 149; funding 146n8; intervention 25, 30, 35, 42, 137–8; regional branches abolished 42; tyranny prevention 155

central government subsidies 117, 120; reduced 41, 102, 159

centralization 129; of candidate selection-procedures 10; dual 138; fiscal 38, 132; of party organization 8–9, 22, 137; state 6, 21, 35, 39; tradition 154; of UK local governments 137

Chandler, W.M. 7, 22, 130, 133

chief executives 6, 9, 11, 52, 62, 80; autonomous 10; directly elected 9, 25; high-profile 152; Labour SNP 146n17; local 7, 47, 49, 74, 85, 97, 101, 112; local LDP-affiliated 94; national associations 109; non-partisan 23; opposed cancellation of Yamba dam 93; progressive 50; from traditional LDP strongholds 91; see also governors; mayors

clientelism, decline in 102, 112

clientelistic 124, 153; links weakened 121; network dissolved 91; redistribution 83; spending reduced 52

come to power 27, 117–18; DPJ 65, 81, 83–4, 89–90, 94, 120; Labour government 140; LDP return 64, 92, 96, 117

community charge see poll tax

competition 35, 85; diverse 136; electoral 45–6, 153; horizontal political 4; inter-regional 159; intra-party 44; lateral 43, 159; party 27–8, 46–7, 77, 131, 135, 152–4; programmatic 4–5; regionalized 141; territorial 129–30, 135, 149

Conservative 139; administration 137, 146n18; Canadian Progressive Party 97n7, 132; centralism 140; government 27, 29, 138–40, 144; governors 116; manifesto 139, 146n11; Party 138–9, 141; Prime Minister 132; support 160n2

Conservatives 132, 139–41, 160n2

consumption tax 42, 69, 76; anti-consumption tax DPJ defectors 94; raising 85, 88, 92

cooperation 2, 8, 14, 19, 129, 142–3; dominant mode 15; inter-governmental 11, 33; within LDP 53; among levels of the same party 21; multi-level 26, 27, 30; party branches 20; politicians 80; reducing 102; in resistance 71; special measure law 42; US Japan defence guidelines 65

dams 29, 83, 124, 125n17, 151; cancelled 114, 117–18; Daidogawa project 117; Kawabegawa project 83, 93, 117–18; national projects 123; opposition movements against 116; policy conflicts 113, 114, 119; promise to cancel 81, 83, 93; Shimouke protests 116, 125n15; successful resistance to 102; Yamba project 83, 89, 93–4, 97, 118

de-integrated 81, 159; LDP 8, 49, 53, 82; party organizations 20

debt 2; issuance 38, 119; local government 41

debt issuance litigation incident (*kisai soshō*) 119

debt-to-expenditure ratio 41

decentralization 1–2, 18, 25, 29, 35, 53n2, 53n6, 110, 145n1, 158; government committee 120; of police and education boards 37; post-decentralization Japan 27, 28, 124; post-decentralization period 119; pro-decentralization scholars 125n8; see also fiscal decentralization

decentralization, administrative 112, 124; administrative authority 32n9; and fiscal 5–6, 35

decentralization reform 7, 8, 9, 30, 36, 39–42, 53, 81, 112–13, 120, 124, 159; fiscal 40, 109; Promotion Law and Committee 42

decentralization under the DPJ 5, 35, 40, 42, 53n6, 81, 111

decentralization under LDP 5, 35, 40, 42, 53, 111

decoupling 6, 39, 75, 102

164 *Index*

delegated functions 38–40, 42

Democratic Party of Japan (DPJ) 5, **8**, 9, 11, 48, 51, **52**, 53n6, 77, 94, 97n3, 97n4, 97n7, 107, 111, 125n19, 153, 160n1; administration 5, **27**, 28, 30, 35, 40, 42, 74, 80–5, *86*, 89, 90–3, 95–6, 106, 111, 120; branches 65, 82, 88, 90, 96; General Election Manifesto 98n11, 125n11; government 64, 72–3, 84, 98n16, 117–18; leadership 80, 83, 88–9, 91, 94–6, 98n16; Noda administration 65, 72, 92–4, 118; policies 85, *87*, 88, 91–2, 96, 103; politicians 91–2, 97n4; prefectural branches 82–3, 85, 90, 92–3; Prime Ministers 103–4

Detterbeck, K. 20, 22, 134–6, 138, 152

devolution 31, 146n17; expansion of local autonomy 144; following 143–4; IGR disputes 142; multi-level conflict following 129; ongoing process 137; referendums for Scotland and Wales 140; regionalized competition following 141; territorial conflicts after 140

devolved 144; powers 40, 140; regional governments 20, 137; regions 28, *29*, 138, 141, 146n9

Diet 61, 71–2, 104, **105**, 160n9, 160n10, 160n13; backbenchers 45, 91, 94; houses 122, 155; Japanese 40; local candidates 75; local members 4, 43–4, *60*, 83, 90, 94, 97n1, 112; members 47–8, 80, 82, 84, 93, 98n25, 100, 103; twisted 154

Diet members 47, 84, 98n25, 100; campaigning and mobilization efforts 80; DPJ 92–3; with experience in local politics 48; LDP 43–4, 90; local 4, 43–4, *60*, 83, 94, 97n1, 103, 112; locally elected 82; pro-TPP position 91; reliance on personal networks 44

DSP 49–50, 97n4

Dyck, R. 20–1

election/elections 3, 6, 17, 32n6, 44, 58, 98n25; Canadian federal 97n7, 132; data **48**, **52**, 53n1, *115*; direct 37; divided 75; divisive policy areas 79n35; fiscal equalization policy 133; funding 25, 76; general 84, 93, 98n11, 110, 120, 139, 141, 153, 158; Greater London Authority 141; gubernatorial 50, 52, 73–5, 101, 116–17; HoR 46; importance of rural/semi-rural districts

46; Japanese 152, 160n1; joint unified 69, 92; leadership 142; LDP backing 118; LDP presidential 84, 96; Lower House 57; manifesto 81, 93, 98n11, 120, 125n11, 146n11, 146n15; municipal legislative and executive 53n1, 54n8; nominations 106; party backing 25, 28; PM-governor meetings 104, **105**; postal privatization 47, 76; prefectural legislative 46; presidentialization 45; regional 134–5, 141–2; results **52**, 80; Scottish parliamentary 141; second-order 135; snap 47, 71; split 62; TPP issue 73, 92; turnout 47; Upper House 57, 72, 74, 123, 146n19; Upper House by-election 69; voter logics/strategies 22; votes 100; win 1, 45, 47; years 5, 46; *see also* re-election

electoral systems cycles 21–2, *29*, 141; majoritarian 24, 45–6, 129–31, 137, 140, 144, 149, 152, 154–6; proportional 24, 140, 144; SNTV 46–7, 54n9

equality, inter-regional 5; *see also* fiscal equalization

Estévez-Abe, M. 11, 45

expenditures 18; debt-to-expenditure ratio **41**; limits exceeded 138; local 38–9; obligatory 41

federal 1; decisions 136; desegregation resolution 16; elections 132; executive 133; judiciary 131; legislation 134, 143, 145n4; policy blockade 135; policy-making 145n5; structure reform 136; systems 6, 20

federal Canada election 97n7; executives *29*, 129; party systems 128, 131

federal governments 2, 20–1, 129–30, 132, 143–4, 151, 155–6; German 128, 133–6

federal parties 15, 32n5, 130, 134; in Canada 128, 131; Conservative 132; opposition 135; in power 133, 143

federal states 18, 137, 145; state relations **27**

federal–provincial administrative functions 143; conferences 131

federalism 155; Canadian 129–33; competitive 133, 136; cooperative 133–4, 136; executive 131; functional 135; German 133–4, 136; jurisdictional 130; literature 15; US 156

Index 165

Filippov, M. 6, 15, 20–1, 32n6, 45
fiscal decentralization 10, 18, 35, 41–2,
  46–7, 52, 65, *66*, 67, 102, 111, 113,
  124, 150; reforms 5, 40, 109
fiscal equalization 39; Canada *29*, 129,
  132–3, 151; Germany 136; Scottish
  executive challenge 142; UK *29*
Flanagan, S.E. 4; *see also* Krauss, Steiner
foreign resident voting rights *29*, 65, *66*,
  67, 84–5, *87*, 88–9, 94–6
Fukui prefecture 83, 88, 92
Fukuyama, F. 156

German 135; bicameralism 143; East
  German communism 135; federal
  government 128; federal–state relations
  27; federalism 134, 136; parties 134;
  provinces fiscal equalization *29*; voter *see
  also* Bundesrat
German Länder 133; coordination across
  136; dissatisfaction over fiscal policy
  143; federal linkage 135; former East
  German 136; governments 134–5;
  influence on federal policy-making
  145n5; opposition parties at federal level
  144
Germany 8–9, 26, 30, 128, 130, 133,
  150–1; cooperative relations 135; East
  and West 136; federalism 129, 131,
  134; incongruence 135, 144; multi-level
  conflicts 129, 143; post-unification 134,
  136; presidential terms 124n4;
  proportional electoral rules 144; second
  chamber 134, 145; tax 146n7
Gifu prefecture 71, 78n20; governor
  Kajiwara Taku 110, 125n8; NGA
  meeting 109; postal rebels 72
government power 31n4, 138; local
  125n11; shared in coalition 24; transfer
  to local 15, 35
Governor Izumida 118, 120
governor meetings with PM 102–3,
  104, **105**, 106, **107**, 108, 112, 125n6;
  informal 103, 113
governor power 119; ascribed to 100;
  executive 113, 123–4; in power 50
governors 7, 25, *29*, 49, 77, 91, 96,
  100–4, 109, 157; association 109–10;
  challenge national policy *114*; criticizing
  PMs **108**; dam project 93–4, 97, 117,
  125n17; directly elected 53; DPJ-
  backed 80; high-profile 2, 101;
  incentives to support 47; independent
  27, 52, 54n13; Japanese 144–5, 152–3;

less fiscal support 111; lobbying 43;
  non-LDP 107, 116, 123; non-partisan
  5, **8**, 50–2, 112, 116; nuclear power
  plants 118, 126n20; opposition-party-
  backed 30; partisan affiliation of **51**,
  124; petition 106; popular 2, 100;
  prefectural 7, 30; progressive 50, 119,
  122; re-election rate 124n3; reformist
  125n13; rogue LDP 123; socialist- and
  communist-backed 4, 35
grants 158; discretionary 41; general 40,
  110; lobbying for 43; local 39; local
  allocation tax system 39; penalties 138;
  reduced 5, 41, 102, 109, 120
Greater London Council (GLC) 139–41,
  144
gubernatorial campaigns 62; candidates
  48–9, 57, 60, 69, 73, 102–3, 106;
  elections 52, 75, 101, 116–17; election
  slogan 50; Okinawa elections 74; posts
  51, 77; race 117; rogue candidate 62,
  75; Saga elections 73

Hashimoto, Toru 84, 101, 110, 119–20,
  122, 125n12, 154; administration 70,
  106; challenges national policy *115*;
  meetings with PM **104**, **105**, **107**
Hijino, K.V.L. 2, 10, 35–6, 42, 47, 49,
  52, 62, 77n1, 85, 106, 117, 145, 159
Holy Trinity reforms **8**, 40
Horiuchi, Y. 2, 10
Hosokawa, M. 35, 101, **104**, **105**, **107**;
  administration 97n3
Hough, D. 2, 135
House Representative **48**
House of Representatives **48**

ideology 65, 94, 154; party 21–2, 150
ikensho see written opinions (WOs)
income: differences 36; per capita 121;
  prefectural per capita **36**; redistribution
  43; tax 140
independence 32n4, 121; Scottish 1,
  11n1, 142; war of 119
inequality/inequalities 39; regional 6, 36,
  37
integrated parties 21, 24–5, 32n5, 32n6,
  32n7, 152; British 138, 143; channels
  lacking 94; German organizations
  134–6; highly 27, 32n5; LDP 45;
  national and local systems 6; not
  integrated 23; weakly integrated 22, 77
inter-governmental conflicts 26, 131, 134,
  142

166 *Index*

inter-governmental relations (IGR) 5–9, 11, 14–15, 17–19, 22, 24, 26, 119, 121, 128, 131, 135, 142–5, 149–50; fused **8**, 19, 26–8, 30, 38; separated **8**, 19, 25, 28, 30, 128
inter-party conflict 135; multi-level *29*
intra-party conflict 6, 21, 62, 70, 74, 135, 144; LDP 77, 78n10, 85; multi-level *29*, 58, 141–2
IRA leaders 139
Ito, M. 83, 90

Japan Agricultural cooperatives (JA) 73
Japan Olympic committee 121
Japan Socialist Party (JSP) 49–51, **52**, 62, 97n4
Japanese Communist Party (JCP) 49, 75
Japanese Society for the Promotion of Sciences (JSPS) 145n1
Jeffery, C. 2, 135–6, 145n5

Kaji, Y. **36**
Kajiwara Taku 110–11, 125n8, 125n11
Kanai, T. 109–11, 159
Kawabegawa dam 83, 93, *114*, 117–18
Kawatake, D. 125n8, 125n13
keiretsu 44
kenren 59, 78n25, 97n1, 97n8, 97n10, 98n17, 98n25; *suisen* **51**, 54n13, 71
kikan innin jimu see delegated functions
Kinnock, Neil 139, 146n12
Kitamura, W. 5, 53n3, 53n6, 83, 111
Koizumi, Junichiro 71–2, 78n18, **104**, **105**, **107**, 125n19; administration 5, 36, 40–1, 64–5, 70, 109, 150
Krauss, E.S. 10, 45, 47, 107
kōenkai 10, 44

Labour 139, 141, 154; administration 146n18; British Labour Party 97n7, 138, 142; council leader 139, 141; General Election Party Manifesto 146n15; government 140, 144; national executive 142, 144; official candidate 142; Scottish National Party 146n17; support 160n2; UK councils *27*, *29*; Welsh 141, 146n18
Laffin, M. 141–2
Lecours, A. 129, 131, 133, 145n3
leftist 139; governors and mayors 4
Liberal Democratic Party (LDP) 3, 11, 26, 47, 77, 78n21, 78n24, *86*, 89, 93, 97n1, 111, *114–15*, 118, 157; administrations 5, 64, 67, *68*, 78n10, 81, 85, 94–5,

97n3, 124; affiliated chief executives 94; branches 82, 84, 95, 153; candidates 160n1; control over two houses 155; decentralization 35, 40, 42; defections 62; dominance 69; dominant organizations 153; dominant party 53; dominant period 30, 44; electoral outcomes **52**; electoral volatility 5; former chairman 158; government 73, 117; incumbents **48**; integration 53n8; internal conflicts 85; leadership 49, 62, 65, 67, 69, 73–6, 83, 92; legislative groups 71; legislators 60–2, 122; local 88; local Diet members 90; local network 59; local politicians 46, 50, 57, 72–5, 80; local resistance 62, 70; loss of seats 80; national leadership 48; national politicians 44–5; official candidates 58, 72, 75; officials 117; in opposition 70, 84, 97n8; organization 58, 60–1; out of power 10, 97n3; parliamentarians 70–1; partisans 58, 60; party manifestos 125n11; period in opposition 51; pork barrel spending 10; prime minister 50; public works 156; re-invention 76; rural 46; rural Diet members 43; seat share **59**; strongholds 91; support 54n13; territorial conflict **27**, *29*; unity in opposition 97n7; vertical integration 4, 7, **8**, 10, 43, 45
Liberal Democratic Party (LDP)-backed 80; candidates 50, 117–18; conservative governors 122; governor 51, 117
Liberal Democratic Party (LDP) controlled legislatures 52; prefectural 9, 65, 78n11
Liberal Democratic Party (LDP) governors **51**; rogue 123
Liberal Democratic Party (LDP) headquarters (HQ) 51, 61, 73, 85, 90, 95, 98n24, 104, **105**, 106, 113; organization staff 78n5, 78n7; postal rebels 71–2; relocation of US Marine Corps Air Station 74–5
Liberal Democratic Party (LDP) national policy 61, 72; inconsistency 57; intra-party conflict 63
Liberal Democratic Party (LDP) prefectural branches 79n32, 84, 97n1, 97n8, 98n25; disciplinary actions 72; executives 62; leadership selection 48–9; national chairmen meetings 60, 73, 78n24, 80; office 59; rebel candidates 71–2; region-specific manifestos 57, 61, 71

Index 167

Liberal Democratic Party (LDP)
  presidential elections 84; rules 96
Lijphart, A. 155
Livingstone, Ken 138, 141
Local Allocation Tax (*chihō kōfuzei* or
  LAT) 39; *see also* grants; subsidies
local autonomy 1, 3, 9, 14, 18–19, 24, 26,
  27, 37, 42, 145, 150; changes in levels
  37; constraints on 40, 53; decreased
  113; exercise of 15; expanded 2, *29*,
  35–6, 102, 144; greater **8**, 22, 28, 31,
  32n5, 128–9, 155; low 26–7, 30, 143
local candidates 141; progressive 50
local democracy 35, 139–40
local elections 10, 45, 47, 79n30, 134,
  152, 158; assembly 54n9; major 5, 46,
  69, 81; opposition to TPP 73, 91–2;
  results **52**, 153; turnout 2, 36, 53n1;
  voter perception 22–3, *29*; voting rights
  for foreign residents 84, 94
local executives 7, 16, 20, 24–5, 28, *29*,
  38, 102–3, 155; conflict 123; directly
  elected 150; high-profile 154;
  independent 30; Japanese 7; partisan
  affiliation 9; resistance on US base
  relocation plans 151; upward influence
  24; *see also* governors; mayors
Local Government Act of 2000 137
local government system 46; British
  146n9; Canadian 28; *dōshusei* 42, 149;
  fused 19, 26, 38–9
local LDP 113; affiliated chief executives
  94; branches 57–8, 69–75, 82, 95,
  98n25, 153; conflict over cancelled
  dams 117; controlled legislatures
  78n10; Diet members 44, 90; dominant
  67, 77; internal conflict over policy 85;
  leadership selection 10, 47; legislative
  groups 71; legislators 58, 60–2, 73–6,
  122; legislatures 123; opposition 70;
  opposition/resistance to national policy
  58, 62, 70, 88, 95, *114–15*; party
  organization 59; politicians 46, 50,
  72–5, 80; representatives 58; submit
  WOs 90; support 117; support of
  constitutional reform 67
local legislatures 2–3, 22, 24, 59, 100,
  149–50, 153, 155; challenge DPJ policy
  88; challenge national policy 67;
  conflicts within 62; control of 97n3;
  controlled by conservatives 117;
  democratic functions 42; DPJ presence
  82; elected 23; local conservative
  dominance 53, 77, 82; opposition from

96, 117, 152; opposition to TPP 83;
  partisan composition 10, 50; partisan
  support 25; pass WOs 61, 63–4, 69, 89;
  regional parties 52
local party organizations 6, 25, 36, 84,
  97n4, 100, 152–3, 155, 259; constraints
  11; DPJ 82, 96; greater autonomy
  delegated 22; support **51**, 54n13
local politics 1–4, 6, 9–11, 14, 17, 23, 31,
  36, 43–4, **48**, 53, 76–7, 81, 100,
  149–52, 154–6
local power 3–4, 11, 18, 37, 43; expansion
  of 7, 25; government 4, 19; regional
  parties consolidating 5; sources 14
local reform 81; contribution system 120;
  government system 46; taxes 40, 144
London Chamber of Commerce and
  Industry (LCCI) 146n8
London mayoralty 142
Lower House 44; chairman 61; dissolution
  158; districts 59; elections 46, 57; LDP
  candidates 72; LDP loss of seats 74, 80;
  LDP parliamentarians 71; member from
  Nagasaki 92; seat share **52**
Lukes, S. 31n3

McElwain, K. 45, 152, 160n1
McEwen, N. 7, 22–3, 142
Machidori, S. 3–4, 25, 50–51, 82, 103,
  107, 155
Maclachlan, P.L. 70–1
majoritarian competition 45–6; electoral
  system 130, 140, 152; government 137,
  144; parliamentarianism 129; politics
  131; systems 24, 149, 154–6
majoritarianism 155
Mallory, J.R. 129, 131
Masuda, H. 36, 125n8, 157–8, 160n4,
  160n6
Masuda report 36, 157
mayoral candidates 49, 141; posts 77
mayors 4, 7, 40; city 49, 75, 153; backed
  by parties on the left 77; city 152;
  directly elected 3, 23, 25, 35, 43, 53,
  80, 140; high-profile 102; independent
  52; lobbying central ministries 43; local
  118; local governor and mayor
  associations 41; London 144; in major
  urban areas 102; Nago 123; Nagoya
  101; Naha 122; National Association of
  Progressive Mayors 50; non-partisan 5,
  51; not backed by the LDP 47;
  opposition-party-backed 30; Osaka 84,
  154; UK 145

168 *Index*

membership: party 32n7, 131; suspension of 62; trade union 138

Metropolitan Councils and the Greater London Council (GLC) 139–40; former Labour Party leader 141; opposition 144

Ministry of Internal Affairs and Communications (MIC) **52**, 109, 125n13, 157; minister 120

Minobe Ryokichi (progressive Tokyo governor) 101, 119

Mochida, N. 39

Morgan, K. 141

Mulgan, A.G. 11, 46, 79n30, 79n31, 91–3

multi-level 22–3, 81, 144; asymmetrical electoral environments 10, 47; challenges 122; channels 7; clashes under dual centralization 138; confrontations 58; congruence 142; cooperation 26, **27**, 30; coordination 10; equation 145; equilibrium **8**, 31; incongruence 9; opposition 69; partisan incongruence 97n3; partisan linkages 30, 150; response of LDP and DPJ 92; stability 134; tensions 123, 132, 140

multi-level conflict 8, 14–16, 22, 24–8, 49, 63, 69–70, 77, 81, 83, 89, 97, 103, 112, 121–2, 124, 128–32, 137, 140, 143–5, 149–51, 154; under the DPJ 94, 96; intra-party 141–2; intra-party policy 9, 58, 75; partisan 30–1; policy 7, 19–20, *66*, 67, 113

multi-level dynamics 9, 11; inter-executive 24; inter-party 22; intra-party 20; LDP 58

multi-level interactions 8, 20, 22, 24, 26, 31; under DPJ administration 85; over policy 10

multi-level party politics 11; conferences *60*; congruence 43, 150; incongruence 50, 52–3; integration 128; system 133

multi-level relations 8, 14, 23–4, 30, 53, 81, 83, 145, 150, 152; conflictual 22, 129; cooperative 33n10, 128

municipal coalitions 157; elections 53n1, 53n8; governments 38, 65; LDP legislative groups 71; legislators 3, 43, 47, 59, 75; legislatures 54n12, 59, 61, 65; local politics **48**; mergers 5, **8**, 10, 46, 48; opposition movements 118; politicians 44, 48

municipalities 17; Japanese 39–40, 54n9, 157; passed WOs 71; at risk of

extinction 36, 157, 160n5; safety agreement 126n21

Muramatsu, M. 3–4, 10–11, 18–19, 32n4, 38, 40, 43–4, 47, 49–50, 159

Nagano winter Olympic Games 117

Nakajima, M. 93–4

Narumi, M. 35, 53n2

National Association of Chairpersons of Prefectural Assemblies *68*, 69, 78n10, *86*

national elections 16–17, 32n4, 46, 74, 141, 104; LDP defeat 80; mobilizing voters 82; privatization conflict 71; quality candidates 77; TPP issue 73; turnout 2, 47; volatility 58

national executives 20, 24, 103, 155

National Governors' Association (NGA) 102, 109–12, *115*, 119–20, 125n11, 125n13; homepage **110**

National and Local Government Dispute Resolution Council 113, *115*, 120, 123–4

national politics 1, 4, 17, 43, 49, 82

nationalization of Japanese politics 149, 151; partial 126n24; thesis 152–3

New Frontier Party (NFP) 51

New Labour 141

Nishio, M. 39–40, 42

non-cooperation 15; over community charge 140; of local governments 16; threats of 133

non-partisan 25; actors 159; candidates 30; chief executives and legislators 23; governors 5, 50–2, 112, 116; voters 101

nuclear power *29*, 64, 126n20; campaigning against 118; DPJ internal division over future use 83; DPJ local branch support *87*; operator 126n21; plants 81–3, 85, 88, 93, 96, 102, 113, *114–15*, 118, 151, 155

Oil Shock 50

Okayama prefecture 71; governor 90, 96; LDP stronghold 91

Okinawa **52**, 58, 61, 79n32, 79n34, 79n35; challenge to national policy *115*; conflict with central government 123; dependent on central government transfers 113; ethno-territorial conflicts emerging 132; governors 42, 75, 102, 106, **107**, 120, 122–3; gubernatorial elections 74; non-LDP governor 116;

US base 2, *29*, 42, 70, 74, 81, 93, 121, 123, 151, 155; WOs passed *68*
Onaga Takeshi, Governor 75, 79n32; challenge to national policy *115*, 122–3
opposition party 9, 51, **52**; control of governments 49; control of urban areas in Japan 28; federal 135; strength **59**
Osaka 58, 61, 67, 82, 84, 88, 95, 100–1, 113, 121; governor 2, 5, 50, 52, 110, 119–20, 154; governor challenge to national policy *115*, 117–18; progressive local governments 49; support for key national policies *87*; University 53n3; WOs passed *68, 86*
Osaka Restoration Association 84, 154

partisan 133, 137–8, 140; background 113; channels 128, 131, 151; control 154; forces 143; links 124; multi-level conflict 129; neutrality 110; opposition 122; swinging dynamic 122
partisan affiliation 81, 100, 112–13, 133, 150; of governors 51, *114–15*, 122, 124; of local executives 7, 9, 25
partisan challenges 31; channels 6–7, 20, 26, 37, 43, 53, 67; composition of legislatures 3, 10, 20, 50, 95; conflicts 27, 28, *29*, 30–1, 97; control 24, 26; divisions 30; dynamic 77; forces 14, 23, 81; group *87*; loyalty 93; opposition 11; outsiders 25; pressures 89; strategy 27
partisan congruence 6–7, 23–4, 26, **27**, 28, 81, 142; lack of 20, 128; multi-level 22
partisan incongruence 7, 9, 24, **27**, 28, *29*, 30–1, 58, 95, 133, 144, 150; across levels 5, 49, 67, 81; multi-level **8**, 23, 97n3
partisan linkages 26, 129, 143, 145, 145n5; between levels of government 8–9, 14; multi-level 128, 150; weakened 30
partisans: co-partisans 16, 44, 67; local 5–6, 9, 11, 27–8, *29*, 69, 81–3, 93–6; local LDP 58, 60
partisanship 122
party integration 7, 20; intra-party 4; multi-level 128; vertical 21, 128; weakened 75
party organization 153; decentralized 142; intra-party conflicts 149; multi-level conflict 150; vertical de-integration 152
party organizations 32n7, 91, 135; adapted to challenge of regionalized competition 141; centralization 76,

137; decentralized 44, 62; DPJ 82; DPJ meltdown 97n7; focused on territorial interests 136; highly integrated German 134; integrated 135; internal conflicts 14; intra-party multi-level interactions 20; LDP 49, **51**, 54n13, 82; LDP reform 97n8; regional 137–8; socialist 97n4; structure 21, 129; UK 137; UK Labour and Conservative 138; vertical integration 6, 8–10, 14, 21–2, 26, *29*, 133

Pekkanen, R. 10, 47
petition/petitions 84, 96, **105**, **110**; central government 112; for local projects 103, 106; local 90; new method 90; NGA collective 119; PM meetings with governors concerning 106; practices 91; presented 109; right of 90; system *29*; traditional LDP system 83; traditional season 91; unifying 85, *86–7*, 88–91, 94; war 43, 94
policy conflicts 11, 113; intra-party 9, 58, 61, 63, 75; multi-level 7, 14, 19–20, 58, *66*, 67; territorial *29*; over TPP 92
political elite 130; local 131, 153
poll tax 138, 140, 144
pork barrel 10; *see also* clientelism
post-devolution UK **27**, 31, 129
postal privatization 5, *29*, 46, 65, 74; law 72; LDP opposition 57, 70–1, 76; multi-level policy conflict *66*, 67; opposition among rural residents 78n16; protests over 150; reforms 70; snap election 47
power/powers 6, 15–16, 26, 32n7, 100, 125n8; administrative 25; balance of 17; bargaining 111; candidate nomination . 76; chief executives 47; collective bargaining 109; competence to act over local issues 137; concentrated 129, 131, 144, 149, 155; decentralizing 159; decision-making 21, 42; deconcentrated 155; delegation 15, 21; devolved 40, 144; discretionary 30, 40, 76; dispersed 131; to dissolve elected legislature 124n2; divided 24, 156; DPJ losing 72; DPJ term in 106; dynamic 82; executive 150, 156; expansion 137; formal and informal 123, 152; formal legal 151; imbalance of 96; impact on national policy 100; informal 124; over initiating and blocking policy 100; of intervention 142; Japanese local executives 7; LDP

170 *Index*

power/powers *continued*
 holding 96; LDP out of power 97n3;
 legal and administrative 53, 118;
 legislating 19; legislative 140, 144;
 levers of 31n3; limited 140; limited
 revenue-raising 38; over local council
 decisions 139; national 16, 47, 80–1;
 national levers of 21, 84; party in power
 30, 58; policy-making 18, 24; power-
 concentrating majoritarian systems 24;
 safety agreement 126n21; to Scotland
 and Wales 140; second and third faces
 of 31n3; separated 19; stripped from
 party leadership 96; sub-state 145n2;
 subnational state 15; taxing 109; unitary
 42; veto 24, 93, 123, 134, 154–5; *see
 also* come to power; government power;
 governor power
power share 15; coalition governments 24;
 lack of 130
prefectural 116, 145; dam projects *114*,
 117; governments 38, **41**, 65, 117,
 124; governors 7, 30, 37; LDP
 legislator 75; legislators 3, 43, 47, 59,
 72–3, 122; legislatures 5, 9, 49, 54n12,
 58, **59**, 61, **63**, **64**, 65, 67, 69, 78n11,
 82, 84–5, *86–7*, 95–6, 97n3, 109, 153;
 organizations 57; per capita income **36**;
 politicians 44, 48, 90, 92, 95; seat share
 52; WOs 63
prefectural assemblies 54n9, 57, **64**, 71,
 80, 95, 122; elections 47
prefectural branch 48–9, 57, 60–1, 71–2,
 79n32, 80, 82–3, 97n1; chairmen 73,
 78n24; DPJ 85, 90, 92–3; executive 62;
 LDP 74, 84, 97n8, 98n25; office 59
prefectural elections 53n1; assembly 47;
 legislative 46
prefecture 59, 64, **107**, 116–17, 122; fiscal
 strength 113, *114*; Gifu 109; home 106;
 host 126n21; hosting US military bases
 74; Ishikawa 88; island 121; large-scale
 dams 83, 93; Niigata 120; nuclear power
 plant 83, 118; Okinawa 2, 74–5, 123;
 Osaka 84; representatives 100; Tottori
 78n21; WOs 67, 78n10, 85, *86*, 88
presidential systems 7, 23–4, 124n2
privatization 46, 65; bill 71–2;
 programmes 141; of public services 5;
 WOs opposing 71
progressive 88, 95; candidates 49–50;
 chief executives 50; government era
 102; governors 50, 101, 119; Japanese
 27, 49; local governments 51, 77; local

partisans 94; parties on the left 97n3;
 partisan opposition 11; period 30, 35,
 49–50, 53; policies prevented 156;
 policy programmes 50
progressives 50, 122
public works 81, 89, 124; abolished 83;
 bid-rigging of 117; by-laws regulating
 123; cancellation of 93; conflicts over
 113; cuts to 92; LDP expanded 156;
 manager dismissed *114*; national
 projects 126n28; obligatory local
 contributions 119; opposition against
 102, 116–17; petitioning for 90;
 projects *29*; restarting 92; spending 5,
 46, 84, 156–7; termination or revival of
 projects 151; wasteful 118, 125n19

Radice, G. 141, 160n2
rate-capping 139; opposition from
 Kinnock 146n12; rebellion 139, 144
re-election 21, 25, 44, 69, 71–2, 102,
 116, 118; rate 124n3
Reed, S.R. 3, 10–11, 15, 38, 44, **48**,
 49–50, 92
reform/reforms 65, 77, 154;
 administrative 5, 39, 45; British finance
 system 138; campaign finance 45;
 constitutional 64–5, *66*, 67, 94, 132;
 difficult 76; DPJ 97n7; electoral 4, **8**,
 10, 30, 45, 53, 60, 65, 152, 155;
 federal structures 136; of finance system
 138; fiscal 5; fiscal equalization
 programme 132; implementation of 72;
 institutional 8, 149, 156; LDP party 84,
 97n8; national-level 76; party fortunes
 84; to political institutions 65; postal
 privatization 70–2; pro-reform swing
 voters 76; regional sovereignty 83;
 resisted by dominant local LDP 77; top-
 down 46, 64, 71; undermined over time
 156; *see also* agricultural reform;
 decentralization reform; Holy Trinity
 reforms; local reform
reformist governors 125n8, 125n13
regional inequality 6, **37**; income **36**
Renzsch, W. 20, 22, 134–6
revenues 18, 38, 40–1, 69, 121;
 government 145n2; local corporate tax
 126n24; locally raised **41**; road
 construction 65, *68*; road-related 89;
 self-raised 39, 137
Riker, W.H. 6, 20–1, 155–6
Rodden, J. 2, 18
rogue candidates 62; LDP 58, 75

Index 171

rogue LDP governor 123
Rosenbluth, F.M. 44–5, 152

Saga prefecture 71, 79n29; gubernatorial
elections 73; LDP branch policy 84
Sakurazawa, M. 122
Samuels, D.J. 7, 25
Sasaki, N. 100, 119, 126n24
Sato, E. 50, *114*, 125n13, 126n20
Scheiner, E. 9, 44, 62, 77, 152
Scotland 28, 154; devolution 140–1;
independence 1, 11n1, 142; Labour
stronger 141, 160n2; regional
parliaments 151
Scottish: assembly 142, 146n18;
government 143; independence 11n1;
parliamentary elections 141; regional
government 142, 144
Scottish National Party (SNP) 141–2, 144;
Labour chief executive 146n17; Scottish
assembly seats 146n18
second chamber 20, 32n6; Canadian 131;
Germany 134, 145
second-order elections 135; referendums
2, *29*
Shimizu, K. 10, 48
shinkansen bullet train 120; station 117
Shiro, Asano 109, 125n7, 125n8, 125n9
single non-transferable vote (SNTV)
system 46–7, 54n9
single-member districts 47, 65, 131;
electoral rules 24
Smith, D.M. 8, **48**
Social Democratic Party of Japan (SDPJ)
117
Soga, K. 3–4, 10, 25, 50–1
stability: disruption threatened 134;
governors in office 100; of inter-
governmental relations 5, 26; local **52**
Steiner, K. 3, 11, 39, 49–50, 77
subsidies 83, 121; cut back, reduced 5,
102, 109, 120, 159; dam project 117;
earmarked 5, 110; general 83; local 158;
local government 40–1; national 4, 41,
43, 110; new system 158; rural-area 65;
see also central government subsidies
Sunahara, Y. 3, 10, 32n8, 38, 41, 53n6,
59–60, 83, 90

Tanaka Yasuo 101, *114*, 116–17, 125n16
tariff 92; cuts 73; protection 72; reduced
91
Tatebayashi, M. 11, 21, 39, 42, 49, 60,
82, 97n4

Thatcher, Prime Minister Margaret 138;
administration 28, 151; General
Election Manifesto 146n11; poll tax
140; resignation 140, 144; war on
local government 137, 139, 145n6,
146n14
Thorlakson, L. 21, 32n5
Tokyo 2, 67, 78n7, 90, 95, 104, 113,
116, 125n5, 125n13; average salaries
36; campaigning against 72–3, 76, 124;
DPJ 80, 82, 88; economy 124n1;
electoral outcomes **52**; LDP majority
58; national policy conflicts 57, *68,
86–7*; petition 91; progressive local
government 49; *shinkansen* bullet train
line 120; state funding 146n8; US base
issues 106–7, 122
Tokyo governors 42, 83, 94, 100–1,
126n24; challenge national policy *115*;
gubernatorial election 50; progressive
119
Tokyo Olympics 121; facility costs *115*;
paying for construction of stadium 121;
stadium 2, 42
Tokyo population 157–8; demographic
crisis 160n6
Trans-Pacific Partnership (TPP) free trade
agreement 57, 65, 72, 74, 77n3, 78n4,
78n23, 78n24, 79n31, 79n35, 94,
98n14, 98n15, 98n17, 98n18, 98n19,
155; conflict *29, 66, 68*, 70, 76, *86*, 89,
151; DPJ local branch support *87*;
negotiations 72–3, 83, 85, 88, 91–2,
98n16; opponents 88, 93, 96
Travers, T. 137–8
Tsuji, A. 10, **51**, *68*, 78n11, *86*, **101**, *115*
Tsuji, K. 3, 38

Uekami, T. 10, 47, 97n4
United Kingdom (UK) 1, 8–9, 26, 30,
128, 137, 140, 146n13, 150;
government 142–3; Joint Ministerial
Committee 20; local authorities
decreased 138; local government
centralization 137; local resistance 151;
majoritarian electoral rules 144; mayors
145; multi-level tensions and conflicts
140, 143; national ruling parties 28;
partisan incongruence 144; post-
devolution 129; riots 140; tax 146n7;
tensions with devolved regions *29*;
territorial cleavages 137, 154;
territorial conflicts *27*, 31, 129; upper
house 145

172 *Index*

United Kingdom (UK) councils 23; Labour 27, *29*; local opposition-controlled 28

United States (US) 130–1; bases 121; conflict over policy 102, 106; congressmen 123; economic support demanded 122; federalism 156; Japan defence cooperation guidelines 65, *66*; LDP intra-party conflict 74; Marine Corps Air Station Futenma 74; military 57, 74, 81, 93; military bases 107, 121–2; multi-level conflicts 124; occupation 121; occupation authorities 35; in Okinawa 42, 70; policy 123; presidents 124n2, 124n4; relocation blocked 2; relocation plans 151; Senate 20; state department official 154; state legislatures 1

Upper House 5; chairman 61; districts 59; elections 57, 72, 74, 123, 146n19; LDP defeat in by-election 69; rural votes 46; veto player 75, 154–5

Van Biezen, I. 22, 142

Van Houten, P. 15, 32n7

vertical integration in party organizations 6–7, 11, 20–2, 24, 26, 43, 128, 145; lack of 20; LDP 7, 9, 45, 47, 53; weakened 21, *29*, 58

vertically integrated party organizations 5, 8, 10, 14, 20, 24, 26, 53, 53n8; German government 128, 133–4; LDP **8**, 10

volatility 100; increased 47; LDP electoral 5, 58; national **8**, 9, **52**

vote/votes 44, 88, 100; DPJ prefectural politicians in rural areas 95; LDP gaining 76; locally 2; majority 110; of no-confidence 117, 141; personal 46; of pro-TPP groups 92; regional 84, 98n25; right of foreign residents 65; rural 46; rural and urban 153; share of 84; SNTV system 46; split 92; winning strategy 124

voters 1–2, 36, 50, 58, 77, 96, 121, 123, 132, 156; behaviour 153; betrayal of 58, 74; dissatisfied non-partisan 101; floating 4, **8**, 45, 47, 153; German 135; hostile 76; incentivize 28; local 61, 74; median 45–6, 152–4; mobilizing 44, 77, 82; opposed base relocation 74; opposition 76, 78n23; organized 5, 45–6; perception of local elections 22–3, *29*; preferences 150–2; pro-TPP 92; rural 45, 91; strategies 24; swing 46, 76; turnout 47; unaffiliated 46–7; unorganized 49; urban 92, 154

voting: behaviour *87*, 152; on candidate characteristics 46; for opposition parties 23; party 54n12; rights of foreigners *29*, 65, *66*, 67, 84–5, *87*, 88–9, 94–6; turnout 36; against WOs 85

Wales 28; devolution 140–1; Labour 141, 146n17, 160n2; regional assembly 137; regional government 129; secondary-legislative powers 140; *see also* Welsh assembly

wasteful 90; *mottainai* slogan (don't be wasteful) 117; public works 83, 93, 116–18, 125n19; pump-priming measures 157; tier of government (GLC) 139

Watts, R.L. 7, 129, 131, 133–4

Welsh assembly 141–2, 146n18; government 143; Labour 141, 146n18; Plaid Cymru party 141; regional legislature 142

Westminster 20; government 142; model state 154; two-party politics 138, 160n2; Westminsterization 11

Wilson, D. 137–8

Wolinetz, S.B. 129–31

written opinions (WOs) 61, **63**, **64**, 65, *66*, 67, *68*, 69, 71, 73, 78n9, 78n10, 78n17, 84–5, *86–7*, 88–90, 92, 94–5, 98n16

Yamazaki, O. 120, 126n25, 126n28

Yamba dam 83, 89, 93–4, 97, 118

Yawata, K. 100, 124n3